Cultivating Copyright

Creators and creative industries are struggling to navigate the digital age. Intellectual property rights, including copyrights, trademarks, and patents, offer invaluable tools to help creative industries remain viable and sustainable. But to be fully effective, they must be considered as part of a greater ecosystem. *Cultivating Copyright* offers a framework for tailoring flexible strategies and adaptive solutions suited to diverse creative industries. Tailored solutions entail change on four fronts: business models and strategies, legal policies and practices, technological measures, and cultural and normative features. Creating strong creative industries through tailored solutions serves critical functions: promoting richly varied artistic endeavors and supporting democratic flourishing.

Bhamati Viswanathan is a legal scholar. She was awarded a Doctorate of Juridical Science (S.J.D.) and a Masters in Law (LL.M.) by the University of Pennsylvania Law School. She holds a Juris Doctor (J.D.) degree from the University of Michigan Law School and a Bachelor of Arts (B.A.) degree, cum laude, from Williams College. She is a member of the New York State Bar and the Copyright Society of the USA. She resides in Boston.

Routledge Research in Intellectual Property

Available:

Cultivating Copyright
How Creators and Creative Industries Can Harness Intellectual Property to Survive the Digital Age
Bhamati Viswanathan

Biotechnology, Patents and Morality
Participatory Democracy and Controversial Patent Decisions
Maureen O'Sullivan

Internet Intermediaries and Trade Mark Rights
Althaf Marsoof

Intellectual Property and Access to Medicines in Africa
A Regional Framework for Access
Olasupo Owoeye

Intellectual Property Branding in the Developing World
Tshimanga Kongolo

Intellectual Property policy, Law and Administration in Africa
Exploring continental and sub-regional co-operation
Caroline Bongiwe Ncube

Intellectual Property Rights and Competition in Standard Setting
Objectives and Tensions
Valerio Torti

Intellectual Property in Global Governance
The Crisis of Equity in the Knowledge Economy
Chidi Oguamanam

For a full list of titles in this series, please visit www.routledge.com

Cultivating Copyright

How Creators and Creative Industries Can Harness Intellectual Property to Survive the Digital Age

Bhamati Viswanathan

Routledge
Taylor & Francis Group
NEW YORK AND LONDON

First published 2020
by Routledge
605 Third Avenue, New York, NY 10017

and by Routledge
2 Park Square, Milton Park, Abingdon, Oxon OX14 4RN

First issued in paperback 2021

Routledge is an imprint of the Taylor & Francis Group, an informa business

Publisher's Note
The publisher has gone to great lengths to ensure the quality of this reprint but points out that some imperfections in the original copies may be apparent.

Library of Congress Cataloging-in-Publication Data
Names: Viswanathan, Bhamati, author.
Title: Cultivating copyright : how creative industries can harness intellectual property to survive the digital age/by Bhamati Viswanathan.
Description: Abingdon, Oxon ; New York, NY : Routledge, 2019. | Series: Routledge research in intellectual property | Based on author's thesis (doctoral—University of Pennsylvania Law School, 2015) issued under title: Creative copyright : tailoring intellectual property policies and business strategies for creative content industries in the digital age. | Includes bibliographical references and index.
Identifiers: LCCN 2019013032 | ISBN 9781138477490 (hardback)
Subjects: LCSH: Intellectual property—United States. | Digital media—Law and legislation—United States. | Cultural industries—Law and legislation—United States.
Classification: LCC KF2985.D54 V57 2019 | DDC 658.4/038—dc23
LC record available at https://lccn.loc.gov/2019013032

ISBN 13: 978-1-03-224082-4 (pbk)
ISBN 13: 978-1-138-47749-0 (hbk)

DOI: 10.4324/9781351104807

Typeset in Galliard
by Apex CoVantage, LLC

Contents

Introduction and Road Map

Introduction

Nange Magro, a Japanese-Italian fashion designer who works primarily with latex, tuned into the 2019 Grammy Awards only to find that the superstar singer Janelle Monae was wearing an outfit that looked highly similar to designs she had made in 2015 for her label Dead Lotus Couture.[1] *Unhappy with the situation, she immediately posted side-by-side images on Instagram, and publicly accused Monae of plagiarizing her original work.*[2] *At the time of this writing, she is still awaiting a response.*

Scientific researchers and academics united in protest against Sci-Hub, a giant rogue site that illicitly disseminates scientific articles but has proven notoriously hard to shut down. In 2017, the American Chemical Society won its lawsuit against Sci-Hub in U.S. District Court.[3] *The judgment included $4.8 million in damages and a broad injunction that requires organizations such Internet service providers, search engines, and domain name registries that are actively associated with the site to censor it. (Sci-Hub is operated on Tor, an anonymous network that is outside the reach of most Internet service providers.) What effect, if any, this judgment will have on Sci-Hub's operations is unclear. When the publishing giant Elsevier won a default legal judgement against Sci-Hub last year, the site's founder ignored the order to pay damages and she has publicly stated that she plans to do the same in this case.*[4] *In addition, even if ACS succeeds in getting*

1 Ben Beaumont-Thomas, Fashion Designer Accuses Janelle Monae of Plagiarism for Grammy Performance, *The Guardian*, Feb. 12, 2019, available at www.theguardian.com/music/2019/feb/12/fashion-designer-accuses-janelle-monae-of-plagiarism-for-grammy-performance.

2 Chantal Fernandez, Designers Take Copyright Infringement Into Their Own Hands, *The Business of Fashion*, June 28, 2017, available at www.businessoffashion.com/articles/news-analysis/designers-take-copyright-infringement-into-their-own-hands.

3 Diana Kwon, American Chemical Society Wins Lawsuit Against Sci-Hub, *The Scientist*, Nov. 7, 2017, available at www.the-scientist.com/news-opinion/american-chemical-society-wins-lawsuit-against-sci-hub-30648.

4 Keith Kupferschmid, Copyright Law in 2017: Big Court Cases to Know About, Copyright Clearance Center, available at www.copyright.com/blog/copyright-law-2017-12-big-court-cases-know/.

American domain name registries to take Sci-Hub down, the site can re-establish itself on domains hosted outside the U.S.

The Danish toymaker Lego is famously beloved for making colorful plastic bricks and figures that have filled many households over generations. They are also famous in IP circles for vigorously defending their copyrights and brand. In 2018, Lego won a landmark copyright case in China against imitators of its colorful plastic toy figures and bricks.[5] *Later in 2018, Lego won yet another case against imitators when the Guangzhou Yuexiu District Court ruled that four Chinese companies had "infringed multiple copyrights of the Lego Group and conducted acts of unfair competition by producing and distributing Lepin building sets," and ordered that the companies immediately cease "producing, selling, exhibiting or in any way promoting the infringing products."*[6] *Damages in the more recent case amounted to around 4.5 million Chinese yuan ($649,735). In 2018, the Beijing Higher Court passed a ruling that recognized the Lego logo and name in Chinese as "well-known" trademarks in China, putting the toymaker in a better position to act against infringement of its trademarks. The $31 billion toy and games sector in China represents an important market to Lego; and Lego has also been working with local education departments, state schools and private education providers in China to encourage children to play with Lego as a way to boost their motor skills, creativity, and attention spans.*

In 2012, Ipek Irgit launched a fashion sensation: a colorful, crocheted, skimpy bikini that she branded the "Kiini."[7] *In 2014, the Kiini was featured in Vogue, People, and Conde Nast Traveller. By 2015, it had brought in approximately $9 million. The Kiini quickly became the model for copycat bikinis. In 2015, Ms. Irgit expressed outrage over what she saw as the proliferation of knock-offs or imitations of her original work. She brought suit in federal court in the central district of California against Victoria's Secret, accusing the company of copyright infringement of her original work, which was eventually settled. In 2018, Ms. Irgit filed another federal lawsuit, this time in federal district court in the Southern District of New York, against Neiman Marcus and PilyQ, a swimwear company that supplied crocheted bikinis to Neiman Marcus, accusing them of unfair competition and violating Kiini's "trade dress." But Ms. Irgit's lawsuits brought her to the attention of Maria Solange Ferrarini, a self-described street artist in Trancoso, Brazil, who since at least 1998 was widely known as*

5 Christian Wienberg, Lego Wins Intellectual Property Lawsuit in China, Nov. 5, 2018, available at www.bloomberg.com/news/articles/2018-11-05/lego-wins-intellectual-property-lawsuit-against-lepin-in-china.

6 Lego Wins Court Case in China Over Copyright Infringement, *Japan Times*, Nov. 6, 2018, available at www.japantimes.co.jp/news/2018/11/06/business/corporate-business/lego-wins-court-case-china-copyright-infringement/#.XGNwatF7ndc.

7 Katherine Rosman, The Itsy-Bitsy, Teenie-Weenie, Very Litigious Bikini, *New York Times*, Dec. 20, 2018, available at www.nytimes.com/2018/12/20/business/kiini-bikini-lawsuit-ipek-irgit-solange-ferrarini.html.

the designer and maker of crocheted bikinis that were virtually identical to the Kiini. Ms. Ferrarini's work had earlier been spotted by PilyQ, and in 2016 Ms. Ferrarini had entered a nonexclusive licensing arrangement with PilyQ. Ms. Ferrarini and PilyQ were outraged by what they perceived as Ms. Irgit's copyright infringement of their original work. In 2018, on behalf of Ms. Ferrarini, PilyQ sued Ms. Irgit and Kiini in federal court in the Central District of California, citing unfair business practices and asking for a public apology. In return, Ms. Irgit filed motions to dismiss and to have Ms. Ferrarini's lawyer disqualified. As of this date, the actions are still pending.

What do all these cases have in common? They span multiple creative industries, and they involve highly original creative works—fashion designs, scientific papers, children's toys, and video games—that require serious effort and investment by their creators. They all appear to have been targeted by enterprising individuals or firms that want to make use of creators' works, or to make those works freely available, without compensating the original creator. And in all these cases the original creators appear to have reasonable arguments that their copyrights were infringed.

Where do these cases differ? Most obviously, they vary in scale and economic impact. Infringement may have serious financial consequences on an individual level, such as keeping an emerging fashion designer from breaking even. They may have large consequences for major firms and startups, tolling millions of dollars in damages, as when renowned toys and popular games are imitated. And they may have significant economic impact on creative intermediaries, such as inflicting large costs on publishers, while having less of an immediate financial impact but more of a significant reputational impact on creators, such as circulating academic papers without the consent and control of scientists, researchers, and scholars.

They also differ in the remedies sought: whether seeking monetary damages, attribution or acknowledgement, or preventing competitors from encroaching on commercial advantage, all the creative firms and individuals in these cases are looking to be recognized and compensated for the unauthorized use of their work. All of these remedies are important and valuable, although their value may vary depending on circumstances of the case.

Lastly, and perhaps most importantly, all of these cases show that creators and creative industries value copyright in their creative works. They want to be recognized for their original efforts, and they want to be rewarded for their work as they see fit. They also understand that American copyright law gives them not only the basis for their rights, but also the structure, the provisions, and the tools to enforce those rights. As the Director of Communications for the American Chemical Society (ACS), stated when the case against Sci-Hub was favorably resolved:

> What we were seeking was to get an affirmative ruling from the court upholding U.S. copyright law. We have laws, and we, in a civil society,

expect those laws to be abided—here, we have clear evidence that, not only did they steal content, but they actually created a spoofed ACS website to further add false legitimacy to their operation.[8]

This book speaks to creators and creative industries who want and need to bring works to fruition. Copyright is an important tool in implementing creative goals, but it is not the only one. Copyright is embedded in creative industries, which are complex machineries with many moving parts and many instrumental players—not just people, firms, and institutions, but also technologies, as well as practices, norms, and cultures. Creators and creative industries make choices that involve both economic and intangible features: earning rewards may be necessary for survival, but garnering reputational benefits, seeing one's work properly attributed, and contributing to the greater good are also often as critical as monetary returns. And the recipients of creative works are also vital players: consumers, audiences, users of creative works, all have a deep-seated interest in seeing creativity be supported and thrive.

The copyright landscape is rich with debates over the particular nature of copyright protection, its scale and scope, its impact on various industries, its history, and its increasing centrality to creative production. This book does not seek to engage directly with those interesting concerns. Rather, it has a far more practical goal: to equip creators and creative industries with the concepts and tools they need to prosper in a radically changed world. That is not to say that the book is blindly "pro-copyright"; creators also benefit from limits on copyright protection, and cannot and should not ignore the public interest. However, it is creators, not users, who are currently facing a crisis, and this book focuses on the practical response to that crisis.

The Road Map

This book constructs a road map for change, enabling creators and creative industries to navigate the changed landscape of the digital age, and to find a path to prosperity that suits their particular needs, ambitions, and goals. It divides into four parts. **Part One**, consisting of **Chapters 1 through 5**, lays out the problem, flags the risks ahead, and considers some initial strategic options. **Part Two**, consisting of **Chapters 6 through 10**, presents the tailoring framework that is the basis for forming solutions that fit the needs of creative industry constituents. **Part Three**, consisting of **Chapters 11 and 12**, examines the effects of Big Tech on creative landscapes, and explores innovative approaches that are emerging to contend with the changes Big Tech has wrought. **Part Four**, consisting of **Chapter 13**, situates the importance of

8 Diana Kwon, American Chemical Society Wins Lawsuit Against Sci-Hub, *The Scientist*, Nov. 7, 2017, available at www.the-scientist.com/news-opinion/american-chemical-society-wins-lawsuit-against-sci-hub-30648.

tailoring solutions for creators and creative industries in the greater context of democracy and human flourishing.

Chapter 1: What Is the Problem: Copyright and Creativity in Crisis, lays out the problem by outlining how the advent of the Internet has thrown the creative industries into a state of crisis that persists to the present day. The Internet has developed, grown, and become accessible to anyone with a cable or broadband connection, and is increasingly enmeshed in the lives of ordinary people. It enables users to find their way to information, resources, and content with unprecedented ease and at relatively low cost. This has transformed entire industries almost overnight, and the creative industries are no exception. Suddenly people have access to more creative works than at any time in history. But they also have new ways of consuming creative work. This has led to profound changes in creative industries at every stage of content generation, production, delivery, and remuneration.

The changes wrought by digitization are so significant that their impact is still being felt and measured today. One of the best explanations of how these processes work, and what kinds of problems they have led to, is the theory of disruptive innovation. For disruptive innovation to merit its name, it has to involve both the transformation of markets and the disruption of business models and paradigms in established industries. **Chapter 2: What Is Causing the Problem: Disruptive Innovation** delineates how creative industries have been deeply affected by digitization and its aftermath. It examines how disruptive innovation has played out in a number of commercial sectors, as well as how it is changing the landscape in the creative sectors.

Creative industries are well aware of the fact that technology raises a host of new risks and facilitates a range of new behaviors on the part of competitors, users, enterprising actors and unscrupulous actors, investors, underwriters and supporters, and industry participants. **Chapter 3: What Are Creative Industries Afraid Of: Known Risks** crystallizes those risks and concretizes the potential challenges. Commercial realities can make these risks readily identifiable, and the success of managing them clearly quantifiable.

But there are qualitative and intangible risks that are harder to pinpoint precisely because they do not always have more immediate or evident bottom-line effects. These risks can put into jeopardy some of the most valuable aspects of creative production, such as the need to have open spaces for idea generation, collaboration, generational support, and foundational work. **Chapter 4: What Should Creative Industries Be Afraid Of, But May Not Be Aware Of: Unseen Risks** explores what some of those less obvious risks look like, and why they are equally important to confront and conquer as those that are well known.

When faced with large, complicated risks, many industries tend to start with two basic premises. One proposition is that changing business models is a direct route to correcting losses of revenue and market share. Another proposition is that increasing IP protection ensures that a portfolio of IP assets will retain its value and possibly reveal new revenue growth potential. **Chapter 5:**

What Doesn't Work: Focusing Exclusively on Business- or IP-Based Solutions explains why trying to address only one piece of the problem is likely to leave creative industries in a suboptimal position in the long run.

From the point of view of an individual creative firm, or even a slice of a creative sector, both of these strategies would seem to be rational and to show good business sense. From a more macroeconomic sense, they also seem to offer forceful ways of making industries adapt to new technologies and changed environments with strong and concerted measures, rather than with incremental solutions. Indeed, some of the calls for expanded legal protections,[9] sweeping regulatory protections,[10] or broad commercial overhauls are grounded in this sense that drastic times call for drastic measures.

In some cases, overhauling business models may be a necessary step to renewed growth. When consumers prefer streaming content online to purchasing it in hard copies, shifting to expand licensing rights is essential to reaching the new revenue flows. At the same time, when online advertising pays less than traditional media advertising, but reaches wider audiences, diversifying ad-supported content and advertising plays may be one solution, but other solutions may involve more innovative business ploys, such as introducing new forms or formats of content, creating differentiated pricing, and adding merchandise tie-ins.

Equally, reshaping legal policies, amending regulations, and encouraging new practices may be helpful, even essential, to ensuring that copyright functions fairly and effectively, supporting the production and commercialization of creative output as it was intended and designed to do. Copyright and other IP rights create stable markets in creative work. Strong rights, and returns that are well-administered, help creative industries prosper and grow. Legal rights that also help to ensure that creative content providers have real and effective means of flagging and shutting down potential copyright infringers are important to protecting their valuable properties.

But there are limits to both business and legal strategies, and those limits exist at both the individual level of creative enterprises and at the systemic level of creative industries. Individual creators may require access to a rich array of creative works on which to build. Creative industries may require a measure of openness to encourage collaboration, sharing, and creative exchange. **Chapter 5** considers some of these tradeoffs that creative individuals and industries will want to balance when shaping their vision for change. In sum, **Chapters 1–5** stake out the questions facing creative industries today and show that the interplay among these questions is as important as each specific one.

9 See, e.g., Stephen Carlisle, Copyrights Last Too Long! (Say the Pirates): They Don't, and Why It's Not Changing Anytime Soon, Nova Southeastern Univ., July 15, 2014, available at http://copyright.nova.edu/copyright-duration/.

10 See, e.g., Josh Tabish, The Copyright Barons Are Coming. Now Is the Time to Stop Them, *Wired*, Jan. 31, 2017, available at www.wired.com/2017/01/copyright-barons-coming-nows-time-stop/.

Chapter 6: What Does Work: The Tailoring Framework begins to engage in the dauntingly complex analysis that faces creative industries in the throes of disruptive innovation. This undertaking requires asking critical questions, making a great many assessments, weighing them in the balance, and devising a workable solution. Further complicating the matter is that a good solution will most likely depend on what creative industry is under discussion: what are its particular qualities, strengths and weaknesses, challenges, needs and objectives?

The hardest part of devising a strategy for creative industries may simply be knowing where to start and how to organize the problem and the solution. A proper framework and a readily applicable test will help lay the groundwork for shaping well-crafted strategies and long-term solutions. **Chapter 6** puts into place the essential framework for action. The myriad questions for analysis are broken down into four major factors, each with its own set of inquiries and evaluations. The four-factors test looks at each of the main categories of analysis in turn: business strategies and models, legal policies and practices, technological measures, and behavioral and normative concerns. The four factors test may seem highly detailed, but its fine-grained nature enables creative industries to come up with structured solutions that are tailored to their measure. And, like tailoring a suit or dress, it requires some effort to come up with the perfect fit.

Chapters 7–10: Tailoring Business Models and Strategies; Tailoring Legal Policies and Practices; and Tailoring Cultural and Normative Features assess each of the four factors in turn, and offer a point-by-point set of solutions and prescriptions that are available to creative industries. These are not mandates but suggestions, and they are by no means comprehensive. Rather, they are intended to indicate the varied, multi-faceted, and individualized possibilities that can arise from the use and application of the four-factors test and the tailoring approach. These solutions may not be perfect or without some drawbacks. They may not wholly overcome the challenges a creative industry faces; or they may solve some problems and create others. Where discernable, these possibilities are raised. More importantly, though, the solutions presented here are intended to encourage creative industries to use both their analytic and imaginative faculties when taking on the challenges of the digital age.

The tailoring framework is dynamic: it assumes an ever-changing universe and calls for an ongoing balancing act. But disruptive innovation can occur in waves, and some of those waves can be tsunami-sized in proportion. The recent rise of dominant actors in the technology sector, known familiarly as Big Tech, represents the kind of change that is massive, market-disrupting, and game changing. While the scale of change is hard to fathom, the impact is even harder to discern, and the consequences virtually impossible to foresee. **Chapter 11: What Is Exacerbating the Problem: Big Tech: The Thumb on the Scales** looks at the exacerbating effect that the major technology companies are having on the viability of creative industries going forward. It takes a hard look at the rise of Big Tech and its ownership and control of four vital concerns: pipelines, pricing, policing, and populism. In light of the emerging hegemony of Big Tech, it further considers some of the consequences that are looming before the creative industries.

The presence of Big Tech may be game changing, but it does not necessarily undercut the efficacy of the tailoring framework. In some instances, however, its cumulative effect on creative markets may be very hard to check or to counter (particularly given the dearth of antitrust actions that have characterized responses to Big Tech to date). Major, possibly risky, new efforts may be called for, which may involve vertically integrating to create more powerful and market-dominant players; calls for increased regulation; or new, outside-the-box strategies and solutions. **Chapter 12: What to Do When Tailoring Doesn't Suffice: Countervailing Strategies** explores some promising endeavors that have recently been launched, as much to give creative industries encouragement that action can be taken as to suggest what that action might be.

The initial question of this book may seem straightforward, and is encapsulated by the latter part of its title: how can creative industries harness IP to survive, and even thrive, in the digital age? But answering that question reveals a critical paradox at the heart of copyright. Why, after all, does protecting copyright in the creative industries matter? Is it solely to secure creators' livelihoods and ensure creative industries' viability? The answer lies in a concern that is equal to creativity in its importance and merit: copyright's paradox is that protecting the property rights of creators serves to both protect and strengthen democracy.

Chapter 13: Why This Matters: Copyright, Democracy, and Art sets out the argument that copyright is essential to democracy because it secures serious artistic expression and underwrites artistic professionalism at all levels of creative production. When artists have rights in their work, they can make a living from selling those works in the market, rather than having to seek a patron, as in former eras, or by relying on government subsidies, as in other regimes. By distributing the cost of paying for copyrighted materials over many consumers, creative works remain relatively accessible to a great many audiences, users, and future creators.

This runs counter to the intuition that making works free and freely accessible to all is good for democracy because it maximizes access. The problem with that position is that creative works of a certain level of quality, seriousness, and aesthetic merit will not get made if an original creator does not know she can get paid for the risk she is being asked to take. Some creative work will still get made: amateurs, people who have primary means of income or support systems, and superstar artists who can make money from a number of sources, may well still produce creative work. But professional artists of modest means will not be able to continue to make art without the promise of making even a subsistence-level living from their work. What these mid-tier artists produce is important, however, and enriches culture in immeasurable but important dimensions. Eventually, their artistic works will enter the public domain, constituting part of the cultural heritage that seeds future artists and artistic aspirants. The richness of the public domain depends on having a broad base of creative output, and that too is compromised when artists are deprived of the fruits of their labor by inattentiveness to—or worse, denial of—copyright's critical work.

1 What Is the Problem

Copyright and Creativity in Crisis

The creative industries are in crisis. Multiple factors have contributed to disrupt their business practices on such a scale that they are now facing unprecedented struggles to survive. Any one of these industries—music, entertainment, publishing, journalism, and fashion, to name but a few—has faced turmoil in its history, and most have experienced cycles of growth, disruption, uncertainty, and eventual recovery; but it is hard to point to a time when *all* of them have struggled at once, and with such broad economic swings and reversals. It remains to be seen whether the change is irreversible—but what is clear is that it urgently requires reform.

Addressing the current state of affairs requires understanding how the creative industries arrived here. The crisis that faces us is long in the making, and tracing out the path that brought us to this juncture would require a book of its own. But the roots of copyright law and the economic realities of creative industries are well-established and enduring foundations on which that path is laid. Exploring their basic principles, and tracing their development to the new digital age, is a fitting place from which to start and launch the inquiry: how can creative industries survive the digital age?

1.1 The Germination of Copyright

Creativity has always been an expression and a sign of human flourishing. In music, art, and storytelling, expression began with communal traditions that were only occasionally preserved in recorded form: a handful of scribes laboriously transcribed musical plainsong, some artists made devotional paintings and sculptures that adorned places of worship, and storytellers learned oral narratives that they recounted to live audiences. Eventually, works began to be recorded, and recordings started to become valuable. The introduction of the Gutenberg Press made books available for readership and circulation on a previously unimagined scale. The development of the recording disc, the innovation of the phonograph, the progress to magnetic tape recording, and all the iterations that followed made sound recordings available to listening audiences first in public venues and music halls and then at home. As these recordations of creative works gained wide circulation, they became increasingly sophisticated, their fidelity to the original work improved, and they grew increasingly popular with enthusiasts and ever-larger audiences.

The advent of copyright law grew from these bursts of creativity—not just in creation, but also in the production, refinement, and delivery of creative works. It is vital to bear in mind that copyright was born of the impetus to make creative works but also to make them available to others. Naturally, one part of that drive to create access was commercially motivated: creators and producers wanted to get paid for their work and to ensure that in the future they would be compensated if that work proved valuable in their creative market. But another part of that drive to create access was shared, if not perhaps universally recognized: to add to the cultural heritage shared by society, and to inspire, feed, and give future artists the materials and resources that would help them in turn add to culture's creative capital and its bounty.

Doubtless competitive interests drove copyright law as well. The history of copyright in U.S. book publishing makes this eminently clear. The advent of copyright law in the U.S. was hastened by the contentious relationships between British publishers, American upstarts, and brash entrepreneurs who sought to engage in a kind of literary arbitrage by buying works in England and selling them at a discount in the U.S. Even the first instance of U.S. copyright law was written to protect American publishers' rights and returns. But under the influence of Noah Webster, American authors and publishers came to learn the value of copyright, and to understand that it could pay dividends that compensated for the initial risks taken to bring a book to market.[1] The early contentiousness over copyright in book publishing led to the creation of agreed-upon federal copyright law. But it also serves as a reminder that battles over the control of creative works have deep and lasting roots in commerce that resonate to the present day.

1.2 The Economic Justifications for Copyright: The Appropriability Problem; The Production, Structural, and Expressive Functions of Copyright

Early tussles over the rights to bring creative works to market and to reap their value laid the groundwork for the development of copyright. Many scholars have sought to justify the grant of copyright on various philosophical grounds.[2] One proposition is imported from John Locke's views on real property, and holds that property rights are natural rights earned as the rightful fruits of one's labor and investment in tending to, developing, and stewarding

1 See James N. Green, The Rise of Book Publishing in America 1782–1830, Library Company of Philadelphia, available at http://www-management.wharton.upenn.edu/raff/documents/Green_2.pdf.

2 See generally William Fisher, Theories of Intellectual Property, in *New Essays in the Legal and Political Theory of Property* 168, 170–3, 184–94 (Stephen R. Munzer ed., Cambridge University Press, 2001).

one's property.[3] That natural rights view has been the subject of much dispute with respect to both real property and intellectual property, but it still has a powerful appeal to those who believe that originality takes great investment on the part of creators, and that their investment deserves to be rewarded accordingly.

The philosophical underpinnings of copyright law are too vast and disputatious to canvass here. But there is compelling ground to justify the grant of copyright on economic grounds alone. The economic justification of copyright gives a cogent framework for understanding why copyright arises and how it effectively functions. A fundamental principle underlying copyright in creative works is solving the appropriability problem of public goods. Creative works are generally agreed to fall into the category of "pure public goods."[4] Public goods have two key characteristics. First, public goods are *nonexcludable*, in that producers cannot provide their benefits to one consumer without simultaneously providing those benefits to other consumers. Second, pure public goods are *nonrival*, in that the consumption of goods by one consumer does not reduce the supply available for consumption by others.[5] Nonrivalry is predicated on the assumption that the marginal cost of making an additional copy of a copyrightable work is zero.[6] Together, these assumptions imply that creative markets will provide insufficient incentives to produce copyrightable works and will provide insufficient access to those works that are produced.

3 See John Locke, *Second Treatise of Government* (1690), available at www.gutenberg.org/ebooks/7370.

4 For the seminal statement tying intellectual property to the theory of pure public goods, see Kenneth J. Arrow, Economic Welfare and the Allocation of Resources for Invention, in *The Rate and Direction of Inventive Activity: Economic and Social Factors* 609, 614–16 (Nat'l Bureau of Econ. Research, ed., 1962). In the copyright literature, see Stephen Breyer, The Uneasy Case for Copyright: A Study of Copyright in Books, Photocopies, and Computer Programs, 84 *Harv. L. Rev.* 281 (1970); William W. Fisher III, Reconstructing the Fair Use Doctrine, 101 *Harv. L. Rev.* 1659, 1700–5 (1988); Wendy J. Gordon, Fair Use as Market Failure: A Structural and Economic Analysis of the Betamax Case and Its Predecessors, 82 *Colum. L. Rev.* 1600, 1610–11 (1982); William M. Landes & Richard A. Posner, An Economic Analysis of Copyright Law, 18 *J. Legal Stud.* 325, 326 (1989); Mark A. Lemley, The Economics of Improvement in Intellectual Property Law, 75 *Tex. L. Rev.* 989, 994–9 (1997). For overviews of the economics of public goods, see Richard Cornes & Todd Sandler, *The Theory of Externalities, Public Goods, and Club Goods* 143–239 (2nd ed., 1996); William H. Oakland, Theory of Public Goods, in *2 Handbook of Public Economics* 485, 486–99, 502–22 (Alan J. Auerbach & Martin Feldstein eds., 1987).

5 See R.A. Musgrave, Provision for Social Goods, in *Public Economics: An Analysis of Public Production and Consumption and Their Relations to the Private Sectors* 124, 126–9 (Julius Margolis & Henri Guitton eds., 1969).

6 See Yochai Benkler, An Unhurried View of Private Ordering in Information Transactions, 53 *Vand. L. Rev.* 2063, 2066, 2070, 2078 (2000); James Boyle, Cruel, Mean, or Lavish? Economic Analysis, Price Discrimination and Digital Intellectual Property, 53 *Vand. L. Rev.* 2007, 2013 (2000); Timothy J. Brennan, Copyright, Property, and the Right To Deny, 68 *Chi.-Kent L. Rev.* 675, 698 (1993); Mark A. Lemley, Property, Intellectual Property, and Free Riding, 83 *Tex. L. Rev.* 1031, 1053–4 (2005); Neil Weinstock Netanel, Copyright and a Democratic Civil Society, 106 *Yale L.J.* 283, 292 (1996).

They also imply that any attempt to alleviate the problems of underproduction will exacerbate the problems of underutilization.[7]

In the digital world, creative goods approach the classic characterization of pure public goods: one person's consumption does not diminish their availability to others, and they can be perfectly reproduced at essentially zero marginal costs.[8] Thomas Jefferson expressed the essence of this concept more poetically:

> If nature has made any one thing less susceptible than all others of exclusive property, it is the action of the thinking power called an idea, which an individual may exclusively possess as long as he keeps it to himself; but the moment it is divulged, it forces itself into the possession of every one, and the receiver cannot dispossess himself of it. Its peculiar character, too, is that no one possesses the less, because every other possesses the whole of it. He who receives an idea from me, receives instruction himself without lessening mine; as he who lights his taper at mine, receives light without darkening me.[9]

The nonrivalrous and nonexcludable nature of creative goods makes the problem of appropriability central to creative industries, and only more pressing in the digital age. The main concern that public goods present is the degree to which industry participants can recover up-front investments in creative works. Following the traditional economic analysis of appropriability,[10] the public good nature of creative works means that they may not clearly indicate that investing in their creation and production will lead to adequate returns on investment. Thus, industry participants will lack adequate incentives to invest in their production.

The grant of intellectual property (IP) rights in creative work, of which copyright is a part, neatly solves this appropriability problem. Under the U.S. Constitution, Congress is empowered to grant authors and inventors an exclusive right to their writings and discoveries.[11] While expressly limited by time, the grant of rights by Congress can be expansive, as long as it serves

7 Christopher S. Yoo, Copyright and Public Good Economics: A Misunderstood Relation, 155 *University of Pennsylvania Law Review* (2007), available at https://ssrn.com/abstract=948229.

8 Lee Davis, Is Appropriability a "Problem" for Digital Information Goods? (2001), available at https://openarchive.cbs.dk/bitstream/handle/10398/6819/wplefic012002.pdf?sequence=1.

9 Thomas Jefferson, Letter to Isaac McPherson, Aug. 13, 1813, available at http://press-pubs.uchicago.edu/founders/documents/a1_8_8s12.html.

10 Kenneth J. Arrow Economic Welfare and the Allocation of Resources for Invention, in *The Rate and Direction of Inventive Activity: Economic and Social Factors* 609, 614–16 (Nat'l Bureau of Econ. Research, ed., 1962).

11 U.S. Const. Art. 1, Section 8, clause 8, available at https://fairuse.stanford.edu/law/us-constitution/.

"to promote progress in science and the useful arts."[12] The grant of IP rights offers creators and innovators a palpable incentive for undertaking risks and bearing costs, assuring them that they will receive a "bundle of rights" in exchange for their productive efforts and output. The holder of a copyright is entitled to exploit, or monetize, her rights in her work, rewarding the venture she has undertaken and ensuring that she will be encouraged to venture again, secure in the knowledge that she can continue to benefit from copyright ownership if the work is deemed valuable in the creative market.

Copyright is designed to be both a tradeoff and a balancing act. The tradeoff exists because creating original works tends to be a costly and risky undertaking. When professional creators and creative industries consider the task ahead of them, they require assurance that if they create a valuable work their risks will be rewarded and their costs compensated. In order to face the prospect of earning a living through creative work, they also look for incentives in the prospect of positive returns—royalties from sales, licensing fees, positive asset valuation—which both support their efforts and affirm their projects' commercial worth. Under the U.S. Copyright Act, creators have a broad range of compensable rights over their original works, including: the right to reproduce the work; to distribute copies of the work; to publicly perform the work; to publicly display the work; and in the case of sound recordings, to perform the work publicly by means of a digital audio transmission.[13]

The rights granted by IP are limited, however, in nature, scope, and time length. In copyright law, only some works are copyrightable: works that are "fixed in a tangible medium of expression," are eligible, making it relatively easy to secure copyright in books, movies, and music scores, while less easy (although not necessarily impossible) in comedy routines. Moreover, important exclusions protect some works: for instance, the fair use doctrine offers parodies a defense to copyright infringement. The scope of a work can also be limited, so that while cookbooks that describe how to make delicious recipes are protectable, the recipes themselves are not. The time that copyright lasts is limited, as intended by the Founders; and while it seems to some critics overly susceptible to being extended, it cannot be made to last forever.[14]

The limitations on copyright are part of its balancing act: optimally, copyright is meant to enable rightsholders to extract ample value from their creative output, but not to encroach upon non-propertizable work and not to exceed a reasonable span of time. Copyright's balancing act also weighs the importance of incentivizing creators against the equally compelling importance of ensuring access to consumers, users, and future creators. This is one

12 Id.

13 17 U.S. Code §106, available at www.law.cornell.edu/uscode/text/17/106. See also, available at www.dmlp.org/legal-guide/rights-granted-under-copyright.

14 And there are other constraints on the grant of copyright, such as contextual concerns: if the work was made by an employee in the scope of her employment, copyright may be granted to her employer. That is not a limitation on the grant itself, however, but rather on the ownership of copyright.

of the rationales for limiting the duration of copyright: when the time of copyright protection tolls, creative works are released to the public domain to ensure that their access is available both to those who wish to enjoy them and to those who will use them as the building blocks for future works or, as was famously said, for "seeing further by standing on the shoulders of giants."[15]

Giving creators adequate incentive to generate original creative work fulfills the production function of copyright. A second purpose has been called the structural function of copyright.[16] The grant of rights stems from a historic understanding that serious artistic work, undertaken over time, free from constraints (such as being dictated or suppressed), made either by an individual or collectively, is a costly, risky, and innately unpredictable endeavor. By promising artists that they will receive payment for their valuable works, copyright eliminates the need for earlier systems of support, such as wealthy patrons, government subsidies, familial backing, or random acts of kindness. Although some of those supports may still exist, such as university subsidization of academic research and scholarship, they tend to stand alongside copyright, rather than supplanting it. More importantly, copyright gives artists considerable independence from government influence or authority, and enables them to look to the creative markets for financial reward and sustenance.

Creative work has historically been best served when it is made free from the pressures of patronage, government oversight, or outside influence. The importance of creative freedom cannot be overstated. The Supreme Court underscored this understanding in the seminal case of *Harper & Row v. Nation Enterprises*, in which Justice O'Connor stated: "it should not be forgotten that the Framers intended copyright itself to be the engine of free expression. By establishing a marketable right to the use of one's expression, copyright supplies the economic incentive to create and disseminate ideas."[17] This has been called the expressive function of copyright: By sustaining creative authorship, copyright not only encourages the production of new and original contributions but also reinforces their value in the greater discourse.[18]

15 The expression "standing on the shoulders of giants" has a storied history. For some of its famous iterations, see Isaac Newton, *Letter from Isaac Newton to Robert Hooke* (Historical Society of Pennsylvania, Feb. 5, 1676), available at https://discover.hsp.org/Record/dc-9792/Description#tabnav; see also Robert K. Merton, The Normative Structure of Science, in *The Sociology of Science: Theoretical and Empirical Investigations* 267 (Norman W. Storer ed., 1973).

16 See Neil Weinstock Netanel, *Copyright's Paradox* (Oxford University Press, New York, 2008); see also Neil Weinstock Netanel, *Is Copyright the "Engine of Free Expression?"*, available at www.oxfordscholarship.com/view/10.1093/acprof:oso/9780195137620.001.0001/acprof-9780195137620-chapter-5.

17 *Harper & Row v. Nation Enterprises*, 471 U.S. 539, 558 (1985). See, available at www.law.cornell.edu/copyright/cases/471_US_539.htm.

18 This view is not without controversy, particularly when considered in light of the sometimes-thorny relationship between copyright and the First Amendment. See Neil Weinstock Netanel, Is Copyright "the Engine of Free Expression?" available at www.oxfordscholarship.com/view/10.1093/acprof:oso/9780195137620.001.0001/acprof-9780195137620-chapter-5.

1.3 The Varied Nature of IP Regimes: High-IP Regimes, Low-IP Regimes, and Hybrid IP-Regimes

When copyright does the heavy lifting required to clear the costs of creative production, it secures the viability of a creative industry that would otherwise be at risk of market failure.[19] Music rights, film and television rights, book publishing and journalism rights, are just a few high-IP regimes in which copyright makes creative production possible, scalable, and manageable even when very large, complicated and/or collaborative creative works are involved. It is impossible to imagine films being successfully produced without key licensing agreements for copyrighted input and output—not just materials used, such as music scores, but also materials produced, such as tie-in merchandise. In these high-IP regimes, copyright drives and operationalizes creative production.

But some creative industries seem surprisingly less reliant on copyright than others. Fashion, for instance, is often regarded as a low-IP regime, as it has historically had very little copyright available for limited works, such as some print design. The term "low-IP regime," also sometimes known as a "negative space," turns out to be somewhat deceptive in the context of fashion, however, as trademark plays a central role in securing rights in goods, protection of original work, and enforcement rights against potential infringements of protected works—for instance, fighting counterfeits is a major part of the battle waged by fashion against trademark infringers. As will later be explored, there are other features of fashion that support the vitality and productiveness of the industry. Copyright has more than once been proposed as an additional layer of protection to buttress the coverage that trademark offers.[20] To the present, though, copyright has not represented a critical support to the production and exploitation of original design.

There are also hybrid-IP regimes, in which copyright protects some creative work but is not imposed upon other kinds of creative output. In education, certain activities and areas of production, such as scientific research and discovery, and academic scholarship, are treated as important copyrightable, and in some cases patentable, work.[21] Other pedagogical activities and output, however, such as courses and course materials, have not historically been propertized, and only recently have come into consideration as potentially copyrightable work.

19 Wendy J. Gordon, Fair Use as Market Failure: A Structural and Economic Analysis of the *Betamax* Case and Its Predecessors, 82 *Colum. L. Rev.* 1600 (1982), available at https://open.bu.edu/handle/2144/22971.

20 See Innovative Design Protection and Piracy Prevention Act, S. 3728, 111th Cong. (2010). *See also* Susan Scafidi, F.I.T.: Fashion as Information Technology, 59 *Syracuse L. Rev.* 69 (2008).

21 This has been facilitated, and to some extent precipitated, by the Bayh-Dole Act of 1980. *See* Michael W. Carroll, One Size Does Not Fit All: A Framework for Tailoring Intellectual Property Rights, 70 *Ohio St. L.J.* 1361, 1412–13 (2009).

As will become apparent, the long-standing rationales for encouraging copyright in some work and minimizing copyright in other work are based on myriad factors, including institutional choices, value judgments between kinds of creative work, and social and behavioral norms, all of which may be subject to reappraisal and change. Regardless, it is necessary to recognize that hybrid-IP regimes can function effectively and profitably, leaving room for nonpropertized resources and materials, while still ensuring that valuable creative work is protected, rewarded, and fostered.

1.4 Creators *versus* Creative Intermediaries

Creators and creative industries have historically been interdependent, at least since the era of artistic patronage has disappeared, and state sponsorship of the arts has been greatly diminished. Creators allow creative industries control over commercial aspects of their works in order to focus on artistry and craft. Creative industries rely on creators for their "content" (a term that is used broadly here to comprise creative output) and typically take ownership of copyright in artists' creative works in order to manage the risks and oversee the payments flowing from the monetization of creative work. While some advocates of artistic independence have argued that the Internet is making the role of creative intermediaries obsolete, many artists still recognize the value of handing off commercial responsibilities to outside entities that are skilled in marketing, producing, distributing, and other activities that are necessary to making an income from art but that can take precious time and resources from the actual work involved in making art.

Copyright binds creators and the industries that bring their works to market by establishing mechanisms for the production and dissemination of works at scale and for profit. If artists are to be professionally successful—that is, if they seek to make a living from their work—they need rights in their work that they can enforce and exploit for pecuniary gain. Entire industries have been built around the role of middlemen who manage artistic production to ensure that creative copyright maximizes such returns.

Creative industries are structured upon the idea that artists will outsource the management of rights and revenues and cede a percentage of profits to creative intermediaries, which can include managers, agents, promoters, and other middlemen. In the best of circumstances, these intermediaries serve as facilitators throughout the creative and productive process, from finding and nurturing talent to bringing creative works to fruition and then to commercial markets. This is not to say that the relationship is always perfect: the history of the arts is sadly littered with instances of exploitation of artists, the unfair allocation of royalties and other revenues, and tensions over the division of labor and profits between artists and industry figures. But generally, the survival of creators, the input of middlemen, and the health of the creative industries in which they operate is a mutually dependent proposition.

At the same time, however, the rights and interests of creators and other participants in the creative industries are not always aligned. For instance, when intermediaries such as publishing houses, music labels, and film studios are rightsholders, their interest in maximizing copyright revenues ought to benefit the artists they represent—at least to the extent that greater total revenues should result in increased royalties paid out per creative work. As intermediaries seek changes in policies that result in increases in copyright revenues, it should logically follow that they are serving the interests of the artists they represent. But there are changes in policies that might result in increases in copyright revenues to artists, but not to intermediaries. At that point, intermediaries may not have adequate incentives to seek changes to the system, even if it means that the artists they represent would be benefited.

Further, some changes may benefit artists to the detriment of intermediaries—whether by cutting them out of the payment stream (for instance, by direct payment to the artists that obviates the use or need for intermediaries) or by promising a larger cut of royalties to artists without an increase to the revenues of the intermediaries. In these cases, artists and intermediaries may find themselves adversaries in the division of total revenues, rather than allies in the fight against diminution of the revenue pool as a whole.

Illustrative is the divide facing the book publishing world. Traditional publishing houses have been forced by market realities to accept Amazon as an important, if not dominant, distributor of their published works. It is hard to forego distributing books through Amazon, as they are the largest marketplace for book selling, and owner of a significant secondary market via their subsidiary, AbeBooks. They are also aware that Amazon allows authors to self-publish on its site, and further incentivizes authors by offering a significant share of royalties—greater, on average, than royalties garnered through traditional publishing houses.

The lure of self-publishing, coupled with the promise of royalty-sharing, makes Amazon a formidable adversary to book publishers. Yet Amazon's competitive presence in the book distribution market creates a dilemma for book publishers that is not readily resolvable. It can pit writers against traditional book publishers, or at least undermine writers' incentives to take the traditional path to publishing their works.

There has been much conflict in how publishing houses approach the question of which policies should be set if Amazon is to be regulated. This is one case in which the interests of publishers and authors may run in tandem in some respects and in tension in others. It is further exacerbated by a marked decline in authors' incomes, which has led many authors and their representatives to speak out against Amazon for "devaluing content," undermining profits for the sake of distribution, and reducing the profits that publishers make and the royalties that they pass on to their authors.[22]

22 See, Alison Flood, Crashing Author Returns 'Threaten Future of American Literature,' *The Guardian*, Jan. 2, 2019, available at www.theguardian.com/books/2019/jan/08/crashing-author-earnings-threaten-future-of-american-literature.

The tensions that are arising between Amazon and the book world are only one example of those that divide creative industries internally. But the divide between creators and creative industries is one of the most important divisions, and one of the hardest to breach. Nonetheless, in the battle to preserve content value, major stakeholders in the creative industries—foremost of whom are creators and creative intermediaries—remain allied. And it is to their interest that this book speaks.

This book cannot address every instance in which the rights and revenues of creators and intermediaries are aligned, divergent, or opposed. What it offers instead is an in-depth examination of creative ecosystems in which creators and creative industries are both challenged by outside forces—commercial, technological, social, and so on—that challenge their viability and their potential for universal creative enrichment. Creators, middlemen, and creative industries have enough grounds in common for tackling these challenges communally, cohesively, and systemically, with a view to ensuring that creative professionalism can be rewarded and creativity, whether undertaken by professionals or amateurs, can be sustained.

2 What Is Causing the Problem
Disruptive Innovation

2.1 How Disruptive Innovation Works

The Internet is one of the clearest examples of disruptive innovation in modern times. It is impossible to measure the impact it has had on almost every aspect of all of our lives. It is also hard to overstate the technological advancement it represents. But the term "disruptive innovation" actually means something more specific, and more relevant to our purposes, than simply "life-altering" or "new technology." It describes the effect on *business models* that technology-driven innovation can have. That effect drives changes in entire *markets* and *value networks.* To understand the disruptive force of the Internet on creative markets, it is necessary to understand just how disruptive innovation works.

Disruptive innovation is a term ascribed to Clayton Christensen[1], who described how a new technology, and its changing application, could arise within an existing industry and radically shift its core business model and value proposition.[2] Christensen's contribution to the idea of disruptive technological

1 J.L. Bower & C.M. Christensen, Disruptive Technologies: Catching the Wave, 73 *Harvard Business Review* 1 (Jan.–Feb. 1995). The idea of disruptive technologies as drivers of economic change predates Christensen: much earlier, Joseph Schumpeter adapted the idea of creative destruction from Karl Marx. Id.

2 Christensen's theory addresses how small-but-nimble firms can integrate current technology with newer innovation to create competitive advantages in their sector. The resulting products and services may not immediately appeal to existing customers, but they are designed to attract new sets of customers and to expand the firm's market base. While established firms may be aware of these innovations, they may not pursue them when they initially arise, either because they are not immediately profitable or because their development can draw on resources needed for sustaining innovations that keep them competitive in the current marketplace. Christensen posits that a firm's existing value networks insufficiently value the disruptive innovation, preventing the firm from pursuing it when it emerges. But startup firms embrace a different value network, and are able to take advantage of disruptive innovation to challenge the traditional value networks of established firms. If the disruption is successful, it places established firms at a great disadvantage. At that point, established firms in the network can at best only defend their market share with a second-to-post effort, which may allow them to survive, but not to thrive, in the newly disrupted environment.

change was observing that it changed not just firms or products but entire markets. His basic example was the automobile: early automobiles were revolutionary but not disruptive technological innovations. When first introduced, they were luxury goods that did not disrupt the market for horse-drawn vehicles. The market for transportation remained essentially intact until Henry Ford introduced the Ford Model T in 1908.[3] Ford designed the Model T to be a lower-priced, mass-produced, and mass-marketed automobile, well within the reach of ordinary consumers who flocked to purchase them. This, as we know, transformed not just the nature of transportation but the entire transportation market. In other words, it was not the innovation alone—not just the automobile—but rather the application of the innovation—the mass-produced automobile—that was the disruptive innovation.

The digital age is certainly rife with disruption, and many of its greatest technological advancements could be called contenders for the disruptor role. That is not, however, always the case. A mobile device such as an iPhone (or its competitors) seems plausible: it allows consumers unprecedented access to enormous amounts of personal data, entertainment, access to the Internet, and a range of resources that seemed inconceivable not that long ago. It is arguable that the iPhone has disrupted specific markets: some have argued that despite the earlier emergence of the digital camera, it was the iPhone that disrupted the world of personal photography, and that its built-in camera has affected markets in a broad range of photographic goods (cameras, film) and services (film development, professional photography, even photojournalism).

It is not clear, however, that the iPhone has drawn away consumers from the photography industry; nor that it has reached a new pool of previously unserved, or underserved, consumers. It may well have turned casual Polaroid users into iPhone users; it may have eroded in-store film developing and encouraged users to print their photos at home; and it may have turned avid amateur photojournalists into competition for professional photojournalists. But these are examples of existing photographers and enthusiasts who may move from one technological device to another, or who may choose to have multiple devices for various purposes. Some of them have also not been moved: many serious photographers still remain committed to traditional single-lens reflex (SLR) cameras or digital single-lens reflex (DSLR) cameras.

The iPhone may have been a driving force in the decline of the sale of traditional cameras to amateur photographers or the casual user who is relatively unconcerned with the quality of prints. But many professional photographers and high-end camera makers argue that the market for serious cameras will not shift to the iPhone. Rather, they argue that new innovations in the camera market, including the development of the mirrorless camera, sensor tech, and

3 See, Henry Ford: Model T Collection, The Henry Ford, available at www.thehenryford.org/collections-and-research/digital-collections/sets/7145.

AI-capable devices, will continue to keep avid users and professionals in the market for ever-improving versions of the traditional camera.[4]

The parallel development of the iPhone and its competitors in the camera market is an emerging story. It may be that at some point iPhone camera technology develops to a level of sophistication, cost effectiveness, and ease of use that the iPhone renders traditional cameras wholly obsolete. But at this point, the existence of the two markets existing side-by-side argues against the idea of the iPhone as a paradigm of Christensen's theory of disruptive innovation: with respect to photography, iPhones may have marked effects on the market, but they do not yet fundamentally transform it.

The Internet, on the other hand, is a textbook example of disruptive innovation. It did not begin as one: it was first conceived as a scalable means of communication and access to information goods and resources. It was only when the technology was expanded to reach personal computers, and designed to be accessible to ordinary users and consumers, that the Internet began to have a disruptive capacity. But when that occurred, it began to transform markets at rapid pace, and to transform them across the board.

The swift pace of change that characterizes the digital landscape is not due to the Internet alone. Innovations in related technologies, including the development of broadband and cable, and related growth in other sectors of telecommunications, contributed as well. The build-out of infrastructure was essential to deliver the Internet to users worldwide, and facilitated the movement of data, information, resources, and goods and services in every imaginable area of activity and commerce. But these technological advances are most disruptive in the sense that they enable networks like the Internet to grow and scale. It is the Internet that operates to disrupt and resettle creative ecosystems.

The Internet creates new market venues through e-commerce, and only digital connectivity is required to bring universal access to physically remote vendors and consumers.[5] Some of those markets may be similar to established ones. For instance, eBay is modeled on standard auction sites and practices. Amazon follows many aspects of the business model of traditional brick-and-mortar stores, only larger by many orders of magnitude. Business-to-business (B2B) and business-to-consumer (B2C) transactions have always existed. But the Internet scales existing markets, creates new market capacities, and

4 See Steve Huff, The Future of Cameras, Gear and Photography. The Mirror Is Dying, Steve Huff Photo, June 7, 2018, available at www.stevehuffphoto.com/2018/06/07/the-future-of-cameras-gear-and-photography-the-mirror-is-dying/; Nasim Mansurov, The Future of Digital Cameras, Photography Life, 2012, available at https://photographylife.com/future-digital-cameras.

5 Granted, not everyone has digital connectivity. But the rate of adoption is still rising, and already represents significant penetration: over 4 billion people, or more than half the world's population, uses the Internet. See Simon Kemp, Digital in 2018: World's Internet Users Pass the 4 Billion Mark, We Are Social, Jan. 30, 2018, available at https://wearesocial.com/blog/2018/01/global-digital-report-2018.

facilitates new entrants to an extraordinary degree. It transforms the pace, the scope, and the nature of competition.

At some point, scale really does matter: it brings together participants across markets that were previously isolated or stand alone. Scale allows for efficiencies that aren't possible when ventures remain smaller and more constrained in marketing and distribution reach. Scale also enables network effects that are self-perpetuating: social media sites such as Facebook work better when they attract and retain more users. Similarly, electronic marketplaces such as Facebook Marketplace, Craigslist and eBay function optimally when they garner more traffic. And the scale of Internet markets is so large that it is not comparable to its predecessors. Whether these markets are structured vertically like a "cathedral," or horizontally like a "bazaar," the Internet creates a landscape of its own.[6]

2.2 How Disruptive Innovation Impacts Rights in Digital Creative Works

The disruptive innovation of the Internet has some of its greatest impact in the creative sectors. Due to its vast reach, the digital world enlarges the demand for creative content by making creative works immediately available to anyone with connectivity. The other side of the coin is that it increases the demand on creative producers to make more works and to disseminate them more widely and rapidly. Further, it multiplies the ways in which creative works can be both consumed and disseminated. Creative consumers are no longer tethered to fixed physical spaces or devices—they are no longer tied to theaters, television sets, libraries, or cinemas. They can carry entire libraries of works in their pockets. Indeed, they expect to be able to have their preferred works at their fingertips, and at all times. Taken together, these features mean that content producers are not facing shrinking markets in terms of demand. Quite the opposite: they can develop products at full capacity knowing that at least the potential for enormous audiences is ready and waiting. Whether or not they are able to make sales to those audiences profitable may be an open question, but the potential is there.

But while the ubiquity that the Internet promises is an expansion of goods available, it is not an expansion of *rights* in those goods. Far from it: from the outset, digital works have been differently treated from physical ones, both legally and contractually; and producers have worked to ensure that the rights they grant in digital works meet their specifications. Rights in creative works were traditionally treated as rights stemming from the ownership of physical goods, known generally as personal property: books, CDs, the newspaper, and so on. This meant an owner of a creative work embodied in a piece of

6 Eric S. Raymond, *The Cathedral and the Bazaar: Musings on Linux and Open Source by an Accidental Revolutionary* (O'Reilly Media, Inc., Sebastopol, CA, 1999).

personal property could do many of the same things with their work as the owner of, say, a piece of land: hold it, share it, or alienate it. Those rights in tangible creative works still exist. If you own a book, for example, you can lend it, photocopy it for your own purposes and use it, sell it (although under the first sale doctrine your rights in that copy of the book are then "exhausted," meaning you can sell it once, but you cannot copy it and sell the copies[7]), keep it forever, or give it away.

Those rights change when digital works are involved. If you "purchase" an e-book, you are unlikely to be able to copy it more than a few times and then only for reading on your own devices; you may not sell it; and you might be surprised to find that your vendor can delete it without your knowledge or permission.[8] Other rights may be limited too: you may be able to borrow it from a circulating library, but if rights in an e-book are still contested, as is sometimes the case, you may not be able to borrow it until the library obtains permission. In other words, the "purchase" may be more limited than the purchase of a physical product: you have obtained the e-book not by an outright sale but under license, and the license governs what you can do with the e-book and, more to the point, what you cannot do. The bundle of rights is different, and just by downloading the e-book you have consented to those changes.

Another major change lies in the ways in which works are disseminated, and the ways in which they are consumed via the Internet, moving away from the traditional model of ownership of physical works and toward the digital distribution of streamed content. Digital streaming services design their interfaces primarily to allow users to consume content but not necessarily to download content or to otherwise make it a permanent part of their collected works. This is another movement away from constructing creative works as personal property. It is also another movement away from treating rights in creative works as rights in personal property. Streamed content is distributed under licenses that circumscribe access to creative works via bundles of rights that are defined by licensors alone. Some of those rights may be contractually defined to be more limited than rights in physically embodied works, as determined and governed by the license.[9]

Unlike the case of digital works that can be retained by consumers, streamed content is not designed to be permanent or to be owned. Licenses in streamed content occur at several levels. First they are made between content owners and content distributors: record labels owning copyright in musical works will license their content to online radio and consumers will be the beneficiaries of the contract. Then consumers who want to listen to the musical works will

7 17 U.S.C. §109. See also, available at www.justice.gov/jm/criminal-resource-manual-1854-copyright-infringement-first-sale-doctrine.

8 Aaron Perzanowski & Jason Schultz, *The End of Ownership: Personal Property in the Digital Economy* (MIT Press, Cambridge, MA, 2016).

9 Id.

join streaming services under the terms of the contract to which they consent upon joining. The streaming services set the terms of licensing in every aspect of participation and listenership. Those rights might involve the ability to listen to a certain number of works per month, under a subscription agreement, or the ability to assemble works in a personal playlist that can be stored and retrieved via the streaming service. But they are not likely to involve anything resembling the rights of ownership in traditional works that were historically taken as a given.[10]

For many consumers, this is perfectly fine. People have been listening to the radio, watching television, and otherwise consuming some content without needing to own it. But historically, traditional media and entertainment audiences have also not wanted to do anything with the content they consume. The Internet enables, and even promotes, interactivity with content. Users can make YouTube videos and GarageBand musical works in their home, and by uploading their works to the Internet make them available to millions of users. They can write fan fiction; and they can self-publish fiction and nonfiction. This has resulted in an extraordinary proliferation of user-generated content (UGC). Users can also avail themselves of newly emerging 3-D printing to make all manner of physical works, including remarkably faithful copies of artworks and literary works, which they can then repurpose as they choose. Firms can also avail themselves of the same technology; and they can go further in creating databases, libraries, and catalogues of creative works. They can disseminate creative works by outright sales, or they can license and stream creative works. All of these activities are not entirely new, but they are rapidly growing in sophistication and reach.

From the perspective of consumers, the Internet seems to promise access to huge troves of free and engaging content. It also seems to promise to make content available at all times, under any circumstances, and without constraint. Some consumers believe that the availability of content implicitly comprises a "right" to download creative works and to have those works permanently stored in a personal repository. These promises are false, as copyrighted creative works are indeed governed and curtailed by the laws that govern copyright. Whether they exist in the digital space or in physical space, the rules of copyright are not suspended. But paradoxically digital licensing of works can go further in constraining the rights of users than the sale of physical works. Digital licensing may not spell out its restrictions, but it is far from an unrestrained grant to consumers of free access and free use.

There is an inherent paradox of the Internet, which is that digitally licensed works appear to the casual consumer to be more freely available and accessible, but the rights underlying those works are often more strictly limited than those held in personal property. The disparity is not at all clearly conveyed or

10 See John Herrman, You Don't Own Anything Anymore, *Buzzfeed News*, April 25, 2012, available at www.buzzfeednews.com/article/jwherrman/you-dont-own-anything-anymore.

understood, which means that most consumers do not recognize the move toward purely licensed content. Nor do they consider its consequences. This can be problematic, as when consumers find they want to do more with creative content than simply have access to it on a one-time basis. The march toward universal licensing may also mean that consumers forfeit even a modicum of bargaining power over the future use of content online. The current pace of change suggests that consumers are not particularly concerned with the curtailment of their rights. As in the case of privacy, however, they may eventually awaken to those concerns, only to find that once rights have been ceded, they are extremely hard to regulate and restore.

Privileging licensed rights in digital works is inevitable, and increasingly prevalent. The commercial and cultural shift away from ownership is clear, and creative industries are jumping on the bandwagon. But moving away from ownership can have hidden costs, not just in rights but also in pricing, autonomy over works, access, and privacy. Ownership comes at a fixed cost: buying a book is a one-time transaction at a fixed and known price. The resale of the physical object of the book is possible, but the resale of its contents (if it were to be photocopied or otherwise reproduced) is not permissible under the first sale doctrine. While there are secondary markets in book sales, such as used bookstores, the terms of resale are clearly defined and widely recognized and accepted.

Licensing of creative work, particularly in the digital world, is generally less transparent and clear-cut. The terms of digital licenses are set by licensors who own and control the works and who distribute or provide them to consumers. Those terms include pricing, the length of time that the work is held (even if the work is purportedly owned, a digital distributor can have the right to remove the work from a device, as users famously discovered in an early dispute with the Kindle device[11]), the number of times the user can access the work, and so on. Terms can vary, and can be adjusted at the provider's discretion. Providers can engage in price discrimination by setting prices for any given group of users, and can vary prices at will based on features that consumers have no control over, such as fluctuations in demand (such as when a work launches and is in popular demand), changes in content ownership or control, or public controversy or protest. Consumers are liable to find that they are unable to determine what price they will be charged for the content they desire. Such a lack of predictability, and variations in pricing, may be suboptimal for consumers of creative content, and as knowledge of these variations becomes more widespread, may lead to consumer dissatisfaction or behavior that seeks ways to avoid, take advantage of, or otherwise engage in arbitrage in creative works.

11 See Bobbie Johnson, Amazon Kindle Users Surprised by 'Big Brother' Move, *The Guardian*, July 17, 2009, available at www.theguardian.com/technology/2009/jul/17/amazon-kindle-1984; Jared Newman, Amazon Kindles Settles '1984' Lawsuit, PC World, Oct. 1, 2009, available at www.pcworld.com/article/172953/amazon_kindle_1984_lawsuit.html.

Providers can vary prices based on consumer data, and but they can also use the sale and delivery of creative content as a means of gathering further data from consumers. The Internet facilitates such data gathering, analytics, and decision-making, and the results are applicable to both fixed and variable pricing decisions. This may compel consumers to decide how much they are willing to pay for content—not just once, but many times over. It can also limit consumers' ability to choose whether or not to pay for content—as in the case of students assigned required material for a course, or journalists who must have access to news in order to do their own journalism.

When pricing is wholly variable, fluctuating, and controlled by producers and distributors, and when consumers may not have the choice to "vote with their dollars" and opt out of payment, the rights that attach to licensed works start to look more curtailed, and less satisfactory, than the permanent rights that attach to ownership of property. In a world that offers both property and licensed works, this may not be a problem. But if physical property is eliminated altogether, it may lead to real losses for consumers of creative content that cannot easily be recuperated or substituted with offsetting gains.

2.3 How Disruptive Innovation Transforms Markets and Business Models in Digital Creative Works

From the start, the Internet and its markets have grown and developed rapidly and to an extent organically, as companies coming online learn through trial and error to adapt their products to a new ecosystem. This requires flexibility in the face of new demands of digitization and newly expanded markets. Consumers too are compelled to learn the ways of e-commerce as online markets expand their scope and reach. Creative companies, whose works are constantly in demand, are forced to wrestle with how to generate, produce, and distribute works online. The biggest challenge for creative industries is not how to get products into the pipeline but instead how to monetize them: how to sell digital products—whether creative content, goods, services, or resources—and how to make those sales profitable.

Some of the challenges of monetizing creative content remain similar to those faced in brick-and-mortar stores, such as pricing, advertising, reaching targeted bases, branding, and building customer loyalty. But some challenges are complicated by features specific to the digital realm, such as how to make content widely available but also protected from easy appropriation, how to support content-rich sites with online advertising, whether to price discriminate among audiences in order to maximize rent extraction,[12] and how to convince online audiences that content is valuable and worth paying for.

12 See "Price Discrimination," *Economics Online*, available at www.economicsonline.co.uk/Business_economics/Price_discrimination.html.

These questions often have dimensions that are specific to the digital space. For instance, online advertising rates are generally lower than print advertising rates, although differences can vary by industry and advertising sector.[13] On the other hand, digital advertising, particularly on social media, can reach more viewers than print, and may result in higher returns on investment.[14] Digital advertising is growing rapidly, which would seem to be a boon to creative industries disseminating increasing amounts of content online. But the growth is increasingly concentrated in, and controlled by, two hugely dominant companies, Google and Facebook, which currently comprise more than 65% of the advertising market.[15] Being subject to duopoly control is a prospect that may trouble creative industries, and that can roil their markets to a considerable degree.

Creative industries strive to meet the challenges of monetizing digital space through iterative efforts: industry participants continue to try successive improvements to their practices, and hope to move closer to a business model that can remain profitable even as the environment changes and new incursions on their territories arise. Flexibility and the ability to recalibrate in the face of unexpected challenges, innovations, or new entrants and new competition, remain the hallmark of success in the disrupted digital landscape.

Creative industries are not the only entities struggling to remain profitable as they disseminate content online. But they continually face the need to prove to consumers that their goods and services are worth investing in and paying for. This challenge is unique, and it compounds their fraught enterprise. If digital space is to be monetized, creative industries will have to remain engaged in the search to find business models that satisfy consumers, maintain profitability, and compensate creators for their work.

2.4 How Disruptive Innovation Enables Piracy and Radically Undermines Markets in Creative Works

The advent of the Internet has realized two seemingly oppositional changes. On a favorable front, the marginal costs of production[16] of creative goods and resources have been radically lowered in many industries. For the most

13 See, e.g., "Traditional Media vs. Social Media Advertising," Lyfe Marketing, available at www.lyfemarketing.com/traditional-media-versus-social-media/.

14 See, e.g., Grant Cooper, Social Media vs. Traditional Media, Social Vantage, Oct. 2, 2017, available at www.socialvantage.com/social-media-vs-traditional-media/.

15 See Matthew Ingram, How Google and Facebook Have Taken Over the Digital Ad Industry, *Fortune*, Jan. 4, 2017, available at http://fortune.com/2017/01/04/google-facebook-ad-industry/.

16 Marginal cost is the additional cost incurred in the production of one more unit of a good or service. It is derived from the variable cost of production: given that fixed costs do not change as output changes, no additional fixed cost is incurred in producing another unit of a good or service once production has already started, see "Marginal Cost," *Economics Online*, available at www.economicsonline.co.uk/Definitions/Marginal_cost.html.

part, the costs of creating digital goods, such as music tracks, e-books, web 'zines, videos-on-demand, and video games are significantly lower than those required to generate their physical counterparts. Those costs are driven even lower when multiple copies of creative works are made. Further, the cost of distributing digital goods has been lowered equally quickly. Once the goods have been made, they can be disseminated digitally, whether through online sales or licensed streaming. Once distribution platforms are set up, the process can be virtually effortless, frictionless, and relatively inexpensive.

These lowered costs of production and reproduction can be a boon to creators and creative industries, enabling them to make more creative works available without having to factor in the usual expenses of raw materials, overhead, and other up-front outputs that add to the initial investment costs, and riskiness, of bringing creative works to market. In some cases, the lowered cost of production has led to lower pricing of goods—digital music tracks, for instance, are holding at historically low prices per song—enabling creative producers to charge consumers reasonable prices for creative content. In other words, digital delivery is almost infinitely scalable at almost no additional cost. The sale of reasonably priced digital goods has several positive features: content is accessible to a broad range of consumers; production costs can be distributed across a large consumer market; and content owners can realize adequate revenues through large volume sales rather than having to rely on low volume sales of highly priced goods, enabling them to make a greater and more diverse range of creative content.

But the decreased costs of digital production can prove a mixed blessing. The costs of reproducing and disseminating creative goods have indeed dropped precipitously—but this is equally applicable to the licit and illicit circulation of creative works, and to good and bad actors alike. Online piracy has grown exponentially as an outgrowth of the Internet, primarily because digitization of creative works makes them much easier to reproduce and disseminate on a large scale and at virtually no cost. The scope of online dissemination was initially evident in the development of "file sharing" platforms and services, which enabled ordinary digital users to participate—often enthusiastically—in the appropriation and dissemination of creative work.

The single most powerful disruptive force that the Internet enables is piracy: the wholesale appropriation of creative works. The appropriability problem that copyright is intended to solve is upended when online appropriation is made easy, low-cost, rapid, and frictionless. Moreover, using the Internet to copy and distribute works entirely bypasses copyright, which both undermines its incentive scheme and eviscerates its remuneration of creators, producers, and distributors of creative works.

Online appropriation, like many facets of the digital world, is readily scalable. Music sharing sites such as Napster and its progeny have repeatedly demonstrated the ease with which multitudes of users can both upload and download digital files, creating huge user bases and facilitating the exchange of creative outputs. Napster and some of its followers have been challenged, and it and many of its cohorts have been shut down, but imitators continue to proliferate online. Since the basic concept of file sharing was planted and took root, sites designed to circulate creative content and to circumvent copyright altogether have continued to operate with impunity and to evade authorities.[17] Not just music, but books, movies, television series, and many other creative works are collected and disseminated by file-sharing sites and services. The ubiquity of file sharing shows not only how easy it is to circumvent copyright in creative works via the Internet, but also how popular it is.

The Internet facilitates both legal and illegal uses of creative works, making it a double-edged sword: it offers the promise of new markets, but it also opens the threat of market failure.[18] Online music and entertainment providers bring content to a whole range of users who want to consume creative works on their laptops, mobile phones, or tablets. Streaming services add to the range of content availability, turning personal computers and handheld devices into virtual radios, but with the added feature of user-controlled playlists. These are all new markets in creative industries, and they give creative industries new spaces for reaching wide consumer bases.

At the same time, however, a seemingly endless array of illicit sites continues to emerge, offering content that has not been licensed or paid for, completely circumventing copyright protections. These sites create illicit markets in content that are analogous to black markets in physical goods, in which products are illicitly obtained and purveyed at cut-rate prices, typically without any compensation to the original maker of those goods. As in the case of black-market goods, there is often no quality control, and the consumer buys at his or her own risk. In the digital world, this may mean downloading content at the risk of being infected by a virus or having software corrupted.

Digital piracy may also leave consumers host to other digital woes, such as malware, phishing scams, and credit card fraud. Ultimately, it also leaves the consumer of illicit works open to copyright infringement lawsuits, as some users found to their shock and dismay when sued by the Recording Industry Association of America (RIAA) for illicitly using and sharing copyrighted musical works.[19] The threat of litigation also continues as illicit digital activity evolves, and new means of appropriating content emerge: for instance, a host of litigation is currently threatened against users of "conversion" sites that enable YouTube users to copy or "rip" digital music tracks from videos on YouTube, thereby circumventing copyright in the underlying music.[20]

17 See, Steven Caldwell Brown & Thomas J. Holt, eds., *Digital Piracy* (Routledge, Abington, Oxon 2018), available at www.routledge.com/Digital-Piracy-A-Global-Multidisciplinary-Account-1st-Edition/Brown-Holt/p/book/9781315158679.

18 See Wendy J. Gordon, Fair Use as Market Failure: A Structural and Economic Analysis of the *Betamax* Case and Its Predecessors, 82 *Colum. L. Rev.* 1600 (1982).

19 See Andrew C. Humes, The Day the Music Died: The RIAA Sues Its Consumers, 38 Ind. L. Rev. 239 (2005).

20 See, e.g., YouTube MP3 Converter Loses Court Battle But the Battle Plays On, Torrent Freak, Oct. 23, 2013, available at https://torrentfreak.com/youtube-mp3-converter-loses-court-battle-but-the-music-plays-on-131023/; Eve Peyser, YouTube to MP3 Converter

Users are often ambivalent about sites that offer illicit works for obvious reasons: on the one hand, their prices are temptingly low, but on the other hand, the risks that attach are perilously high. But creative artists and creative industries are almost universally opposed to illicit sites precisely because they undercut legitimate markets in creative works, driving down profits throughout creative industries and making it significantly harder for artists to get paid for their creative efforts and output.

Illicit markets in creative works drive down the price of those works to a point at which the costs invested in creating the work cannot be retrieved, leading to marginal losses that are fatal to creative industries' prospects. Equally, they are fatal to creators' livelihoods, as creators only get paid in royalties that are only collected when copyright is protected and exercised. Perhaps the most pernicious aspect of the problem is that many illicit sites offer creative works for free, leaving no margin at all for compensation in creative works. As more than one commentator has observed, it is virtually impossible to compete with free.[21] How can creative industries and creative artists function in such a landscape?

Monetization of creative content may seem on first glance to be a profit-making motive that primarily benefits creative industries owning copyright in creative works, including large corporate entities: in music, record labels such as Warner and Sony Music; in entertainment, media companies such as Disney and Fox; in journalism, Gannett and News Corp; in broadcasting, the Sinclair Broadcast Group; and in publishing, Hachette, Simon and Schuster, and HarperCollins. These entities own large portfolios of copyrighted creative works, and are likely to be the first to realize the royalties, payment streams, and rewards that flow from monetizing creative works. Large corporate industries, even in creative fields, may not seem particularly sympathetic when their profits are eroded by online disruption, even of an illicit nature such as file sharing that circumvents copyright. Some users also feel some of these entities had a history of exploiting artists for gain, and that they do not deserve to reap the profits of artists' creative efforts. Indeed, this argument is often used to justify illicit file sharing—a kind of Robin Hood impulse to take from the rich companies and share among users who simply want to enjoy creative works.

There are several critical flaws in this perspective on creative copyright. First, creative industries assume risks when supporting artistic endeavors, including paying up front for the production, development, and marketing of original works. In certain cases, such as movies and television shows, those up-front

---

Site Sued by Major Record Labels, Gizmodo, Sept. 27, 2016, available at https://gizmodo.com/youtube-to-mp3-converter-site-sued-by-major-record-labe-1787166928.

21 See, e.g., Chris Anderson, *Free: The Future of a Radical Price* (Hyperion, New York, NY, 2009) available at https://hbr.org/2011/06/competing-against-free; Dorie Clark, How to Fight Back Against Disruption and Compete With Free, *Forbes*, Feb. 22, 2013, available at www.forbes.com/sites/dorieclark/2013/02/22/how-to-fight-back-against-disruption-and-compete-with-free/#72937a62787e.

costs can be astronomical. In other cases, the costs are very large but often hidden, as in the costs that investigative journalism incurs. Other costs are systemic, such as the outlays that publishing houses are required to make to build and support databases, search engines (and the underlying algorithms that make searches effective and useful), catalogues, and print services.

In some cases, the costs are obvious to users, such as the evident costs of building video games with popular licensed characters, such as the Marvel "superheroes" or Star Wars characters, or products, such as animated Lego figures. Also evident are the ongoing costs of developing, improving, and expanding the underlying software, consoles, equipment, facilities, and other video game products, resources, and services. The vast majority of these costs must be borne prior to the sale of original creative works; and the ongoing costs must be invested during the life of creative works and their support systems. Without the mechanism of remuneration that copyright affords, there would be little to no incentive for creative companies to assume these risks and underwrite these investments.

Further, creative artists, not just creative industries, are engaged in the risk-taking that copyright promotes and incentivizes. By promising artists that they will be compensated for creating new works that are demanded and consumed in the creative market, copyright sustains artistic production and supports artistic livelihoods. Stories abound of creative artists who were able to make a living prior to the era of rampant appropriation, and who were driven from creative work altogether when their livelihood was undercut by piracy.[22] Work that is not compensated or is undercompensated (that is, the initial investments cannot be recovered) is commercially unviable, and it cannot serve as the source of a livelihood by creative artists.

Critics of this postulate argue that some creative artists prefer to forego the rewards of copyright by making their work freely accessible by using a Creative Commons license, sharing their works openly and distributing them freely, or otherwise making their works available on open access sites. Why would artists forego royalties? Reasons include building an audience, reaching users who are unable to pay for content, rewarding loyal patrons, or reaching out to fans in order to secure their loyalty. But a crucial distinction remains: creative artists who make their works freely available are making a choice, and are exercising control over their works in ways that copyright makes entirely possible. Indeed, the bundle of exclusive rights that copyright law bestows on copyright holders is the right to do what one wants with the work—and that implicitly includes giving it away.

Similarly, creative firms may choose to make works freely available for various reasons, including offering loss leaders that will help seed their customer base and consolidate their first-mover advantage, or that will help grow audiences'

22 See Jonathan Taplin, *Move Fast and Break Things: How Facebook, Google and Amazon Cornered Culture and Undermined Democracy* (Little, Brown, New York, NY, 2017).

presence and retain loyal audiences over time with sporadic rewards. Again, it is the copyright owner's choice not to charge users for access to works, and not to reap royalties from use of works, that is the critical feature of this retreat from monetization. Whether called choice or private ordering solution, the underlying point is the same: copyright is not circumvented, but instead exercised in ways that are wholly consistent with the underlying grant of copyright ownership and control.

The Internet may make it easier for creators to choose on what terms they want to make their works available, and may make it easier for them to exercise their choices. But digital technologies are also rife with the potential for abuse, and the proliferation of sites that facilitate illicit copying and distributing of copyrighted works makes it impossible for creators to determine the market value of their works and to reap those rewards if they so choose. These sites create unpredictability, instability, and a race to the bottom with respect to the pricing of creative goods. In the face of disruption, creative industries find it harder to justify making initial investments in risky creative works. Creators find it harder to make a livelihood from their efforts, and sometimes decide that they cannot pursue creative work on a professional basis. The result is a world of entirely embattled industries and ultimately a world impoverished of creative goods. The short-term effects of piracy may appear to offer cheap or free creative resources to users. But the long-term results are diminished creative productivity and a hollowed-out creative class. This is the backdrop for our inquiry and the reason it is urgent that creative content be protected and creative industries be given the tools and strategies to survive digital disruption now and in the years ahead.

2.5 How Disruptive Innovation Affects the Nature of Creative Content

The Internet may also be changing the nature of works being created. In a world where "binge watching" of television series is becoming increasingly popular, entertainment companies are considering what kinds of shows are best suited to being watched in one continuous viewing, even if they are initially released in serial format.[23] Music producers talk openly about creating popular songs with very strong "hooks," catchy musical phrases that are instantly recognizable, in order to appeal to audiences that may be sampling the song on iTunes prior to purchase.[24] Writers are experimenting with various formats, genres such as fan fiction, and interactive works. And video gamers

23 See, Nolan Feeney, When, Exactly, Does Watching a Lot of Netflix Become a Binge?, *The Atlantic*, Feb. 18, 2014, available at www.theatlantic.com/entertainment/archive/2014/02/when-exactly-does-watching-a-lot-of-netflix-become-a-binge/283844/.

24 See, John Seabrook, The Song Machine, *The New Yorker*, March 19, 2012, available at www.newyorker.com/magazine/2012/03/26/the-song-machine.

are creating games, characters, and sporting events that are designed to bring real space action into the video game purview.

These are just some of the ways in which the Internet may not merely touch upon but may also transform the very nature of creative content. It vastly exceeds Christensen's paradigm of disruptive innovation. Here, not just markets but the content these markets carry are affected. These changes make it increasingly clear that the Internet is just as transformative as it is claimed to be. For the creative industries, this is the takeaway: the digital world presents challenges that are an order of magnitude different from those that came before and that will require new strategies and solutions to overcome.

3 What Are Creative Industries Afraid Of

Known Risks

3.1 Introduction

Creative industries are overwhelmed by the challenges they face in the digital age. They are left reeling by the one-two punch of disruptive innovation, brought on by the Internet and its capacity for massive-scale piracy, combined with the ever-increasing power of Big Tech companies, whose appetite for content is matched by their drive to keep content prices at a minimum and their apparent indifference to the up-front costs and risks that creative entities must assume in generating content.

Creative firms increasingly compete with each other for consumer attention and demand. This may be a boon for consumers, who are able to choose from an array of creative output that is accessible at virtually any place, time, and price. But it is a challenge for creative firms, because while the demand for creative work remains high, the willingness to pay for it remains stubbornly low. And while arguably consumers are always reluctant to pay for content, they now have new ways to obtain content that may help persuade them that content is not particularly valuable or not worth paying for.

Some competitive pressures are exogenous to creative fields, arising from external conditions such as the growth of free resources and materials on the Internet, some of which may entice consumers away from paid content. Others are endogenous, such as the drive to make complicated, expensive works—television series, elaborate video games, serious investigative reporting—that increases the riskiness of creative endeavors. Both kinds of risks are being heightened by rapid shifts in the commercial environment, and both require creative firms to demonstrate their ability to respond, adapt, and re-align their resources and priorities when facing immediate demands for change.

Illegal copying inflicts a huge toll on creative industries.[1] Although it is often argued that digitization drives down marginal costs, any gains that are

1 It is hard to get an accurate view of the monetary effects of piracy, but in 2014 alone, it was estimated digital piracy resulted in $275 billions of unmonetized demand. See Intellectual Property Theft: A Threat to U.S. Workers, Industries, and Our Economy, Department for Professional Employees, available at https://dpeaflcio.org/programs-publications/issue-fact-sheets/intellectual-property-theft-a-threat-to-u-s-workers-industries-and-our-economy/#_ednref17.

made from making production more efficient are liable to be erased, if not outpaced, by the costs of fighting digital piracy. The resulting challenge for creative firms is that it can be hard, if not impossible, to "compete with free."[2] Creative firms need to invest in the inherently risky business of building and licensing content. They need to keep prices high enough to recuperate their initial investment and be rewarded for their effort. But they cannot afford to alienate consumers by pricing their products excessively—that is, at levels that the market will not bear.

Creative firms want to meet and fulfill consumer demand, and they need to keep and grow their audiences in markets at home and abroad. Customer satisfaction is key to their success. But when competing with digital pirates, creative firms are at a loss: it is hard to imagine a price that will seem reasonable when compared with no cost at all, particularly to consumers who may not realize or care that a world of cost-free products will ultimately prove to be unsustainable.

Illicit digital copying is detrimental in undermining creative firms' business plans, and its appeal to consumers is even more harmful and hazardous. By offering creative content at artificially low prices, digital pirates dupe consumers into believing that cost-free goods are not only attractive but also costless. Moreover, they undermine consumers' understanding that creative goods have, and should have, real value. The changes in consumer behaviors and attitudes in response to the lure of digital piracy has been strikingly clear: since the days of Napster, a regrettable portion of creative content consumers have actively engaged in seeking and obtaining illicit content.

Creative firms face a difficult dilemma: how do they respond when consumers turn to illegally infringing sources of copyrighted material? Creative firms cannot allow their customers to engage in activities that divert resources, circumvent copyright, and undermine profitability. When digital users resort to illicit copying, distributing, and partaking of content, creative industries must decide how to address their activities, where to draw the line, and whether to pursue those activities with threats, litigation, sanctions, or other highly publicized responses.

All of these strategies, however, are likely to strain public relations and cast creative firms as villains—not merely to the disinterested observer, but more cogently to actual and potential customers. Moreover, these strategies have the potential to backfire further, pushing ambivalent consumers to embrace an ethos favoring sharing, copying and disseminating works by whatever means possible, and blurring their sense of a distinction between legal and illegal uses of content.

While creative industry players are acutely aware of the risks that potentially antagonizing their consumer base entails, they may also feel that they have no

2 Chris Anderson, *Free: The Future of a Radical Price* 208–15 (Hyperion, New York, NY, 2009).

other recourse than to take measures that signal the seriousness with which they regard illicit file sharing. The ultimate problem that they face, however, is a loss of the connection and trust that they have worked hard to build with their audiences, and an erosion of understanding among consumers that content is worth paying for and should be paid for—and that without payment, certain kinds of content may simply not be made.

Creative industries try not to act too zealously when managing consumer relations, in part because their actions are likely to be magnified by public opinion, circulated in social media, and prone to spiral out of their control. What they can better address are the commercial risks, necessities, and driving forces that are within their command: pricing choices, business decisions, and economic realities that can pose immediate challenges but can also open new opportunities for revenue growth.

But by focusing on commercial risks, creative firms can overlook entire areas of "soft" risks. In many ways, creative industries are rich ecosystems that operate both by making money and by promoting activities and value systems that are not so profit oriented. Some of the finest ways that creativity is sustained involve interpersonal activities such as sharing and exchanging, collaborating and co-authoring, mentoring and teaching, all of which build creative communities and foster creative output.

It is possible that these activities can occur when licenses and formal arrangements are put into place. But not always: licenses can be costly and complicated; not all licensors want to license their works, or place too high a value on licensing their works; and not all licensees are well situated to manage such formalities or negotiate fair and reasonable terms. Many times creative work happens best when it is untrammeled by property rights, especially at the outset of creation or when creative exchanging and learning is taking place.

Intellectual property rights, including copyright but also trademarks and patents, do not always curtail creative production. But in some cases they do not need to extend over work that is operating free from rights and that does not require property rights for protection or support. Importantly, privileging intellectual property rights can overshadow the value of nonpropertized work, and overzealous application of property rights can stifle or throttle it. And not only creative work can suffer, but creative output can suffer as well.

Creative industries are not always aware of risks to their ecosystem that cannot be easily identified and quantified. Nor are they always aware of the value of what is not readily propertized, particularly when that creative work and its output do not yield obvious or lucrative returns. Copyright law too can offer only some guidance, protection, and support to such work: it is, after all, intended to bolster rights in intellectual property, not to affirm the value of non-property. But by carefully limiting the rights it grants and protects, copyright law does leave creative industries ample room to support and sustain the nonpropertizable work that they value. It behooves creative industries and their participants to recognize both those parameters and the value of what lies both within and outside of its expansive borders.

3.2 Unfair Skewing of the "Innovation Lottery"

Creative industries always face a fundamental concern: whether the risks they assume in creating new works will be satisfactorily compensated by adequate returns.[3] Even without IP protection, they would be confronted with the basic commercial need to clear their costs. With IP, they are at least assured that they can capture the returns from creative work.

The nature of creative work raises the threshold of risk for two reasons: first, creative work can be more easily appropriated than, say, industrial output, and second, the consumption of creative work is generally taste-driven, and taste is notoriously hard to predict. Fashion, music, entertainment, television, and video games: it is hard to name a content-rich industry that is not dependent on consumer taste. All these industries must gauge the receptivity of their audiences to new output, and must rely on popular appeal to remain competitively strong and profitable.

Further complicating matters, creative industries must constantly issue new works, as audiences gravitate to fresh and original creations, and as audience tastes often prove unpredictable. In somewhat less-volatile fields, such as education and nonfiction publishing, taste may be somewhat less of an arbiter of preference, and may be less subject to change. But even in these fields taste can be differentiated: in fiction publishing, popular appeal is much harder to pinpoint.

Generally, consumers are constantly seeking new outputs, and sometimes new outlets, for the works these industries produce. They may also substitute criteria of taste with equally subjective notions of quality, experience, value, and associative goods[4]—such as the benefits of interchange with members of the creative community—for assessing whether the industry's offerings are worth their while.

Taking these risks is known as the "innovation lottery"; and creative industries play the innovation lottery game for high stakes to remain commercially viable.[5] This calculus is compounded when disruptive technologies emerge. On the positive side of the equation, change can open up entire new venues, facilitate new means of production, alter delivery streams, and fundamentally change consumer and user practices. But on the other side, change can completely alter traditional business practices, interfere with established industry players, and compromise industry norms. Change driven by disruptive

3 William M. Landes & Richard A. Posner, An Economic Analysis of Copyright Law, 18 *J. Legal Stud.* 325, 333 (1989); Edmund W. Kitch, Elementary and Persistent Errors in the Economic Analysis of Intellectual Property, 53 *Vand. L. Rev.* 1727, 1728 (2000).

4 2 Henry Hansmann, *Higher Education as an Associative Good* (Yale L. & Econ. Working Paper No. 231, Sept. 1999), available at http://ssrn.com/abstract=192576.

5 See generally F.M. Scherer, The Innovation Lottery, in *Expanding the Boundaries of Intellectual Property: Innovation Policy for the Knowledge Society* 3 (Rochelle Cooper Dreyfuss, Diane Leenheer Zimmerman & Harry First, eds., 2001).

innovation can also erode or eliminate necessary sources of revenue that creative firms have long depended on and worked hard to maintain.

3.3 High Fixed Costs of Production

For major content producers such as media, entertainment, and video game companies, record labels, fashion houses, newspapers, and educators, making content is an expensive proposition. In the music industry, finding and producing the next big act in pop or rock music still costs a record label a significant initial outlay, coupled with an uncertain payoff.[6] The high fixed costs of production must be at a minimum recouped and preferably exceeded if music producers are to remain successful.[7]

The need to clear margins can steer music producers toward certain business strategies and plans: selling their product at certain price points (seeking best sellers or hits that generate the highest volume of sales or downloads); relying on advertising support; being beholden to outlets such as broadcasting or online streaming for product delivery; searching for the greatest number of venues for the release of new product; pursuing new revenue sources such as secondary rights; seeking cross-licensing deals; seeking royalties for recordings played in smaller venues, such as restaurants, bars, and gyms; seeking merchandising and ancillary rights; and seeking to lock upcoming or best-selling artists into long-term contracts. These decisions are typically calculated to maximize the returns from music production in order to offset its considerable up-front costs.

The high fixed production costs that underpin the business models of music and other creative industries are not uniformly negative. They spur pro-competitive behaviors, foster profit maximization, amply reward talented creators and diligent producers, and perpetuate the generation of new content that satisfies consumer demand. But these factors also steer creative industries in the direction of value-maximizing practices: compelling a high volume of sales and licensing, focusing attention on immediate success as opposed to nurturing developing talent over a longer career, concentrating resources on known and marketable entities, and concentrating on immediate gains.[8]

These necessities can potentially affect the quality and nature of creative work that is being produced. In music, it has been argued that producers seeking to maximize returns are liable to favor high-selling acts, which

6 See *Navigating the Music Industry: Current Issues & Business Models* 183–201, Dick Weissman & Frank Jermance, eds. (Hal Leonard, Milwaukee, WI, 2003); see also *Death of the Middleman, Living Economics*, available at https://livingeconomics.org/article.asp?docId=278.

7 Raymond Shih Ray Ku, The Creative Destruction of Copyright: Napster and the New Economics of Digital Technology, 69 *U. Chi. L. Rev.* 263, 295–6 (2002).

8 See *Navigating the Music Industry: Current Issues & Business Models* Dick Weissman & Frank Jermance, eds., 275–99 (Hal Leonard, Milwaukee, WI, 2003).

encourages a certain uniformity of products that are bland yet satisfying to mass audiences.[9]

The mandates of traditional music production may not change anytime soon. But technology is opening up new realms of content production to more innovative and nimbler generators of content, who are creating output that is less expensive to produce and deliver, yet still satisfying to music audiences and consumers. This is posing a direct challenge to the established industry that is only likely to escalate as newer, more savvy musicians emerge with greater awareness of the Internet and increasing abilities to tap its resources and tools for creating, mixing, editing, releasing, and delivering music product to global audiences.

There are several instances in which new artists have shown they can ably use technology to self-produce, self-promote, and self-market. Justin Bieber is now a classic example of a popular musician who wrote and recorded his own songs, and then uploaded videos of his performances on YouTube.[10] He developed his name recognition to such an extent that he was signed by a major record label, which now produces his music commercially.[11] Bieber's initial efforts at self-promotion saved up-front costs for the record label, which did not have to make an initial outlay to make, package, market, or nurture the artist. But Bieber did eventually sign with the label.[12]

Other musical acts, such as the heavy metal band Metallica, rely primarily on direct sales of music online, streaming, and live ticket sales to sustain themselves.[13] Metallica assumes much of the costs of production, which are greatly reduced by technology. Recently, the band announced that it had repurchased copyrights in its earlier catalogue and that it intends to be solely responsible for the dissemination of that previously recorded work.[14] While these steps do not offset high production costs, they mitigate them by garnering lucrative rights that pay out over time, potentially offsetting future expenditures.

Similarly, in the case of journalism, newspapers make large outlays, primarily on the labor of investigative journalists, reporters, foreign correspondents, and

9 See Lenika Cruz, In Music, Uniformity Sells, *The Atlantic* (Jan. 4, 2015), available at www.theatlantic.com/entertainment/archive/2015/01/in-music-uniformity-sells/384181.

10 See Desiree Adib, Pop Star Justin Bieber Is on the Brink of Superstardom, *ABC News* (Nov. 14, 2009), available at http://abcnews.go.com/GMA/Weekend/teen-pop-star-justin-bieber-discovered-youtube/story?id=9068403.

11 See Monica Herrera, Justin Bieber—The Billboard Cover Story, *Billboard* (Mar. 19, 2010), available at www.billboard.com/articles/news/959001/justin-bieber-the-billboard-cover-story.

12 Id.

13 See #57: Metallica, *Forbes* (Jul. 16, 2018), available at www.forbes.com/profile/metallica/#f475178439f7.

14 See Rolling Stone, Metallica Launch New Record Label, *Rolling Stone* (Nov. 30, 2012, 5:35 PM), available at www.rollingstone.com/music/music-news/metallica-launch-new-record-label-174244/.

other writers, as well as on editing, printing, and delivery costs. Technology enables their new emerging competitors to occupy the news space via online dissemination, rather than through print media. Online newspapers and media sites can generate their own work at lower costs by pooling resources, soliciting poorly paid or unpaid work from freelance writers, or writing follow-on works that may not amount to much more than rewrites of previously published materials. In other words, they can engage in classic free rider behavior by aggregating preexisting news sources and putting out a competitive product at a lower cost of production. Particularly where such online sources are reputable and cost nothing or next-to-nothing to use, they can offer a truly competitive alternative to the business model of traditional journalism.[15]

Education is another creative industry in which production costs are high, fixed, and relatively immutable.[16] Consumers—that is, students and the parents who usually financially support their education—typically want and demand real-space institutions that will direct and mediate their education. Such institutions are extremely expensive to operate and maintain, and their educational model is based on charging high prices (that is, tuition plus fees and room and board) to compensate for those high costs.

The Internet disrupts this model by presenting an alternative model of production. The online educational model can reduce costs dramatically, in part by eliminating real-space constraints, and in part by achieving economies of scale by teaching more students in more concentrated courses and programs.[17] Online education can entail major startup costs.[18] Once such costs are allocated, however, they may be amortized, offset with budgetary or operating earmarks, or separately funded.[19]

As the initial production costs of online education drop, ongoing costs stabilize, and business models are likely to become self-sustaining.[20] As these cost savings occur, and as their development is undertaken by nontraditional

15 Joshua Benton, The Leaked New York Times Innovation Report Is One of the Key Documents of This Media Age, *Niemanlab* (May 15, 2014) (describing the New York Times' leaked internal report, which discussed other company's "repackaging" of New York Times content while outperforming the New York Times).

16 See, e.g., Rita Kirshstein & Jane Wellman, Technology and the Broken Higher Education Cost Model: Insights from the Delta Cost Project, *Educause Rev.* (Sep. 5, 2012), available at www.educause.edu/ero/article/technology-and-broken-higher-education-cost-model-insights-delta-cost-project.

17 See Alistair Inglis, The Changing Costs of Delivery of Distance Education Programs, in *Handbook of Distance Education* 507, 509–13, Michael Grahame Moore, ed., 3rd ed., (Routledge, New York, NY, 2013).

18 Id.

19 Id.

20 See Kevin Carey, Here's What Will Truly Change Higher Education: Online Degrees That Are Seen as Official, *New York Times* (Mar. 8, 2015), available at www.nytimes.com/2015/03/08/upshot/true-reform-in-higher-education-when-online-degrees-are-seen-as-official.html. 23 See Robert Neuwirth, *Stealth of Nations: The Global Rise of the Informal Economy* 86–113 (2011).

institutions (such as for-profit institutions and startups), new business models with lower costs of production, greater volume, maybe lower quality (maybe not), and at a much cheaper price offer a new paradigm for education delivery to certain segments of the market. This model already exists for certain kinds of programs, such as technical training and practical certification.[21] Where this new model may radically disrupt the higher education industry is when online education begins to offer degrees and credentials that are substitutable for traditional education equivalents.

3.4 Devaluation of Content

Innovative technologies can devalue both invented devices and creative content. Photography was changed forever when the daguerreotype was displaced by the introduction of the mass-market box camera, the Kodak, and the Brownie, making photographic equipment portable.[22] This was followed by the invention of the portable and affordable single-lens reflex (SLR) camera, allowing amateur photographers to take high-quality photographs, and challenging professional photographers to work harder to obtain steady work.

In the era of SLRs, film development required costly darkrooms, equipment, and production skills. Most nonprofessional photographers took their photographs to film development and print shops, which kept the price of photographs relatively stable and high. The invention of cheap, mass-marketed, and fairly disposable instant cameras was coupled with the development of a chemical process that could rapidly produce finished prints. This changed the value of film, the use of film development, and the worth of permanent photographs. It was a great benefit to consumers, who could now choose among an array of options. But it forced the makers of cameras and film, and the owners of film development shops, to be adaptive and proactive.

The introduction of digital cameras proved another game changer. Digital cameras do not use film, but instead capture and save photographs on digital memory cards or internal storage, lowering operating costs considerably. As film development was no longer a necessity, cameras requiring chemical film development, and film itself, became relegated to niche markets. Digital cameras became equipped with wireless communication capabilities (such as Wi-Fi or Bluetooth), and were seamlessly integrated into mobile phones. These changes again benefited consumers, who were able to carry and use their cameras everywhere, and to produce photographs without the need for external resources or services. But it had a profound impact on professional photography, turning professionally staged photographs into "special occasion" works, such as photographs of class pictures, weddings, and other milestone events.

21 See City Tech Online, available at www.citytech.cuny.edu/citytechonline/; Devry University, available at www.devry.edu.

22 Stephen Dowlings, The Most Important Cardboard Box Ever? *BBC* (Jan. 5, 2015), available at www.bbc.com/news/magazine-30530268.

The development of the camera demonstrates that while content can still be important to consumers, its value proposition to content producers can be changed. Photographic content was not devalued in the sense that consumers still greatly value photographs, but it was devalued as a steady income source for professional photographers. Professional photographers have had to search for new revenue streams that distinguish professional content from amateur works, and have fought to convince consumers that professional work is worth paying for. Photojournalism has also been affected, as amateur photographers who capture significant current events are becoming increasingly successful at selling their works to news outlets and media sites.[23]

The changes in the photography industry described here have been driven by technological innovation and changing markets. But another major driver of change is when illicit copying becomes a major factor, undermining markets and driving down the value of content. Photography is far from immune to this concern: rampant piracy of original photographs, counterfeiting of photographs, and sites dedicated to photograph file sharing abound.[24] Across creative sectors, illicit uses of creative content drive down content value and push industries toward market failure.

Music offers a now-classic example of the potential technology can have for devaluing content and undermining traditional sources of revenue. Online file-sharing services enable users to copy music files, which are shared freely and often illicitly among innumerable users, at no cost. Such file sharing evades payment for the use and reuse of music tracks to both artists and copyright holders. In so doing, it decreases revenues across the industry.[25] While the exact amount of the decline in music sales is debated in music circles,[26] many agree that such music "theft" is rampant.[27]

While alternative revenue streams, such as live performance ticket sales and merchandise sales, may compensate somewhat for these losses, the depreciation of the value of recorded copyrighted material remains problematic.

Publishing also suffers from the devaluation of content when its work is circulated outside standard channels. Online file-sharing sites for e-books, such

23 See Christina Zdanowicz, "Miracle on the Hudson" Twitpic Changed His Life, *CNN* (Jan. 15, 2014, 3:47 PM), available at www.cnn.com/2014/01/15/tech/hudson-landing-twitpic-krums/index.html (interviewing Janis Krums, whose tweet with a photo of US Airways Flight 1549 floating in the Hudson River went viral, resulting in Krums receiving opportunities he credits with his current success).

24 Olivier Laurent, Google Accused of Enabling Photography Piracy, *Time* (Apr. 26, 2016), available at http://time.com/4307769/google-getty-images/.

25 23 See Robert Neuwirth, *Stealth of Nations: The Global Rise of the Informal Economy* 86–113 (2011).

26 Indeed, some believe concerns are inflated and do not reflect healthy changes in the world of content. See, e.g., Lawrence Lessig, *Remix: Making Art and Commerce Thrive in the Hybrid Economy* 143–55 (The Penguin Press, New York, NY, 2008).

27 Raymond, supra note 7.

as Scribd, eat into e-book sales.[28] As in the case of digital music, such copying makes written works inexpensive or free, and distributes them easily and rapidly to large audiences. Sites such as Scribd also enable large-scale infringing activities, but creative industries can find it hard, and costly, to challenge them in court and to eventually force them out of business.

The film and television industries are facing a similar threat of devaluation of content from technology-enabled file sharing. Film, TV, and video content are uploaded daily onto online sharing sites and networks, such as YouTube, BitTorrent, and Gnutella. The legality varies widely among sites and content. Whereas YouTube will remove illegally shared content if it is brought to their attention, sites such as BitTorrent are unlikely to take the offending material down.

There are also gray areas in which technologies may not exist solely or primarily to enable illicit activities but may still facilitate content sharing in ways that devalue content. In some cases, such as the now-defunct Aereo, these technologies have been recognized by courts as primarily enabling infringing uses of copyrighted work, and have been forced to shut down.[29] In other cases, such as the Kodi device and similar set-top boxes, the verdict is still out as to the degree to which infringing activities are enabled, and as to whether courts will allow them to remain in operation.[30]

What these technologies have in common is the ability to deliver content to users at greatly reduced cost. While popular with users, they vex content producers by stripping value from creative works. But because they are potentially lucrative to their developers, these devices are likely to proliferate. If they do, they will continue to challenge legitimate distributors of copyrighted creative content and to exert pressure on the value of content and the business models of content production.

Journalism is facing similar challenges with respect to changing user practices and preferences that lead to the substitution of some newsprint for free online materials. This change is enabled and supported by the emergence of blogs, group sites like *Talking Points Memo*, *Politico*, *The Huffington Post*, and so on, which are generally produced at lower costs than traditional media, in part because they rely upon the lower-cost labor of freelancers or writers who will forfeit payment in exchange for exposure. While these pressures arise from legitimate competition in the market, there are news aggregators that are able to free ride on investigative journalism without consequence.[31]

28 Alison Flood, "*We're Told to Be Grateful We Even Have Readers*": *Pirated Ebooks Threaten the Future of Book Series* (Nov. 6, 2017), available at www.theguardian.com/books/2017/nov/06/pirated-ebooks-threaten-future-of-serial-novels-warn-authors-maggie-stiefvater.

29 Benton, supra note 15.

30 See Brian Barrett, The Little Black Box That Took Over Piracy, *Wired* (Oct. 27, 2017), available at www.wired.com/story/kodi-box-piracy/.

31 See Saul Hansell, Start-Up Plans to Make Journalism Pirates Pay Up, *N.Y. Times* (Jul. 26, 2009), available at www.nytimes.com/2009/07/27/technology/start-ups/27attributor.html.

The support for such online news sites may be a mix of private funds, cheap labor, and venture capital funding. The challenge is also exacerbated by the ease with which such sites, as well as individual readers, can copy and re-distribute articles that traditional print media companies post on their own websites, via the simple tool of deep links that make materials available to users at no cost. The use of links to published materials offers an end-run around any means of compensation print media companies might pursue; and it presents a clear free rider problem to these entities.[32]

Further, the loss of dues-paying readership, particularly subscribers and newsstand purchasers, is currently posing a real threat to newsprint, magazines, and other traditional media companies. Traditional newspapers and news sources, even as venerable as the *New York Times*, struggle with dropping subscription rates, which makes them lose vital advertisers and so makes them less sustainable. Finally, user practices can once more be seen to change, as readers increasingly refuse to pay for material that is placed behind paywalls; only in the exceptional case, such as the *Wall Street Journal*, has the existence of paywalls actually proved effective.[33]

As in the other creative industries discussed, these factors devalue original content, and help to exert downward pressure on advertising rates, which are the backbone of journalism's business. Some future revenue streams may emerge, such as the monetization of ad-streaming online, and tie-ins with live events (festivals and symposiums, TED talks, and so on). But the devaluation of the content of journalism itself does not lend itself to such obvious solutions.

3.5 Devaluation of Intermediaries

Among the many stakeholders of content-rich industries, intermediaries or middlemen serve multiple purposes in producing the raw material of artistic creation into finished, credentialed products that are brought to market.[34] Technology can enable creators to take on some of these intermediary functions, and it can help creators deliver commercially finished products to users.[35] This threatens the fundamental business model of intermediation. Although intermediaries still exist in many creative industries, and in some cases may not be at risk of disappearing anytime soon, many are still threatened by the prospect of impending technologically induced obsolescence.

32 See Nicholas Carlson, Ban Blogs from Linking to Newspapers, Says Judge, *Business Insider* (Jul. 2, 2009), available at www.businessinsider.com/blogs-should-be-barred-from-linking-to-newspapers-says-judge-2009-7.

33 See Drizzle, *Paywalls Are on the Rise with Many Success Stories* (Nov. 22, 2016), available at https://medium.com/@getdrizzle/paywalls-are-on-the-rise-with-many-success-stories-3a7101f55bea (finding the Wall Street Journal had 550,000 paying online subscribers).

34 See generally Antoine Hennion, An Intermediary Between Production and Consumption: The Producer of Popular Music, 14 *Sci. Tech. Human Values* 400 (1989).

35 Ku, *supra* note 7, at 306–11.

Intermediaries abound in the mature music industry. Record labels, talent scouts, marketers—all play multiple roles in finding new talent, representing composers and performing artists, producing commercially packaged albums and songs, marketing and promoting the work of songwriters and musicians, and enabling and assisting with the production of live performance concerts.[36]

Intermediaries are typically paid through up-front signing fees, royalty streams, and contractual payments. In the case of record labels, they hold the copyright in the original compositions created by their artists, and they often retain rights in the catalog of artists' prior works.[37] Some intermediaries function as agents, signing artists to contracts that give them the ability to negotiate performances, rights, and revenues. Others specialize in recorded works, managing rights in recently recorded works as well as back catalogs.

Intermediaries have been well entrenched in the music industry. But some composers and musicians are beginning to take control of their own output, and to retain their rights, royalties, and related revenues.[38] Artists can use digital technology from the production of work through its delivery, and can assume professional roles that they once outsourced to others. At the production stage, they can create, edit, and finalize their work product. They can sell copies of recorded work such as albums and songs, as well as tickets to live performances. They can also build websites that facilitate the sale of merchandise (such as t-shirts and other promotional materials) and other products that help build brand loyalty. Through their websites they can promote their work, reach and interact with audiences, announce dates and recount newsworthy stories, and share promotional materials.

Musicians and songwriters can also take on work that more directly lies in the area of expertise of intermediaries. Digitization can enable them to manage their royalty streams via performing rights organizations, to draft contracts and licensing agreements, and to manage their brand. These practices can reduce dependence on intermediaries, which can be cost-effective, especially for emerging artists. As musicians become more comfortable with taking on these responsibilities, they often become more accustomed to the idea that they can dispense with intermediaries altogether, and they become eager to take control of both the creative process and their creative output.[39]

3.6 Devaluation of Credentialization

Some intermediaries in creative industries play important roles of credentialization, identifying creative works for audiences and confirming that they are

36 See M. William Krasilovsky & Sidney Shemel, *This Business of Music* 340, 10th ed., (Watson-Guptill, New York, NY, 2007).

37 Id. at 341.

38 Id. at 14–20.

39 See Ku, supra note 7, at 308–11.

well regarded as knowledgeable, reliable, and credible authorities and critics.[40] Newspapers, peer-reviewed journals, publishers, libraries, and artistic critics are among the intermediaries whose work comprises identifying and signaling to broad audiences what content is worthy of attention. They can also vouch for creative works, certifying that they meet their standards for quality, authenticity, veracity, and creativity.

But the proliferation of creative output available online means that users can find resources everywhere, and creators can make their work directly accessible to large audiences without such work being vetted, agented, or otherwise intermediated. Some of that work can still be high quality, possibly causing some creators and audiences to doubt the value or need for credentialization by traditional sources.

Technology is giving rise to a host of online critics, such as bloggers, desktop publishers, popular websites, and others who express their views on an array of creative works. When these self-directed, and sometimes self-appointed, figures review creative content online, they can bypass standard channels of authority. If they gain audience recognition online, they can begin to usurp the role of traditional intermediaries. They can, whether deliberately or not, contribute to the devaluation of credentializing content by attracting audiences who read them online free of charge, rather than paying for products and reviews offered in newspapers, magazines, and other established venues.

The rise of self-appointed critics who bestow credentials according to their own set of criteria raises essential questions about the functional value of credentialization itself. Some current commentators argue that its role has been overvalued, and that audiences can discern value for themselves.[41] Others argue that if its role is undermined, society is more likely allow for the release of sub-par materials that audiences may not take the time, or may not be able, to vet, and that this may lead to a disintegration of quality content in the marketplace.[42]

In the fashion world, the power to bestow credentials and approval lay traditionally among haute couture fashion houses, high-end buyers, magazines, and a few well-known authorities. These arbiters of tastes and trends are now being challenged by online critics, bloggers, street fashion artists and photographers, and other newly minted, sometimes self-styled, tastemakers. While beginning to acknowledge the power of some of these newcomers,[43] some of

40 On the usefulness of intermediaries, see Robert P. Merges, Contracting Into Liability Rules: Intellectual Property Rights and Collective Rights Organizations, 84 *Calif. L. Rev.* 1293 (1996); Mark A. Lemley, Intellectual Property Rights and Standard-Setting Organizations, 90 *Calif. L. Rev.* 1887 (2002).

41 See generally Ku, supra note 7.

42 See generally Anthony Horowitz, Do We Still Need Publishers? *The Guardian* (Feb. 27, 2012), available at www.theguardian.com/books/booksblog/2012/feb/27/anthony-horowitz-do-we-still-need-publishers.

43 See for example the acceptance and incorporation of the blogger Tavi Gevinson into the fashion establishment. See generally Christopher Borrelli, Teen Fashion Maven

fashion's established authority figures openly say that they are learning how to respond to, and perhaps learn from, the challenge that online contenders represent.[44]

The publishing industry also illustrates some of the challenges to credentializing agents in a mature industry unsettled by technology. Historically, publishing houses and literary agents agreed to sign promising authors that they felt would produce a body of work over the course of a career. Whether such work was commercially viable, popularly appealing, or critically acclaimed, the publishers and agents agreed the work would represent their brand, and in turn they would represent the author. They vetted manuscripts prior to publication, offered editorial support, marketing and promotional support, and commercial production, and stood behind their writers in the publishing marketplace.[45] Some publishing houses or imprints were so highly regarded that they cast a positive glow, and just the fact of being signed by a well-regarded publisher could attest to an author's ability, status, regard, and salability.[46]

In contrast, digital technology is now contributing to the growth of self-publishing, particularly through Amazon, the largest distributor of published work.[47] Budding authors can now bypass the middlemen, the publishing agents and houses, and bring their work directly to their chosen audience. Audiences gain increasing control over their ability to express their response to works, whatever the means of publication may be (i.e., self-published or via a publishing house). Audiences can, as always, express their acclaim by purchasing copies of the book and increasing its commercial success. And they can enter the credentializing process by leaving comments on their own websites, on the "reader reviews" sections of such vendors as amazon.com, barnesandnoble.com, or through postings on blogs, online reviews, and other critical outlets.

A case in point is the well-known story of E.L. James, who self-published her novel, "Fifty Shades of Gray" in 2001, putting it online as an e-book and selling it on a print-on-demand basis.[48] Due to aggressive viral marketing by

---

Tavi Gevinson Is 16 Going on 30, *Chi. Tribune* (Sept. 18, 2012), available at http://articles.chicagotribune.com/2012-09-18/; Brianna Wellen, *Catching Up with Tavi Gevinson, The Rookie of the Year*, available at www.chicagoreader.com/Bleader/archives/2015/10/15/catching-up-with-tavi-gevinson-rookie-of-the-year.

44 See, e.g., Sarah Jones, How Much Influence Do Fashion Bloggers Have? *Luxury Daily* (Nov. 26, 2014), available at www.luxurydaily.com/how-much-influence-do-fashion-bloggers-have (noting collaborations with bloggers by Marc Jacobs and Estee Lauder).

45 See William Germano, *What Do Publishers Do?* (University of Chicago Press), available at www.press.uchicago.edu/Misc/Chicago/288447.html.

46 Id.

47 Jeffery A. Trachtenberg, "They Own the System": Amazon Rewrites Book Industry by Marching into Publishing, *Wall Street Journal* (Jan. 16, 2019), available at www.wsj.com/articles/they-own-the-system-amazon-rewrites-book-industry-by-turning-into-a-publisher-11547655267.

48 See Natasha Bertrand, "Fifty Shades of Grey" Started Out as a "Twilight" Fan Fiction Before Becoming an International Phenomenon, *Business Insider* (Feb. 17, 2015), available at www.businessinsider.com/fifty-shades-of-grey-started-out-as-twilight-fan-fiction-2015-2.

the author, and the enthusiastic response of book and e-book purchasers, the book proved an enormous success that topped the bestseller lists and, with its sequels, sold in hundreds of millions of copies.[49] The book and its sequels were eventually assumed by Vintage Books. The success of the "50 Shades" series has inspired countless authors to follow suit by self-publishing on Amazon. Amazon also enhances the appeal of self-publishing on its platform by offering attractive royalty rates that match, and sometimes surpass, traditional rates.[50] This has upended the publishing market, and the strength of self-publishing is only likely to grow over time.

3.7 Loss of Traditional Sources of Revenue

Content industries have typically relied on bread-and-butter sales of hard copy products that are bundled, marketed, and sold as production units with built-in markups (for example, the costs of an album are typically higher than the cost of its individual song sales) and often-generous margins. Digital technology enables the disaggregation of some of these products, such as the sale of individual music tracks rather than of entire albums, which tends to reduce revenues by erasing the added value of bundling.

But the greater impact on hard copy sales is the ability of digital users to gain access to online reproductions of such materials, such as digital tracks of songs recorded on CDs.[51] The online version of such works lends itself to easy copying and dissemination: as has been repeatedly evinced in the case of music, downloading digital music tracks has become commonplace practice and, notably when coupled with uploading music for other listeners to share, such practices have had a marked impact on the profit margins across the entire sector.[52]

The Internet clearly has an impact on both the uniqueness and the value of the original work, as well as helping ensure that readily accessible future copies have much less value than they might otherwise be able to retain. The secondary sales market of creative goods remains a complicated question: courts have not fully resolved whether the first sale doctrine applies to the resale of digital goods, although the recent case of *ReDigi* seems to indicate that at present digital resales are not favorably viewed.[53] Still, secondary markets are bound to re-emerge online, possibly with technological advances that obviate the need to reproduce copies of works. These new versions may also be challenged in court, but it is possible that a viable digital market in secondary work will survive review.

49 Id.

50 Digital Price Page, *Amazon* (last updated Mar. 25, 2018), available at https://kdp.amazon.com/en_US/help/topic/G200634500#70%25.

51 See Ku, supra note 7 at 272–3.

52 Id.

53 Capitol Records, LLC v. ReDigi Inc., 910 F.3d 649, 664 (2nd Cir., 2018).

The ease of copying that digital means afford also applies to journalism and print media. Users can cut-and-paste an entire article, or can place a link to the article on a website, enabling the reader to consume the original article for free and depriving the original writer or copyright holder the right to collect any returns from consumption of the original work. Challenges have been made to linking in the E.U.,[54] but at present the practice is widespread and accepted practice in the U.S. Similarly, aggregator sites collect articles and offer them to users, typically paying the originating host a fraction of a share of the cost of the article.

Advertising is another area in which creative industries are faced with a loss of revenue due to the advent of digital technology.[55] These losses arise for multiple reasons.

Digital audiences may be numerous, but they are hard to target; also, it is generally harder to get readers to click through advertisements online than it is to get readers to browse through print advertising. Traditionally well-paying areas of advertising have moved online, but their ad rates tend to be lower. This applies broadly to real estate listings, resale and auction sites, and classified ads. Across the board, online advertising may reach more viewers than print and traditional media, but the increase in volume is often not enough to offset a decline in online advertisement rates.

Some traditional industries are looking to leverage social media and online-oriented advertising and marketing. Recently, fashion companies have paid independent movie directors to make short feature films that mention their brand (and, it is hoped, lend it credibility by association). However, these efforts have not yet been seen to have any measurable payoff in terms of purchasing consumers.[56] These kinds of efforts are meant to stave off losses from traditional sources of revenue, such as ad placement in fashion magazines, whose declining circulations mean loss of advertising dollars. It remains to be seen whether digital sources can return to the advertising returns of earlier years.

3.8 Competing With Free

Some consumers who use digital technology resist having to pay for content and are willing to circumvent copyright, especially when it is easy and penalty-free to do so. Even knowing that content creators will be deprived of their

54 James Wilson & Russell Brandom, Everything You Need to Know About Europe's New Copyright Directive, *The Verge* (Sept. 13, 2018), available at www.theverge.com/2018/9/13/17854158/eu-copyright-directive-article-13-11-internet-censorship-google.

55 Rebecca Greenfield, The Decline of Google (and the Internet's) Ad Business, *Wired* (Jul. 20, 2012), available at www.thewire.com/technology/2012/07/decline-google-and-internets-ad-business/54835.

56 Charles C. Mann, The Heavenly Jukebox, *The Atlantic* (Sept. 2000), available at www.theatlantic.com/issues/2000/09/mann.htm.

rights and rewards when their copyrights are violated may not be enough of a barrier to some consumers' infringing behaviors, as "free" is a price that can be irresistible when there are no obvious costs involved.

Various commentators have argued that this trend began with the initial willingness of certain content providers to make their content available for free online.[57] Several creative industries began with free digital content, often finding to their consternation that later moving to a paid model would become a formidable challenge.

At the advent of the Internet, certain prominent newspapers began by offering their entire news content online at no cost.[58] Finding that their newsprint sales and subscriptions were plummeting due to increasing online readerships, these newspapers then tried to impose for-pay mechanisms on consumers who had enjoyed untrammeled access to content.[59] In recent years, a few premium newspapers have been able to find success with some combination of paywalls, subscription models, aggregator sites, and loss leaders. *The Wall Street Journal*, the *New York Times*, and the *Washington Post* are leaders in the field, and have enjoyed surprisingly strong and growing subscription-based revenues.[60] Smaller newspapers, even reputable ones, have found success harder to reach. To date, most consumers still seem unwilling to pay for online news, and the decline in sales of print media continues apace.[61]

A consistent theme in the digital world is the prevalence of piracy and large-scale copyright infringement. Many digital content distributors still follow the precedent set by Napster, which began as a means for digital music tracks to be reproduced, uploaded, and shared among listeners for free.[62] While Napster was eventually dismantled, its progeny, such as BitTorrent, continue to make content freely available to audiences on the Internet.[63] Some of the content may be legitimately available, but often at least some is illegally shared. This new model of content sharing has spread to various other entertainment and cultural sectors, but it is digital music sharing that has established the

57 See Chris Anderson, *Free: How Today's Smartest Businesses Profit by Giving Something for Nothing* 101–19 (Hyperion, New York, NY, 2010).

58 Alex T. Williams, *Paying for Digital News: The Rapid Adoption and Current Landscape of Digital Subscription at U.S Newspaper* (American Press Institute, Feb. 29, 2016, 5:00 a.m.), available at www.americanpressinstitute.org/publications/reports/digital-subscriptions/single-page/.

59 Id.

60 Patrick Wagner, *Digital News Subscription are a Potent Revenue Generator, Statisca* (Jul. 13, 2018), available at www.statista.com/chart/14626/subscribers-and-revenue-of-digital-news-publishers/.

61 Kevin Tran, Online News Consumption Habits Are Shifting in 2018, *Business Insider* (Jun. 15, 2018, 10:29 a.m.), available at www.businessinsider.com/oxford-survey-shows-changes-in-how-consumers-read-online-news-2018-6.

62 See Chris Anderson, *Free: How Today's Smartest Businesses Profit by Giving Something for Nothing*, 101–19 (Hyperion, New York, NY, 2010).

63 See Russ Juskalian, 10 Years After Napster, Online Pirates Alive and Well, *ABC News* (Jun. 23, 2009), available at http://abcnews.go.com/Technology/story?id=7913205.

model for free dissemination of content, whether amateur or professional, and whether legally or illegally copied and shared.

Another example of the provision of free content is classical sheet music, which has been cataloged online and offered for free, and is now competing with sheet music stores to such an extent that the latter are being driven out of competition. The few remaining stores are typically subsidized by a larger institution, such as the music store at The Juilliard School.[64] It may be that there is little marginal value to selling sheet music, and that interested institutions must underwrite the costs of providing sheet music to their students or to lovers of classical music. If so, this only serves to underscore the point that when goods or services are made available online, their costs can be driven down to zero and their existence must be supported rather than being able to pay for themselves.[65]

3.9 Competing With Almost-Free

In many cases, the scenario of competing with free can become competing with almost-free.[66] In the fashion industry, knock-offs by lower-end fashion houses that come out almost simultaneously with originals are not free, but are at sold at greatly reduced prices. Similarly, very inexpensive digital versions of content, such as knock-off DVDs and video games, may be offered at such low prices that the original content producers cannot clear the margins of their production costs. This is increasingly proving to be the case with other forms of digital content in fields such as media and entertainment, journalism, and publishing.

3.10 Ability or Inability to Price Discriminate

The digital world is characterized by a plethora of content. A sizeable share of online content is easily accessible, attractive, and available for free or at steep discounts. As in traditional media, much content is supported by advertising, seeming "free" to consumers in that they do not have to pay fees, but instead support advertising through viewership. In this context, it becomes increasingly challenging to persuade consumers to pay even modest rates to support content providers by paying for content, even if consumers know that it is the only way to keep businesses commercially viable. There are also many venues for disseminating content online, all of which are competing for viewership or readership. The diffusion of outlets makes it harder for content producers to

64 See The Juilliard Manuscript Collection, available at www.juilliardmanuscriptcollection.org.

65 See, e.g., Laura Gambino, New York City's Last Classical Sheet Music Shop Closes Its Doors After Eight Decades, *The Guardian* (Mar. 6, 2015), available at www.theguardian.com/us-news/2015/mar/06/new-york-last-classical-sheet-music-shop-closes-frank-music.

66 See Anderson, supra note 2 at 135–62.

charge full rates, or to stagger rates so that they can benefit from long-term payoffs that can help defray the costs of works that take time and exposure to succeed in creative markets.

Moving away from a free model has proven difficult, and only compounds the problem that widespread availability of material affords. It also makes it harder to offer tiered pricing, which provides differentiated rates in accordance with different consumer preferences. Tiered pricing, or rational price discrimination, is a strategy that might otherwise help producers reap the returns that their creative content should earn in the absence of competition with freely distributed goods. Content producers in creative industries can gauge audience interest and extract the maximum rents possible from creative content with finely tuned pricing and release options, while allowing audiences to decide how much they are willing to pay for the works that they want to consume.

Flat pricing prevails even in well-established creative sectors. In music, flat pricing models dominate the market, in part for historic reasons. The originator of digital music pricing plans, Apple's iTunes music, established a model in which the prices for digital tracks are kept artificially low and undifferentiated. Apple has been able to maintain these low rates by effectively cross-subsidizing music sales with the much more profitable sale of its electronic devices. While that strategy may not last forever, it has proven robust.

Music producers and musicians have struggled to find ways to make a profit in an undifferentiated rate environment. Subscription services offer some relief, but their track record is mixed.[67] There is some variation in the price of music CDs, but this is a dwindling market that is unlikely to afford producers any financial relief in the long run. The market segmentation of consumers is hard to maintain in a flat online environment, and harder still when consumers can obtain access to some content for free.

Preferential pricing is not always palatable to consumers. They can view it as unfair price packaging, treating people differently for no apparent reason. But preferential pricing can be an important way for creative firms to derive value from their work, and to enable works to reach widespread audiences over time. In effect, it can be a way for audiences willing to pay higher prices for early releases of popular works to subsidize lower prices for audiences willing to wait for later releases. It is a business strategy that creative industries have long relied upon to extract value from their works.

The movie and entertainment industries demonstrate how successful tiered releases and staggered pricing can work. First-run movies are offered at full price; then prices drop gradually as releases come out on DVD and Blu-ray, in second-run or specialty movie theaters, and eventually in niche markets. Similarly, publishing follows the model of releasing hardcover books at top

67 See Daniel Sanchez, What Streaming Music Services Pay, *Digital Music News* (Dec. 25, 2018), available at www.digitalmusicnews.com/2018/12/25/streaming-music-services-pay-2019/.

prices, then following with paperback books at lower prices, and e-books being offered at various points, depending on the publishers' estimates of their appeal.

Some industries have tried to price discriminate in the digital marketplace with scant success. Journalism has struggled with this problem, as it has tried to charge variable rates to subscribers (premium, discount, weekly, weekend only, etc.), newsstand purchasers, and for different online presentations or packages (print plus online access, iPad edition, etc.). This strategy has only proven successful for premium newspapers. Some familiar magazine titles are now defunct, such as *Sassy*,[68] whereas others, like *Teen Vogue*[69] or *Seventeen*[70] exist only online.

Digital technology is not the sole factor undermining price discrimination, but it has given rise to business models that do not readily accommodate it. This can put creative industries at a loss: varying prices is an important tool in helping make their content attractive and affordable to a broad range of customers.

3.11 Struggling for First-Mover Advantage and Marketplace Position

Gaining first-entrant or first-mover advantage can be an invaluable business tactic, as it is often the lynchpin to building a strong market position vis-a-vis competitors. Obtaining first-mover advantage may allow a company to gain a competitive advantage through control of resources, which can significantly increase profit margins and potentially secure market dominance.

First-mover advantages can enable a creative firm to purchase assets at market prices below those that will prevail when the market matures. In markets that only accommodate a limited number of profitable firms, a first-mover may be able to select the most profitable niches, and may be able to take strategic actions that limit the amount of space available for subsequent entrants. It may be able to establish a dominant position in geographic or product space, effectively making it unprofitable for follow-on entrants to enter main markets or secure niche markets. And it may be able to repel entry by competitors through the threat of price warfare, which tends to be more intense when firms are clustered and one is a standout.

68 See Kara Jesella & Marisa Meltzer, A Woman's Magazine That Tried to Be Otherwise, *N.Y. Times* (Jul. 12, 2007), available at www.nytimes.com/2007/07/12/fashion/12jane.html.

69 Sydney Ember, Condé Nast Ends Teen Vogue's Print Run, Plans to Cut 80 Jobs, *N.Y. Times* (Nov. 2, 2017), available at www.nytimes.com/2017/11/02/business/media/conde-nast-teen-vogue.html.

70 See Torie Bosch, Being Seventeen Magazine's Teen Columnist was a Dream Gig, *Slate* (Nov. 6, 2018), available at https://slate.com/human-interest/2018/11/seventeen-magazine-print-teen-columnist.html.

A creative firm with first-mover advantage may make initial investments that express its commitment to the market and establish its position as a market leader and eventually as an incumbent, which expands its capacity for follow-on market growth. The combined forces of early investment, increased capacity for production, and the threat of price cuts to make follow-on entry unprofitable, can create a virtually unassailable position. As a creative firm secures and builds upon its first-mover advantages, it is likely to achieve economies of scale, further anchoring its dominant position. These benefits may enable a creative firm to offer incentives to loyal consumers to prevent them from switching to competitors' products or services; or it may impose costs or penalties on switching that consumers are unwilling to assume.[71]

Technological changes can either empower or disrupt firms, and can change their position in the hierarchy to an extent that can be hard to overcome. This may lead to irretrievable losses, or to near-monopolistic gains, which can eventually transform entire sectors. Amazon is primarily a retail and technology company, rather than a creative company, but it is a classic example of first-mover advantage.[72] It has gained market dominance in a number of sectors, having used its first-mover advantage to secure its position, and having invested in operations and infrastructure, particularly delivery systems, that cannot readily be matched by its competitors.

The music industry illustrates how first-mover advantage can operate to one company's benefit. Prior to the digital age, the music industry was characterized by the dominance of major record labels, music producers that captured the lion's share of music sales and profits. But the emergence of digital music left the major record labels at a loss for a concerted strategic response.

Apple, a new entrant from the technology sector, entered the music industry and first negotiated, and then with increasing market power, increasingly compelled the record labels to join in a compromise: the licensing and sale of individual digital music tracks over the Internet, via the Apple iTunes Store. The price of digital music tracks was initially set at a very low cost (initially, 99 cents per MP3 download). Although eventually followed by such competitors of online music sales as Amazon, Google Music, and other music services, the first-mover advantage that Apple realized was enormous and still seems virtually invincible.[73]

As mentioned earlier, Apple chose essentially to subsidize its online music sales by charging very low prices per download, and realizing a loss or barely breaking even for several years, instead relying on the sale of its electronic devices—which enabled users to access and listen to such downloads—to

71 See Marvin B. Lieberman & David B. Montgomery, First-Mover Advantages, 9 *Strategic Mgmt. J.* 41 (1988).

72 See Scott Anthony, First Mover or Fast Follower? *Harvard Bus. Rev.* (Jun. 14, 2012), available at https://hbr.org/2012/06/first-mover-or-fast-follower

73 See Music's Brighter Future, *Economist* (Oct. 28, 2004), available at www.economist.com/node/3329169.

compensate for any such revenue shortfalls. The strategy proved enormously successful, and secured Apple's top market position in the computer electronics industry.

At the same time, Apple's success undermined the dominance of record labels. The labels were no longer able to command top prices for music sales, and were no longer able to realize the large share of returns that they had seen in pre-digital times. Several record labels did not survive the transition to digital music.[74] And few retained their influence over the music business.

It is noteworthy that Apple, primarily a technology company and not a creative content company, came to dominate the music industry by securing first-mover advantage and effectively dispossessing the major record labels of their dominant market position. It shows that first movers, even when they are new entrants to an unfamiliar field, can exploit technological discontinuities to displace existing incumbents[75] and thereby establish a dominant position.

In publishing, the example of Google Books follows an analogous model: a large, powerful entity, coming from outside the publishing industry, negotiates a similar arrangement that garners for itself powerful first-mover advantage and market position. As in the previous case, Google was able to disempower existing industry participants, and its new model appears to reduce revenues for the industry across the board.

Google has undertaken efforts to create "the world's largest digital library" via a massive book digitization project.[76] It claims to respect copyright in the books it digitizes, with the exception of some "orphan works" that may be, in some cases, still under dispute. Google claims to show on its website only snippets drawn from books in its database, so that books may not be fully accessed and read by its users.

Representatives from the publishing industry, such as the Authors Guild, have claimed that Google is "stealing" from copyright owners, book retailers, and other industry stakeholders.[77] They have argued that a neutral party, such as the Library of Congress, would have been better suited to such a massive digitization project, as it would not be incentivized to maximize revenue by gaining a virtually monopolistic market share in a single database of digitized books.[78] But litigation has resulted in the courts supporting Google's position and allowing Google Books to go forward.

74 See Eamonn Forde, EMI: The Sad Demise of a Very British Company, *The Guardian* (Nov. 11, 2011), available at www.theguardian.com/music/musicblog/2011/nov/11/emi-demise-british-music-company.

75 Marvin B. Lieberman & David B. Montgomery, First-Mover Advantages, 9 *Strategic Mgmt. J.* 41, 48 (1988).

76 See Miguel Helft, Judge Rejects Google's Deal to Digitize Books, *N.Y. Times* (Mar. 23, 2011), available at www.nytimes.com/2011/03/23/technology/23google.html?_r=0.

77 Id.

78 See Anandashankar Mazumdar, Copyright Office Report Outlines Issues Surrounding Mass Digitization of Books, *Bloomberg BNA* (Nov. 2, 2011), available at www.bna.com/copyright-office-report-n12884904134.

The fight over Google Books reveals the resistance that venerable fields such as publishing can show new entrants when confronted with major, transformative change. But it also demonstrates that a new entrant—again, not a publishing firm, but a technology-based company—can step in where an opportunity to take over a market arises, and where incumbents have not been able to work collectively to drive change.

3.12 Limitations of Technologically Driven Strategies to Thwart Copying and Piracy

Content industries may try to fight fire with fire: that is, to solve technologically induced problems with technology-driven measures. Yet even where content industries try to impose technological anti-theft measures such as digital rights management ("DRM"), they may be limited in their ability to do damage control. The use of DRM is always subject to controversy, and many critics argue that it is a problematic tool when used in conjunction with anti-circumvention legislation, such as the controversial DMCA. Some of its opponents, including copyright critic Cory Doctorow, dislike its perceived overreach.[79] Others question its utility and effectiveness.[80]

DRM has proven largely unpopular with consumers, resulting in a lack of user buy-in that is crucial to retaining customers in an increasingly competitive marketplace.[81] The reasons for user antagonism are varied, but run deep. Criticisms range from technical issues to practical concerns to broader philosophical objections. On the technical side, critics argue that DRM can thwart or complicate interoperability among systems and devices, increasing the likelihood that both entrepreneurs and established firms will be locked out of markets if they are not compatible with the most popular devices.[82]

Another technical concern is that DRM can add to consumer frustration by complicating international connectivity (for instance, CDs or DVDs that are DRM-encoded cannot be played on foreign devices).[83] On the practical

79 See, Cory Doctorow, What Happens When Digital Rights Management in the Real World, *The Guardian*, Feb. 5, 2014, available at www.theguardian.com/technology/blog/2014/feb/05/digital-rights-management.

80 See, Ernie Smith, The Incredibly Technical History of Digital Rights Management, *Motherboard*, Oct. 19, 2017, available at https://motherboard.vice.com/en_us/article/evbgkn/the-incredibly-technical-history-of-digital-rights-management.

81 This has likewise been evinced by the controversy over Apple's digital protection, FairPlay, which Apple eventually removed from its products due in no small part to customer protests.

82 See Urs Gasser & John Palfrey, *DRM-Protected Music Interoperability and eInnovation*, Berkman Center for Internet and Society (Nov. 2007), available at https://cyber.harvard.edu/interop/pdfs/interop-drm-music.pdf.

83 See Carlos Serrão, Victor Torres, Jaime Delgado, & Miguel Dias, Interoperability Mechanisms for Registration and Authentication on Different Open DRM Platforms, 6 *IJC-SNS International Journal of Computer Science and Network Security* 12 (Dec. 2006), available at www.researchgate.net/publication/242406689_Interoperability_Mechanisms_for_Registration_and_Authentication_on_Different_Open_DRM_Platforms.

side, critics note that DRM can complicate Internet content streaming, potentially having a negative effect on innovation in a fast-growing area of content delivery.[84]

Critics of DRM also argue that it can stifle expression and interfere with First Amendment rights to free speech.[85] DRM is criticized by some as changing the balance between protection and freedom without the prior agreement of industry stakeholders, including creative artists, content producers, copyright holders, and end users.[86]

3.13 Limitations of Anti-Copying Strategies

Unlike many other creative industries, fashion does not have significant copyright protection. In IP terms, fashion primarily relies on trademarks to safeguard the value of its goods and brands. But fashion is subject to rampant global counterfeiting. Some estimates show that fashion incurs upward of $1.2 trillion in losses per year.[87]

Fashion strives to curtail copying with anti-counterfeiting measures. This has led to a kind of arm's race requiring fashion firms to invest in protective technologies, such as brand and logo encryption and watermarking, which are expensive and evolving. Fashion firms have also undertaken security measures that involve heavy patrolling of known or potential counterfeiting venues, aggressive litigation tactics seeking sanctions against copyists, and other enforcement mechanisms.[88] The technologies that underlie anti-counterfeiting measures are to a certain extent analogous to the imposition of DRM on CDs that the record industry has tried to use to thwart music piracy. But in both cases, the copyists often seem one step ahead of the creators.[89]

84 See Urs Gasser & John Palfrey, *DRM-Protected Music Interoperability and eInnovation*, Berkman Center for Internet and Society (Nov. 2007), available at https://cyber.harvard.edu/interop/pdfs/interop-drm-music.pdf.

85 While more pointedly aimed at Section 1201 of the DMCA, the concern over technological barriers to speech is the basis of a lawsuit brought by Electronic Frontier Foundation against the U.S. Government and the U.S. Copyright Office. See, Press Release, EFF Lawsuit Takes on DMCA Section 1201: Research and Technology Restrictions Violate the First Amendment, July 21, 2016, available at www.eff.org/press/releases/eff-lawsuit-takes-dmca-section-1201-research-and-technology-restrictions-violate.

86 Id.

87 See, The Counterfeit Report: The Big Business of Fakes, *The Fashion Law* (Oct. 11, 2018), available at www.thefashionlaw.com/home/the-counterfeit-report-the-impact-on-the-fashion-industry.

88 See, Sarah Shannon, Fighting the $450 Billion Trade in Fake Fashion, *The Business of Fashion*, (March 2, 2017), available at www.businessoffashion.com/articles/intelligence/fighting-the-450-billion-trade-in-fake-fashion.

89 See, The Counterfeit Report: The Big Business of Fakes, *The Fashion Law* (Oct. 11, 2018), available at www.thefashionlaw.com/home/the-counterfeit-report-the-impact-on-the-fashion-industry.

In fashion, as in music, user response can be problematic. Anti-counterfeiting measures can be unpopular with the public, despite some recognition that they may be helpful. Many consumers are unable or unwilling to appreciate the utility or necessity of anti-theft devices, watermarks, and other anti-counterfeiting measures. Consumers can also resist by opting out of legitimate creative markets. In fashion even more than in music, many consumers knowingly buy illegal products online,[90] at venues that are understood be counterfeiting havens,[91] and even at times in private residences of willing, well-connected customers.[92] Indeed, consumer preferences and practices have shifted to such an extent that among many fashion customers possessing and displaying a high-end knock-off can even be a point of pride.

Despite the campaigns of the elite designers, who plead with consumers to consider the investment costs and returns of original products, the trend, if any, is toward an increased tolerance, if not embrace, of knock-offs. This is somewhat analogous to the pride that some music listeners evince in amassing music collections that have been gathered from free music distributors online, despite the anti-piracy campaigns of artists, recording industry representatives, and others who decry the effect of music appropriation and its repercussions throughout the industry. And in both the case of music and fashion, it is striking that the creative industries have not been able to make a persuasive case that leads users to change their behaviors and beliefs.

90 See, Chavie Lieber, Why the $600 Billion Counterfeit Industry is Still Horrible for Fashion, *Racked*, Dec. 1, 2014, available at www.racked.com/2014/12/1/7566859/counterfeit-fashion-goods-products-museum-exhibit.

91 Id.

92 See Boonghee Yoo & Seung-Hee Lee, The Buyers of Counterfeit Products in South Korea, 3 *Journal of International Business and Law* 1, Article 6 (2004), available at https://scholarlycommons.law.hofstra.edu/jibl/vol3/iss1/6/?utm_source=scholarlycommons.law.hofstra.edu%2Fjibl%2Fvol3%2Fiss1%2F6&utm_medium=PDF&utm_campaign=PDFCoverPages.

4 What Should the Content Industries Be Afraid of, But May Not Be Aware Of?

Unseen Risks

4.1 Social Norms in Creative Ecosystems: Origins in Guilds and Modern Guild-Like Systems

Creative industries are ecosystems whose capacity for self-regulation maintains internal cohesion and structure. Yet their rules may not be explicit or formalized, but may rather be accepted practice and internalized norms. Self-regulation does not displace, but rather is concomitant with, external or formal regulation.

Creative worlds have self-regulating and self-ordering features that are as critical to their functioning as more formal rules of governance such as intellectual property regimes. These features tend to be developed and internalized by creative community members, and can be such a part of the fabric of the whole that they sometimes run the risk of being overlooked or minimized. Yet they are so integral that without their foundation creative industries would founder, losing some of their capacity for resilience and sustainability.

Understanding the roots of creative norms can help illuminate the role that present-day norms play in keeping creative industries not merely operational, but also innovative and open to creative processes. Many of these norms, built around various kinds of social capital, have some of their earliest origins in the guilds that made up many traditional industries centering on creativity, craft, and artisanship.

Historically, traditional communities clustered in small, tightly knit and highly organized groups that were responsible for cultural production.[1] These groups coalesced into artisanal and mercantile guilds that would eventually formalize practices and policies in their areas of expertise.[2] Membership in a guild was necessary for an artist or artisan hoping to produce and sell their

1 See generally Eric A. Posner, *Law and Social Norms* (Harvard University Press, Cambridge, MA, 2002); Robert P. Merges, From Medieval Guilds to Open Source Software: Informal Norms, Appropriability Institutions, and Innovation (University of Wisconsin Law School, Conference on the Legal History of Intellectual Property, Working Paper, 2004), available at http://ssrn.com/abstract=661543.

2 Id.

works in a given field of practice, whether designing and tailoring apparel, wool dyeing and finishing, silk weaving, or skinning and trading furs.[3] Membership conferred many benefits, including the exchange of expertise and specialized knowledge that were often critical to high-quality production, as well as exclusive rights to buy and sell—not unlike copyright today.

Guild membership required adherence to the terms and conditions set down by the society, whether codified into formal rules or accepted as normative precepts. The structure and operations of many early guilds were remarkably similar, demanding conformity of guild members and rewarding adhesion to their norms with access to a broad range of privileges, including access to specialized learning, trade protections, and enforcement of grievances against encroaching outsiders.

Early guilds were constructed to keep artistic communities thriving and secure. They were premised on the acceptance of shared norms and behaviors that were necessary to assure creators in the community that their work would be recognized and valued, and that their reputation, or good name, would be forever associated with their labors and creations. They were also premised on the understanding that a certain degree of openness within the community was necessary to pass on knowledge and to encourage innovativeness and elaboration. Teaching and nurturing young talent, exchanging ideas, collaborating, and building on the work of fellow members could all safely occur within the confines of the guild.

Guilds inform creative industries today by imparting some of their constructs and carrying forward some of their essential norms. They are perhaps most clearly replicated in low-IP spaces, in which guild-like environments operate without substantial overlays of copyright and related formalities. But they exist equally well in IP-rich industries, particularly when they make room for necessary but nonpropertized work to take place.

4.2 Breakdown of the Norms of Social Capital, Reputational Capital and Cultural Recognition

One of the bedrock norms of creativity is social capital[4], which broadly comprises reputational capital, the value that creative industry participants accord each other for their work, and greater cultural recognition. Reputational capital helps secure positions for creative artists in a field and circulates knowledge

3 See Robert P. Merges *Medieval Guilds Redux: Contemporary Institutions for Collective Invention* (2004), available at www.law.berkeley.edu/17026.htm; Randall C. Picker, *Of Pirates and Puffy Shirts: A Comment on the Piracy Paradox*, University of Chicago, *Law & Economics Olin* Working Paper No. 328 (Jan. 2007), available at http://papers.ssrn.com/sol3/papers.cfm?abstract_id=959727.

4 Pierre Bourdieu, *Outline of a Theory of Practice* (Cambridge University Press, Cambridge, UK 1977); Gary S. Becker, *Accounting for Tastes* (Harvard University Press, Cambridge, MA, 1996); Emanuele Ferragina & Alessandro Arrigoni, The Rise and Fall of Social Capital: Requiem for a Theory? 15 *Political Studies Review* 355–67 (Aug. 1, 2017).

among artists about their standing and stature in their profession.[5] It builds bridges within role creative communities and cements solidarity. It can also foster competitive ties, some of which are positive, motivating artists to create works that they think will be both a statement of their abilities and an influence on their artistic peers and those who follow in their footsteps.

Reputational norms serve signaling roles, highlighting contributions and contributors in a given creative field, bringing to employers' notice promising employment prospects, and informing emerging artists of developments in their area of enterprise. In many fields, building reputational capital contributes to the portfolio of accomplishments an individual can bring to the bargaining table. In the plastic arts, having a portfolio of one's works is a signifier of one's professional worth, functioning much as a recording of work in music, a roster of film credits, a curriculum vitae in education, or a resume in other professional contexts. In education, having a body of publications, some of which are likely to be peer-reviewed or co-authored with esteemed colleagues, also serves as a signal to potential employers of the scholar's proven track record.

Reputational norms can confer positive feedback, such as prestige, prizes, and rewards that are both intangible—such as improved standing among peers—and tangible—such as outright awards of medals, prize monies, and even rights in future royalties. Where such rewards are not linked to IP, they may represent an efficient way of rewarding creative work without incurring the transaction costs that are often entailed in collecting IP-based returns.

Reputational capital can be a strong normative force that rewards artists even when they do not retain ownership in their own creative output. It can help compensate for salaries in the field that are not necessarily reflective of individual mastery of a craft, possibly due to low profit margins, under-rated areas of work, understood tradeoffs between salaries and intangibles such as work-life balance, and autonomy over one's work.[6]

Reputation can support artists, but it can also sanction them when they transgress. The failure of a creator to respect fellow artists and their work may incur communal disapproval, if not outright sanction. In the music world,

5 Stephen M. Maurer & Suzanne Scotchmer, *Procuring Knowledge* 2 (Nat'l Bureau of Econ. Research, Working Paper No. 9903, 2003), available at www.nber.org/papers/w9903.pdf.95.

6 The lack of compensation may occur even in the case of mature, highly respected and renowned fashion designers. For instance, the designer Isaac Mizrahi was been compelled to declare bankruptcy well into the trajectory of his career. *See* Constance White, Mizrahi, Designer Most Likely to Succeed, Doesn't, *N.Y. Times* (Oct. 2, 1998), available at www.nytimes.com/1998/10/02/nyregion/mizrahi-designer-most-likely-to-succeed-doesn-t.html; How Karen Millen Lost the Battle for Her Name—and Her Fortune, *The Guardian* (Apr. 1, 2017), available at www.theguardian.com/business/2017/apr/01/karen-millen-how-lost-battle-name-fortune; John Lippman, Coppola Files for Bankruptcy a Third Time, *L.A. Times* (Jul. 01, 1992), available at http://articles.latimes.com/1992-07-01/business/fi-1253_1_latest-bankruptcy-filing.

bands or other music groups widely agreed to have engaged in blatant copying can experience a direct loss of popularity and regard among their peers when their imitation comes to light.[7] This holds true in the video game community as well.[8] Reactions tend to be equally powerful in the stand-up comedy world when comics believe that one of their members has appropriated comic material.[9]

Reputational capital underlies behavior in other creative industries as well, such as cuisine. Due to chefs' desire for peer approval within the culinary community, norms of paying homage to and crediting fellow chefs prevail. When chefs appear to appropriate the property of their peers—not just recipes, but also techniques, finishes, or distinctive features—their fellow chefs may call them out both to punish their violations and to deter other chefs from following suit.[10] Internet stories and blogs about food can be quick to single out and discredit culinary pirates or copyists, which offers one instance of how technology has facilitated social sanctions against breaches of reputation.[11]

Although most creative industry participants value reputational capital, it is not without its detractors. It is arguable that the stronger rights-based practices are actually to be preferred to norms-based systems: they may be more transparent, less guild-like (that is, less liable to restrict privileges and to impose responsibilities on community members), and more readily quantified, and thus more fairly compared among stakeholders.

On the other hand, however, reputational capital may offer compensatory benefits where rights may not be obtained, or where rewards based in rights are likely to be limited, inaccessible, or otherwise unsatisfactory. Reputational capital may also encompass certain cultural values that are shared by artists, such as the importance of peer approval, the utility of enhanced employment prospects, and the promise of long-term recognition and renown.

4.3 Breakdown of the Norm of Attribution

Attribution is another form of reputational capital that derives from guilds and prevails in many creative fields including fashion, education, music, cuisine,

7 *See, e.g.*, Brian Koerber, *10 Copycats Who Stirred Up Treble in Music History*, available at www.mashable.com/2014/06/05/music-copycats.

8 Dean Takahashi, *Buffalo Studios Blasts Zynga for Copying Bingo Blitz Social Game*, *Venture Beats* (Jan. 29, 2012), available at https://venturebeat.com/2012/01/29/buffalo-studios-blasts-zynga-for-copying-bingo-blitz-social-game/ (TinyTown released an infographic to show similarities between their game and Zynga's game).

9 *See generally* Dotan Oliar & Christopher Jon Sprigman, There's No Free Laugh (Anymore): The Emergence of Intellectual Property Norms and the Transformation of Stand-Up Comedy, 94 *U. Va. L. Rev.* 1787, 1821 (2008).

10 *See generally* Michael Goldman, Cooking and Copyright: When Chefs and Restaurateurs Should Receive Copyright Protection for Recipes and Aspects of Their Professional Repertoires, 23 *Seton Hall J. Sports & Enter. L.* 153 (2013).

11 Id.

and comedy. It is commonly agreed that a creator of original work deserves attribution for her creative work. Many jurisdictions consider attribution a vital part of the rights that authors and artists can assert, as in the case of *droit moral* or moral rights that attach under the Berne Convention. In the U.S., the Visual Artists Rights Act of 1990 (VARA) recognizes moral rights, but they apply to works of visual arts.[12] But, as elsewhere, attribution has normative weight in the U.S.

Attribution frequently comes into play when creators engage with the works of their predecessors, whether by consciously referring to, or borrowing from, earlier works, or by taking inspiration from earlier works in ways that make it clear what those influences are and how they are being incorporated in the creative piece. There is admittedly a fine line in many creative practices between appropriation and creative borrowing. Music offers a rich example of how challenging it can be to make such distinctions. Classical music, jazz, and American roots music are all traditions built on borrowing and sharing, as well as communal and often unattributed music production. But that has often come at a price, particularly to artists who have neither been recognized nor compensated for their creativity.[13]

Copyright law is meant to prevent that injustice by assigning copyright in original work and requiring that creative artists be compensated for that work under the rights they have been granted. But copyright has not always been able to help musicians who were unable to control rights in their original work, or to demand payment for their output. While recognizing the importance of copyright, members of the musical community can still look to attribution as a way of honoring the original musician's contributions, giving credit not in lieu of payment, but as another kind of payment, an honorary act of collective recognition.

Creators appreciate and covet attribution, but not merely for the sake of being recognized and praised. Attribution conveys an artist's standing in the community, and helps to establish and anchor artistic reputation. When an artist's works, style, or influence is acknowledged, it serves to bolster the artist's social worth, esteem, and self-esteem. Many artists express a need for recognition and a profound conviction that recognition is as important to their creative flourishing as more tangible or measurable rewards.[14] Equally, attribution can compensate artists whose works are used by follow-on creators. Attribution may not be an economic reward—it may not stand in lieu of

12 Laura Gasaway, Copyright and Moral Rights, 6 *Information Outlook* 12, 40 (Dec. 2002).

13 Larry Rohter, For a Classic Song About Money, Credit is What He Wants, *N.Y. Times*, Jan. 9, 2013, available at www.nytimes.com/2013/09/01/arts/music/for-a-classic-motown-song-about-money-credit-is-what-he-wants.html.

14 See Jessica Silbey, *The Eureka Myth: Creators, Innovators, and Everyday Intellectual Property* (Stanford University Press, Palo Alto, CA, 2014), available at www.sup.org/books/title/?id=20869.

payment—but it may work alongside payment as an emolument. And in some cases, artists may agree that it is satisfactory to receive attribution alone.[15]

4.4 Breakdown of the Norm of Apprenticeship

Many creative and artisanal fields have long-standing traditions of apprenticeship and homage. Emerging artists hoping to build their reputations will often seek to apprentice themselves with master artists, both to learn and to gain credibility and authority by affiliation. In fashion circles, working at an haute couture design house carries its own imprimatur, and is a well-respected resume booster among young talent.[16] Major fashion designers will create original works that secure their reputation, while emerging designers will strive to create break-out works, and if possible to establish stand-alone boutiques that will garner attention and begin to establish their reputation. While not necessarily highly compensated, particularly at the beginning of the arc of their career, many designers consider the regard of peers, as well as audiences, to be a part of the rewards they earn from the act of creation.[17]

Similarly, in cuisine, apprenticeship in the kitchen of a master chef has long been seen as an essential stage of culinary training (it is in fact called a "*stage*," after the French word for apprenticeship), a rite of passage, as well as a means of beginning to secure a reputation as an emerging chef who has been vetted and approved by the master chef. Chefs describe a "culture of hospitality" that they share among chefs and apprentices in the kitchen.[18] They also attribute and acknowledge priority: credit is given to innovators who create new recipes, culinary styles, and methods of cooking: for instance, molecular gastronomy is widely associated with a handful of famous chefs, including Heston Blumenthal, Ferran Adria, Thomas Keller, Jose Andres, and Wylie Dufresne.[19] Secondary chefs may imitate, appropriate, or riff on the works

15 This can be the basis for works released under some forms of a Creative Commons License. Creative Commons Legal Code, *Creative Commons* (Jan. 9, 2008).

16 Christian Dior Is Ready to Reveal Its Secrets, *EuroNews* (Oct. 23, 2017), available at www.livingit.euronews.com/2017/10/23/christian-dior-is-ready-to-reveal-its-secrets.

17 *See* Constance White, Mizrahi, Designer Most Likely to Succeed, Doesn't, *N.Y. Times* (Oct. 2, 1998), available at www.nytimes.com/1998/10/02/nyregion/mizrahi-designer-most-likely-to-succeed-doesn-t.html.

18 Christopher J. Buccafusco, On the Legal Consequences of Sauces: Should Thomas Keller's Recipes Be Per Se Copyrightable? 24 *Cardozo Arts & Entertainment Law Journal* 1121 (2007), available at https://ssrn.com/abstract=923712.

19 See, e.g., Peter Barham, Leif H. Skibsted, & Wender L.P. Bredie, Molecular Gastronomy: A New Emerging Scientific Discipline, *Chemical Review*, 2313–65 (Apr. 14, 2010). Of course, being associated with a style may not always be desirable. Just as actors do not like to be typecast, some chefs do not like to feel pigeonholed. E.g., Adria, Blumenthal, and Keller have stated that they are not entirely enamored of being associated exclusively, or even primarily, with molecular gastronomy. Ferran Adria, Heston Blumentha, Thomas Keller and Harold McGee, Statement on the 'New Cookery', *The Guardian*,

of master chefs, but attribution where at all possible is de rigueur: even in the case of historic dishes, for instance, a chef will often add "in the style of" to acknowledge the precedent source.

The apprenticeship route to culinary success follows in the traditions of apprenticeship and mastery that began in the private kitchens of France and England and followed in the restaurants that eventually emerged in those countries along strong guild-like lines.[20] These practices enable emerging chefs to accrue reputational capital that would be much more difficult to establish without affiliation, not to mention without the rigorous training that apprenticeships entail. Generally, even the most talented young chefs will first learn to master the cooking vocabulary, or the range of dishes, for which the master chefs are esteemed. When called upon to reproduce these dishes, young chefs are able to demonstrate their mastery of fundamentals of haute cuisine. They are then free to parlay their knowledge into more personalized approaches to their preferred cuisine.

These culinary practices leading from apprenticeship to imitation to mastery are predicated upon the ability of chefs to replicate, and eventually re-master, an entire lexicon of recipes that are neither copyrighted nor otherwise propertized. A proprietary system would necessarily change the access that chefs have to this shared repository of culinary learning, and would require some form of rights clearing, such as some sort of licensing or contractual agreement, prior to recipes being learned, exchanged, and possibly reworked. New recipes that involve intriguing variations on older versions might run the risk of appearing not merely derivative but also appropriative, thereby potentially violating the rights of the recipes' copyright holders. Chefs seeking to bring their creative recipes with them to new employment positions might be curtailed from so doing, most notably if culinary establishments and restaurants chose to assert copyright in their chefs' original works. Thus, not only might reputational benefits be forfeited, but also portability of work might be restricted among itinerant chefs.

The culinary world enables essential productivity to flourish without much propertization of creative output. Recipes and cooking styles are shared and circulated among chefs, and are only brought under copyright when written down in cookbooks or recorded on cooking shows. Although cuisine is a sprawling and international industry, it bears close resemblance to a guild-like system, insofar as its prominent chefs are still limited in number, and their reputations are secure among industry insiders by virtue of their skills in the kitchen, rather than by the copyrighted works that they generate. Other

---

Dec. 9, 2006, available at www.theguardian.com/uk/2006/dec/10/foodanddrink.obsfoodmonthly.

20 The story of the gastronomic legend Auguste Escoffier, and his rise from humble apprentice in his uncle's kitchen to owner of the eponymous restaurant that made his fame, is illustrative. See Biography, Auguste Escoffier, Escoffier Society, available at www.escoffier-society.com/biography.php.

guild-like attributes include a freewheeling culture of sharing, attributing, paying homage by imitating or making riffs on famous recipes, and a strong system of apprenticeship that legitimizes and credentializes emerging talent.[21]

4.5 Breakdown of Economies of Prestige

Creators describe a wide range of motivations and rewards that compel them to work, including the intrinsic pleasures of bringing imagination to life, altruistic rewards of enriching others, and the social payoff of communicating and sharing one's vision with others.[22] Of course, many creators work to get paid for their efforts and output, but many also do not cite payment as their primary, or even their most important, motivation.[23] Creators may be at least as interested in more intangible rewards, such as peer esteem, prizes, and leadership roles, as they are compelled by the need for remuneration. Institutions can offer these rewards, but they can be expensive to fund and administer, and the work that they sustain can be costly to underwrite.[24]

There can also be good public welfare reasons to support creative work, making it more reflective of communal goals, more accessible to diverse audiences, and more available and accessible than propertized work. For these reasons, what leading commentators describe as "economies of prestige" can arise when public sector incentives and rewards substitute for private sector

21 *See generally* Debra First, *Chefs Take the Stage*, Boston Globe Jun. 27, 2012, available at www.boston.com/lifestyle/food/articles/2012/06/27/when_the_chef_becomes_the_apprentice.

22 See Jessica Silbey, *The Eureka Myth: Creators, Innovators, and Everyday Intellectual Property* (Stanford University Press, Palo Alto, CA, 2014), available at www.sup.org/books/title/?id=20869.

23 Id.

24 One way of assessing costs associated with tailoring is to compare them with costs generated by other incentive systems. For instance, some commentators call for a range of institutional forms of direct compensation. *See, e.g.*, Michael Kremer, Patent Buyouts: A Mechanism for Encouraging Innovation, 113 *Q. J. Econ.* 1137, 1146–48 (1998) (discussing auction model as superior to patent system); Douglas G. Lichtman, Pricing Prozac: Why the Government Should Subsidize the Purchase of Patented Pharmaceuticals, 11 *Harv. J.l. & Tech.* 123, 124–25 (1997) (subsidizing buyouts by using a coupon scheme); Steven Shavell & Tanguy van Ypersele, Rewards Versus Intellectual Property Rights, 44 *J.L. & Econ.* 525, 526 (2001) (arguing in favor of optional system that allows innovators to be compensated under current patent regime or reward system); Michael Abramowicz, Perfecting Patent Prizes, 56 *Vand. l. Rev.* 115 (2003). Other commentators endorse prize-based rewards systems in lieu of intellectual property entitlements. See Joseph Stiglitz, Scrooge and Intellectual Property Rights: A Medical Prize Fund Could Improve the Financing of Drug Innovations, 333 *Brit. Med. J.* 1279 (2006); Joseph Stiglitz, Give Prizes Not Patents, New scientist, Sept. 16, 2006, at 21; Steven Shavell, *Foundations of Economic Analysis of Law* 163 (2004). I would argue that institutional compensations and prize- based reward systems, or "economies of prestige", can work alongside intellectual property allocations, and indeed are inscribed in certain creative content industries, such as the education sector. They are not, however, likely to be sufficient on a stand-alone basis.

benefits, and serve as better and more efficient stimuli. Two prominent scholars, Stephen Maurer and Suzanne Scotchmer, argue in favor of economies of prestige, observing that "different models of knowledge creation call for different incentive schemes."[25]

Economies of prestige work particularly well in the case of creative environments "where the social value of an innovation is not appropriable by private firms or intellectual property rights are insufficient to cover costs."[26] Generally, the mechanisms that prevail in economies of prestige can be found in various public sector settings. As Maurer and Scotchmer note,

> mechanisms [other than IP rights] have remained important [particularly in the public sector]. . . . Funding mechanisms used by the public sector routinely include in-house development, procurement through competitive bidding, and research grants to universities and promising scientists. The public sector also uses hybrids that mix sponsorship with intellectual property.[27]

In education, prizes, grants, public sponsorships and funding, and so on have historically supplemented institutional resources, private funding, and revenues flowing from the commercial exploitation of IP rights in academic output, such as patented innovations, or trademarked properties. Some scholars, however, have opposed prestige-based incentives and rewards on the grounds that they are less efficient incentives to innovation than market-based solutions such as property rights and market prices.[28]

4.6 Breakdown of Norms of Knowledge Exchange and Collaboration

While many industries value collaborative work, creative fields have among the most deep-seated affinities for collaboration, sharing, and knowledge exchange. Creative entities or individuals will often agree to co-author works and to share rights in the fruits of their collaboration.[29] Just as often, however, creators will agree in advance not to propertize certain parts of the work, or to reserve rights to propertize at some future point in time in the creative process.

25 Stephen M. Maurer & Suzanne Scotchmer, *Procuring Knowledge* 2 (Nat'l Bureau of Econ. Research, Working Paper No. 9903, 2003), available at www.nber.org/papers/w9903.pdf.95 Id. 96 at 1.

26 Id.

27 Id.

28 See, e.g., Daniel F. Spulber, Prices Versus Prizes: Patents, Public Policy, and the Market for Inventions, available at www.law.northwestern.edu/research-faculty/searlecenter/innovationeconomics/documents/Spulber_Prices_versus_Prizes.pdf.

29 D.B. Resnick, et al., Authorship Policies of Scientific Journals, *J Med. Ethics* (Mar. 2016), available at www.ncbi.nlm.nih.gov/pubmed/26714812.

These kinds of arrangements can help collaboration to proceed untrammeled by complicated rights allocations or burdensome licensing negotiations.[30]

In creative ventures where collaborating often occurs loosely and freely, such as filmmaking, theatrical, musical, and operatic production, and some academic work, room for knowledge exchange, collaboration, and informal engagement may be essential to the development and production of what is often a complex, richly layered piece or body of work. This process can be challenged when at the outset the informal norms that facilitate collaborative practices are replaced by more structured, explicated agreements. The risk in this case is that when propertization becomes the new norm, collaboration can entail new, and possibly onerous, licensing, transaction, and clearing costs. Or propertization may require collaborating parties and related stakeholders to engage in more formalized cost/benefit analyses prior to collaborating. Not only might this have a chilling effect, particularly with respect to small-scale collaborations, where the costs of rights management are likely to be higher than the rewards, but it might also change the open and collaborative nature of creative practices altogether, which risks reconfiguring entire creative industries.

4.7 Breakdown of Commons

Many of the features of guilds also arise in commons, semi-commons, or constructed commons. These features include restricted membership, defined borders, practices and norms, and the internal management of rights and rewards.[31] To a greater extent than a guild, a commons may be a part of an ecosystem that is at least partially proprietary and IP-based. The traditional commons that exist in creative fields are analogous to those that arise in real property contexts, as in the classic cases of cattle ranchers and fish hatcheries.[32]

Driving technological change can put pressure on the commons by accelerating resource exhaustion, changing the balance of powers between stakeholders, and overturning established norms. These pressures may undermine the underlying agreements, constructs, and understanding on which the commons is predicated. In education, the constructed commons[33] is grounded in a proprietary model with respect to scientific research and scholarship, but is less formalized with respect to teaching of courses.

30 See generally Yochai Benkler, Coase's Penguin, or, Linux and the Nature of the Firm, 112 *Yale L. J.* 369 (2002).

31 The classic example derives from Garrett Hardin, The Tragedy of the Commons, 162 *Science* (3859), 1243–8 (1968), available at http://science.sciencemag.org/content/sci/162/3859/1243.full.pdf.

32 *See* Elinor Ostrom, *Governing the Commons: The Evolution of Institutions for Collective Action* (Cambridge University Press, Cambridge, UK, 1990).

33 *See generally Governing Knowledge Commons*, Brett M. Frischmann, Michael J. Madison, & Katherine J. Strandburg, eds. (Oxford University Press, Oxon., UK, 2014).

Where patentable scientific work is concerned, some entities are typically granted greater rights than others, and the division of rights is often built into public-private partnerships among academic institutions and corporate allies. But when important fundamental research is concerned, creating some kind of protected commons in basic materials may be instrumental to advancing scientific process.

One example is the data-sharing of basic genetic materials that are essential to a broad range of scientific work.[34] Technology enables genetic materials to be shared in academia by offering massive databases that are readily accessible, user-friendly, sustainable, and broadly available. But technology also accelerates the rate to patenting, which puts pressure upon research scientists to make the most crucial genetic information less widely available, to confer upon the owner a competitive advantage in the race to patentability.[35] This can put pressure on parties who operate within the IP-based system to emphasize property rights at the expense of academic principles, interests, or goals.

Battles are also being fought in the academic world over rights in scholarly publications and academic journals.[36] The Internet has revolutionized the production of, and access to, academic journals, in part by making the contents of these journals available online via services to which academic libraries may subscribe. Databases such as Google Scholar allow individual articles to be indexed by subjects. Certain specialized journals may be prepared in-house, by specific academic departments, and may be published only online. Alternatively, some academic disciplines permit preprint publication of works in scholarly repositories such as arXiv and SSRN, as well as institutional archives.[37]

Currently, there is a movement in higher education encouraging open access[38], either via a process of "self-archiving," whereby the author deposits a paper in a disciplinary or institutional repository where it can be searched for and read, or via publishing it in a free open access journal, which does

34 Adam Rogers and Eric Niller, A Patent Decision on CRISPR Gene Editing Favors MIT, *Wired*, Feb. 16, 2017, available at www.wired.com/2017/02/patent-decision-crispr-gene-editing-favors-mit/.

35 Andrew K. Cordova Robin Feldman, Universities and Patent Demands, 2 *Journal of Law and the Biosciences* 717–21 (Nov. 2015), available at https://academic.oup.com/jlb/article/2/3/717/1918066.

36 *See, e.g.*, John Willinsky, *The Access Principle: The Case for Open Access to Research and Scholarship* (2006); Bo-Christer Bjork & David Solomon, Open Access Versus Subscription Journals: A comparison of Scientific Impact, 10 *BMC Med.* 73 (2012).

37 See Kalev Leetaru, The Future of Open Access: Why Has Academia Not Embraced the Internet Revolution? *Forbes* (Apr. 29, 2016), available at www.forbes.com/sites/kalevleetaru/2016/04/29/the-future-of-open-access-why-has-academia-not-embraced-the-internet-revolution/#4743250f45eb.

38 For further discussion, see Marc Scheufen, *Copyright Versus Open Access: On the Organisation and International Political Economy of Access to Scientific Knowledge* (Springer International Publishing, Switzerland, 2015).

not charge for subscriptions, and may be either subsidized or financed by a publication fee.[39]

The open access movement may advance certain academic norms. But scholarship has tended to follow a more restrictive model of a commons, in which journals and other scholarly publications are broadly available within the universe of academia.[40] While the materials may not be completely unavailable to the outside world, they are often costly and hard to access, often putting them out of the reach of unaffiliated scholars, independent researchers, or the general public.[41]

The scholarship commons has remained semi-closed due in part to expense: the initial costs of production have been borne by publishing firms, while the costs of subscription have been paid by academic institutions. The privatization of the commons that is visible in these technological times in fact predates the advent of the Internet, and its exclusivity has been a matter as much of pricing as means of access. But technology can serve to make the commons more readily available, encouraging academics to consider making it more readily accessible to all interested parties.

Many publishers are well aware of the costs of academic publishing, yet sensitive to the challenges posed by trying to balance those costs and the need to turn a profit against the need for making academic work accessible. Some publishing houses, such as RELX and JStor[42] are developing approaches that work within their business paradigms and make some works accessible and others works reserved for subscribers to their services.

These models may help make scholarship somewhat more accessible. But they are not perfect substitutes for commons: they are proprietary, and may be changed, reclaimed, or monetized by the decision of their owners. They may not contribute to the breakdown of the commons, but they cannot constitute perfect solutions that will compensate for the loss of commons-like spaces and commons-based norms. Nonetheless, the costs of academic publishing remain high, and it remains an open question as to who might otherwise assume the costs of academic journals in the future.[43]

39 See S. Harnad, T. Brody, F. Vallieres, L. Carr, et al., The Access/Impact Problem and the Green and Gold Roads to Open Access, 30 *Serials Review* (2004), available at https://eprints.soton.ac.uk/260209/1/impact.html.

40 Id.

41 *See e.g.* Jstor, which charges $199/year minimum for individuals accessing the database, available at www.jstor.org/jpass/.

42 See e.g., DeepDyve, which allows scholars to stream scholarly content, available at www.deepdyve.com. Moreover, JStor now offers tiered access plans. See, Robinson Meyer, You Can Now Pay for Access to JSTOR's Trove of Scholarly Articles, *The Atlantic*, Sept. 25, 2013, available at www.theatlantic.com/technology/archive/2013/09/you-can-now-pay-for-access-to-jstor-s-trove-of-scholarly-articles/279998/.

43 See Kalev Leetaru, The Future of Open Access: Why Has Academia Not Embraced the Internet Revolution? *Forbes* (Apr. 29, 2016), available at www.forbes.com/sites/kalevleetaru/2016/04/29/the-future-of-open-access-why-has-academia-not-embraced-the-internet-revolution/#4743250f45eb.

Debates over academic scholarship run somewhat parallel to questions that have been raised by the Google Books venture, in which Google has undertaken to scan and digitize several million volumes of books, and to make them available online through its Google Books service.[44] The Google Books project was undertaken in 2004 in partnership with several prominent libraries and universities.[45] Google Books makes available a "preview" or a "snippet" of the work, and allows a full view of the book if it is in the public domain.[46] Although controversial from its launch,[47] and somewhat uncertain as to its future completion,[48] Google Books remains one of the most significant efforts in mass digitization to date.

Google Books represents an interest—not just on the part of Google, but also on the part of its partnering libraries and institutions[49]—in increasing online access to a vast array of books and magazines. In certain aspects, the Google Books project is similar to a commons or commons-like arrangement. It involves a limited number of parties, primarily universities, libraries, and Google; it provides the terms of access to and use of works; and it creates a restricted source for sharing, with the mechanisms that allow sharing to occur.[50]

Google Books is in fact a proprietary system and database, but it arguably has some commons-like features. Its search functions and results are available to all, and its use of previews or snippets gives users the ability to peruse materials and determine if they are relevant to their interests and needs. Unlike a commons, however, its architecture, its algorithms, its software, and its underlying technology are all proprietary to Google. Its arrangements with the libraries, institutions, and repositories are also exclusive to Google. And its dominance of the universe of online searching is both unique and uniquely in the sole control of Google. Unlike the unowned spaces of traditional commons, the Google Books "virtual commons" is wholly controlled and owned.

Is Google Books the kind of commons that would benefit creative industries? It is a joint venture attempting to make digitized works available on a

44 See, e.g, Dylan Love, An Insider's Look at One of Google's Most Controversial Projects, *Business Insider* (Dec. 2013), available at www.businessinsider.com/google-books-2013-12.

45 *See* Kevin Bergquist, *Google Project Promotes Public Good*, *Univ. Record* online (Feb. 13, 2006), available at www.ur.umich.edu/0506/Feb13_06/02.shtml.

46 *See* Google Books Library Project—An Enhanced Card Catalog of the World's Books, *Google*, available at www.google.com/googlebooks/library/.

47 See, e.g., James Somers, Torching the Modern Day Library of Alexandria, *The Atlantic* (Apr. 20, 2017), available at www.theatlantic.com/technology/archive/2017/04/the-tragedy-of-google-books/523320/.

48 See, e.g., Scott Rosenberg, How Google Books Got Lost, *Wired* (Apr. 2017), available at www.wired.com/2017/04/how-google-book-search-got-lost/.

49 See, e.g., Kevin Bergquist, *Google Project Promotes Public Good* (University of Michigan Record, Feb. 2006), available at www.ur.umich.edu/0506/Feb13_06/02.shtml.

50 The description of Google Books given here greatly simplifies and condenses the controversies over the project as well as its complicated, litigious history. Among other things, it omits the treatment of orphan works, a question that was central to its controversy.

massive scale, involving for-profit companies and nonprofit institutions. It has also relied on a fair use defense to protect the "preview" or "snippets" functions, while preserving copyright in works in their entirety. Google Books is indeed an audacious experiment, and an unprecedented one. It may come to represent the kind of quasi-commons that creative industries can embrace or adapt for making their works available, for preserving their back catalogs and archives, or for collecting and digitizing their body of works. But partnering with an entity that has unequalled technological and market power is an innately risky proposition, and leaves creative owners with many unanswered questions about their long-term prospects of ownership, control, and exploitation of their works. Whether this is the creative commons of the future very much remains to be seen.

4.8 Threat to Negative Spaces

Early guilds were important incubators of creative and artisanal work produced at high quality and often in large volume. They were successful at organizing complex skilled production, and at creating the potential to foster innovation because of the incentives they provided and the rewards they captured. Robert Merges, a leading authority in the field, enumerates three characteristics of guilds that highlight their productive capacity:

> (1) an 'appropriability structure' that makes it profitable for individual entities to both develop new technologies and share them; (2) reliance on group norms, as opposed to formal legal enactments, as an enforcement mechanism; and (3) a balance of competition and cooperation under which group-generic information is shared, but individual-proprietary information is not.[51]

As a mainstay of creative production, early guilds had effective appropriability structures, some of which have effectively been incorporated into modern day practice and adopted by modern firms.[52] Many creative industries and firms today may be called guild-like structures that share the ability to exchange information and know-how, the ability to keep vital information flowing among their members yet protected within their parameters, and the ability to allow the appropriation of knowledge to lead to profitability among the group's members.

51 See Robert P. Merges, *From Medieval Guilds to Open Source Software: Informal Norms, Appropriability Institutions, and Innovation* 18–21 (University of Wisconsin Law School, Conference on the Legal History of Intellectual Property, Working Paper, 2004), available at http://ssrn.com/abstract=661543.

52 Hart, Oliver, Thinking About the Firm: A Review of Daniel Spulber's the Theory of the Firm, 49 *Journal of Economic Literature* (2011); Ronald H. Coase, The Nature of the Firm, 4 *Economica* 386–405 (1937).

These present-day "appropriability institutions,"[53] as Merges calls them, include patent pools, industry-wide standard-setting organizations, academic scientific research and discovery, and some kinds of software development, particularly open-source production. They also include less formalized sites and communities, such as comedy clubs, restaurant kitchens, and many venues in music, theater, writing, and plastic arts, including schools, workshops, festivals, training camps, residencies, and conferences.

Guilds, and guild-like clusters of creators, artisans, and professional makers continue to exist today. Many features of guilds have been carried forward as well. Creative fields share the exchange of expertise and skill among their members within formalized structures, such as schools, conservatories, and training camps, and in informal settings, such as workshops, open lectures, and spontaneously organized groups. Some fields encourage their aspiring practitioners to join guild-like groups, such as performing rights organizations in music (ASCAP, BMI, SESAC, etc.), actual guilds, such as some of the major rights organizations in theater and music (Screen Actors Guild (SAG), American Guild of Musical Artists (AGMA)), or unions that replace and undertake the functions of traditional guilds (International Alliance of Theatrical Stage Employees[54]).

The fashion industry has several guild-like features and practices. Indeed, in the early twentieth century fashion actually had a fairly well-established guild system, the Fashion Originators Guild ("FOGA"), which among other operations created a highly effective system of registering apparel, monitoring potential appropriation of registered apparel designs by outsiders, and attempting to maintain apparel prices that had been threatened by competitors' copying and cut-rate sales (although these practices primarily affected apparel at the higher price end of the spectrum).[55]

According to Randall Picker, a prominent commentator, these practices that stood in the stead of actual IP rights might "suggest that a higher-IP regime was desired by high-end designers."[56] But it is an equally plausible approach to argue that the fashion industry was interested in establishing mechanisms to regulate the behavior and norms of the industry, without recourse to the formalized property rights of IP rights systems and the institutionalized remedies of litigation. The Guild's behavior arguably spurred outside competitors to innovate in the design of less-expensive apparel, rather than to copy high-end designs, when faced with the threat of Guild policing and sanctions.[57]

53 Merges, supra note 1.

54 See Susan Adams, Why Should Stage Hands at Carnegie Hall Make $400, 000?, *Forbes*, Oct. 4, 2013, available at www.forbes.com/sites/susanadams/2013/10/04/why-should-stage-hands-at-carnegie-hall-make-400000/.

55 Merges, supra note 49, at 19.

56 Randal C. Picker, *Of Pirates and Puffy Shirts: A Comment on the Piracy Paradox: Innovation and Intellectual Property in Fashion Design* 3 (The University of Chicago, John M. Olin Law & Economics Working Paper No. 328, Nov. 2007), available at http://papers.ssrn.com/sol3/papers.cfm?abstract_id=959727.

57 It is hard, however, to determine to what extent this impetus was caused by the propertization of rights in apparel, whether via a formal registration system of original apparel

The Fashion Guild itself was eventually challenged and dismantled by the courts on antitrust grounds.[58] This raises valid questions as to whether or not guilds or guild-like practices can keep their members in line without coming up against unfair competition laws. But the more pertinent question in IP terms is what the Guild could accomplish with or without propertization of fashion's original designs. If copyright of apparel were to be legislated into being, and if a registry of original designs were to be made functional, certain critical issues would almost certainly surface. For instance, it is clear in the historic case that copyright in dress design would have best served high-end designers. In the present day, however, high-end designers already enjoy a lead-time advantage in the field, as their works are the first to be issued and then followed. This might increase the market position for high-end designers, thereby concentrating yet more power at the top of the fashion design pyramid.

Further, it is unclear whether copyright in design would benefit independent and/or emerging designers, who might be able to register their original works, but might not have the resources to defend any incursions on their properties. In the case of a guild, defense funds might be pooled and set aside to cover members' litigation costs. But in a competitive marketplace, the smaller stakeholders might not realize the benefits of IP rights that they could not defend.

Copyright in dress design might also invite scrutiny of follow-on works and raise the prospect of litigation where designs were discernably similar. This might have a chilling effect on the churn that a fast-paced and highly competitive market such as fashion depends on for maximizing volume of sales. If the fashion market depends on quick obsolescence and turnover, copyright might present more of a hindrance than a help to market activity. In sum, preserving the guild-like characteristics of a creative field like fashion may prove a complicated balancing act, calling for a careful effort to protect smaller emerging designers while still allowing the "appropriability regime" to extract value from its creative works across the market.

4.9 Undermining of "Negative Space" in Fields Where IP Has Not Traditionally Been Called Upon to Keep Productivity Robust

In creative industries like fashion, cuisine, and comedy, IP steps in to cover essential rights and protections, such as trademark protection of brands, and copyright protection of cookbooks and recorded comic routines.[59] But in these low-IP fields, propertization functions best where it is required to counter and penalize predatory copying. In other respects, guild-like mechanisms

---

designs, versus through the active monitoring and public condemnation that the Guild undertook against its competition.

58 Merges, supra note 49, at 2–3.

59 Buccafusco, supra note 18, at 1122.

can function like private ordering arrangements, obviating the transaction costs or administrative costs that can be incurred in IP-based regimes.[60]

The fashion industry exemplifies the functionality of negative spaces. Although structured as a guild at an earlier point in its history, the fashion industry is now so enormous and multidimensional, spanning international production centers and markets, that it can no longer rightfully be deemed guild-like, as its membership cannot now be meaningfully restricted. Nonetheless, it retains some characteristics of guilds: practices of apprenticeship, rewards bestowed by guild-like trade organizations such as the Council of Fashion Designers of America (CFDA), and informal sanctions of members, such as societal disapproval of outright copying.[61]

Factions within the fashion industry have lobbied to move to a property-based fashion regime, in which some copyright in original design might serve to keep productivity robust.[62] However, as previously outlined, there are considerable costs to such proposals. Copyright in fashion design may lead to claims of infringement that are costly to adjudicate. Independent designers may be hampered by inability to assume such costs, even if it is their work that is disproportionately subject to copying. The administrative costs of "registering" designs, proving originality sufficient to merit copyright protection, and keeping up copyright may be unduly high, especially for new designers. And there may be no equivalent in fashion to mechanical rights or synchronization rights in music, which might help creative artists find new sources of revenue. Lastly, knock-off designers may be entirely shut down, which can throttle the flow of desirable goods to appreciative audiences with modest disposable income. In sum, copyright in fashion may actually undermine fashion's negative space without boosting productivity across the industry.

4.10 Loss of Flexibility That Non-IP or Low-IP Spaces May Afford

The low-IP equilibrium may enable certain creative industries to remain flexible and adaptive. Conversely, increasing propertization may come at the cost of flexibility, growth, and innovation. In creative fields such as music, for instance, the ability to work collaboratively on large musical work, such as musicals, operas, performance art, and other large-scale works, may involve a great deal of collective efforts. High levels of proprietary rights may complicate the negotiation and clearing of rights to the detriment of performance,

60 Raustiala & Sprigman, supra note 3, at 1751.

61 See, What Are the Consequences of Copycats?, *The Business of Fashion*, March 14, 2016, available at www.businessoffashion.com/community/voices/discussions/what-is-the-real-cost-of-copycats/fashions-copycat-economy.

62 Innovative Design Protection and Piracy Prevention Act, S. 3728, 111th Cong. (2010). *See also* Susan Scafidi, F.I.T.: Fashion as Information Technology, 59 *Syracuse L. Rev.* 69 (2008).

reproduction, recording, and distribution goals. Increasingly, music permeates a variety of entertainment products, such as movies, theatrical releases, television shows, and so on. The cross-licensing of musical rights has been known to spiral to such levels of complexity that some promising works have been thwarted or delayed due to hold-out problems and other rights-related obstacles.[63] The problem is only heightened by the increasing globalization of music and entertainment, in that international rights become even more costly to assess and administrate.[64]

There are many low-IP regimes that function well with stringent limits on both copyright and patent rights. In the case of computer databases, for instance, a split between U.S. and European Union practices is revealing. In the United States, such databases are unprotected; whereas in the E.U. they are protected. Tellingly, it is in the E.U. that the number of computer databases has actually declined steadily since protection was extended, whereas such databases continue to thrive in the U.S.

A further example from the computer sector is that of open-source ("OS") software. Here, the underlying source code is indeed copyrightable. However, participants in OS programming construct and engage in a cooperative low-IP regime. According to some prominent commentators, OS projects use the default rules of IP law as a lever to require the code's openness—an end that OS projects pursue for what is described as "a mix of ideological and economic motivations."[65]

A third example, analogous to the copyright industries, is drawn from technology and technology patents, and involves the microprocessor industry. This industry maintains another "contractual" low-IP equilibrium. The microprocessor industry harbors a "charmed circle" in the industry of a small number of dominant firms. These firms engage in portfolio cross-licensing, thus freeing them to pursue architectural and manufacturing innovations without concern for the large number of overlapping and conflicting patent claims that may otherwise arise. Added benefits from the large microprocessor firms' perspective are increased entry barriers that the portfolio cross-licenses impose upon would-be upstarts that lack similarly comprehensive patent portfolios.

In all of these cases, low levels of IP rights, or private arrangements that curtail IP rights, can allow knowledge and information to flow freely, and innovation to occur broadly. When that flexibility is restricted, works that benefit from informal exchanges, such as collaboration and cross-pollination, and

63 Matt Alderton, How Vietnam War-Era Music Fuels Ken Burn's New Documentary, *USA Today* (Sept. 6, 2017, 9:56 a.m.), available at www.usatoday.com/story/news/world/2017/09/06/soundtrack-vietnam-rock-music-pbs-documentary/105090768/ (stating it took five years to get the rights to all the music used in Ken Burn's "The Vietnam War").

64 *See generally* Alaister Moughan, Music with Boundaries: Cross-Territory Licensing Issue & How to Solve Them, *New Music Seminar* (Apr. 23, 2014), available at http://newmusicseminar.com/music-with-boundaries-cross-territory-licensing-issues-how-to-solve-them/.

65 Oliar & Sprigman, supra note 9, at 1771.

formal exchanges, such as licensing and cross-licensing, may be inhibited to the detriment of the entire ecosystem.

4.11 Breakdown of Norms: Stealing Versus Sharing

When large groups of users change how they treat content, they may be expressing changes in preferences, but they may also be revealing changes in accepted norms. Changes in behavioral practices that are adopted over time, and that become widely accepted, tend to indicate basic cultural shifts—changes in what people view as normal, reasonable, and fair. The language that people use to describe their practices reveals how behaviors and norms are viewed, whether positively or pejoratively. These shifts in terminology are not merely semantic: they express how users view and value creative works, and how they relate to creative works as audiences, consumers, and users.

In music, many artists and copyright owners, such as record labels, consider peer-to-peer file sharing to be "stealing" or "piracy," depriving them of much-needed royalties that support their livelihood. Before the digital age, most users who thought about taking music without paying for it—walking into a record store and pocketing a CD instead of buying it, for instance—might well have agreed. The tangible nature of real, physical goods helped to make it clear that taking music without compensation to artists was, in fact, stealing it. The normative view was fairly clear: taking music without permission or compensation was largely unacceptable and unfair to creators.

Yet even in the era of physical, real world goods, some music fans copied and shared music, although usually for personal and noncommercial purposes. Many fans made mixtapes, or bootlegged recordings of live performances recorded on handheld devices, and many felt free to circulate their recordings among friends and peers. Some bands, like the Grateful Dead,[66] openly approved of these practices, while others tacitly accepted that some amount of personal copying could co-exist with healthy commercial profits from sales. The general acceptance of mixtapes and bootlegged music revealed a norm of private, noncommercial sharing that co-existed with the norm of paying for recorded music. That norm persists today: some music fans still believe that when they upload or download music on a P2P site, they are merely extending these earlier practices by sharing access and increasing availability among fellow fans and peers.

Some music fans who engage in P2P file sharing argue that music should be made widely accessible at low or no cost. But they overlook the economic costs of online sharing. Digital technology facilitates the quick, cheap, and effortless reproduction of creative content, whether the work is performed live or already recorded. Digital reproduction can match or exceed the quality of

66 See, e.g., Greg Kott, The Grateful Dead: The Band That Could Save Music, *BBC Culture*, July 1, 2015, available at www.bbc.com/culture/story/20150701-the-grateful-dead-the-band-that-could-save-music.

original. And digital technology facilitates the global dissemination of reproduced works. These features bear little resemblance to the localized and amateur efforts of music fans in the pre-digital era.

The economic costs of P2P file-sharing also greatly exceed the earlier costs of fan copying. When digital music tracks can be shared worldwide, at no cost, and at excellent quality, the incentive to purchase recorded music is significantly reduced. The impact is measurable, and demonstrated by the dramatic and immediate drop in industry-wide music revenues that followed the advent of Napster,[67] and the lack of recovery that has been prolonged while illicit file-sharing sites continue to emerge and persevere online.[68] Nonetheless, the idea that file sharing of the Napster variety is tantamount to the kind of personalized copying that once prevailed among some music fans is a trope that has persisted among defenders of P2P services.[69]

Fundamental differences between the physical world and the digital medium can also make it easier to blur the lines between buying and taking a copyrighted work. The distinction might seem less clear because digital works are often easy to obtain—so easy that one need not consider pesky concerns like "who owns the work" and "who is, or isn't, getting paid when I consume the work." When works are streamed online, the complexities of licensing do not enter the thoughts of ordinary listeners; if they do think of licensing at all, it is likely that they assume the licensing has been arranged by the streaming service. Similarly, many users who avail themselves of peer-to-peer music sharing sites do not consider the underlying copyrights of musical works. If they do, they may assume that the artists do not want or need to protect their copyright—perhaps because they think that artists would prefer exposure to payment, or because they think that artists will not miss the small share of revenues they would make if their works were paid for, or because they think that they would not have paid for the works anyway, so artists are not foregoing any income anyway. Whatever the justification might be, some users simply may want to get creative output for free, and may take it where they can get it. Some users many not want to think of copyright implications, or are unaware that copyright is at issue. And some users may prefer not to dwell upon issues of ownership and payment, reasoning that sordid monetary concerns detract from consideration for the greater public welfare.

Compounding the problem is the fact that many services do not make copyright matters clear, or do not even address copyright at all. Many services

67 Stephen Witt, The Man Who Broke the Music Industry, *New Yorker* (Apr. 27, 2015), available at www.newyorker.com/magazine/2015/04/27/the-man-who-broke-the-music-business (stating "By 2003, global recording-industry revenues had fallen from their millennial peak by more than fifteen percent. The losing streak continued for the next decade. . . .").

68 Smith & Telang, infra note 80.

69 See How Not To Get Sued For File Sharing, *Electronic Frontier Foundation*, July 1, 2006, available at www.eff.org/wp/how-not-get-sued-file-sharing.

currently on offer make it easy to convert the music that is placed on YouTube videos into digital tracks, or MP3s. In many cases, this music conversion likely infringes the underlying copyright, and may place the user who is converting the music into his or her MP3 at risk of being sued for copyright violation.[70] But a user who considers using a YouTube-to-MP3 conversion site may well have no idea that these concerns underlie her choices.[71] The conversion site may not disclose them because it is not in their interest to do so, and may choose to remain silent until they are forced to do otherwise. This can make it hard for users to know whether they are taking music legitimately or not.

The norms of music consumers and fans may remain stubbornly divided; and the norms of artists and users may conflict as well. The blurring of lines between artists and users only reinforce these divisions, as does the proliferation of user-generated content. Artists and users alike are divided over how original creative works can and should be used and repurposed, and their interests and allegiances frequently diverge.

Copyright law allows artists to use works as the basis for their own creative efforts, if the use of the underlying work results in creative output that is transformative.[72] But the extent to which the underlying works can be used, and the point at which creative borrowing becomes appropriation remains contested. Some artists believe that original works should remain intact, and that artists who want to use original works should first clear licensing rights and ensure that the copyright of the original works is honored. In recent years, however, several artists have successfully argued that creatively borrowing from other artists' works can create new forms of art and new traditions.[73] They argue that clearing rights for every snippet of work used is unduly onerous and presents an impossibly high obstacle for creative endeavors that draw on multiple sources. Several high-profile cases have offered ample evidence for this viewpoint,[74] and users' defense of creative borrowing of snippets of work seems to be growing in popular support.

These debates can divide creative industry participants. In fashion, some designers who imitate original designs may call their work "homage." Some

70 See Dani Deahl, Major YouTube Audio-Ripping Site Agrees to Shut Down After Getting Sued by Labels, *The Verge*, Sept. 4, 2017, available at www.theverge.com/tech/2017/9/4/16252348/youtube-mp3-org-shut-down.

71 See Paul Resnikoff, YouTube to MP3 Downloaders: Are They Illegal to Use?, *Digital Music News*, Oct. 10, 2016, available at www.digitalmusicnews.com/2016/10/10/youtube-to-mp3-sites-illegal/; but cf. Paul Resnikoff, YouTube to MP3 Stream-Rippers Aren't Illegal, According to the EFF, *Digital Music News*, Oct. 22, 2017, available at www.digitalmusicnews.com/2017/10/22/youtube-to-mp3-legal/.

72 17 U.S.C. § 107.

73 Olufunmilayo Arewa, YouTube, UGC, and Digital Music: Competing Business and Cultural Models in the Internet Age, 104 *Nw. U. L. Rev.* 431 (2010).

74 Margaret Hartman, Ken Burns Won't Have to Turn Over Central Park Five Footage to the City, *New York* (Feb. 20, 2013), available at http://nymag.com/intelligencer/2013/02/ken-burns-beats-citys-central-park-five-suit.html.

who appropriate designs may call their work "knock-offs" (a term that can have a positive connotation in some circles). Other designers, who feel their works are being detrimentally appropriated, call it a "rip-off" economy. In journalism, blog collectives, RSS readers, and other news and information aggregators argue that they are providing a much-needed service, collecting and disseminating material in varied formats to suit the needs of vast, varied audiences. But many of the content creators and providers of their source materials object to such a characterization, arguing that they "cannibalize" the content that they create, eating at their profits and taking away their readership and subscribers. In photography, several artists have asserted and litigated their "right" to use other artistic works in their photographs, sometimes with minimal changes that they allege render the works transformative. This has given rise to a number of highly publicized cases among well-known artists such as Shepard Fairey[75], Richard Price[76], and Hank Willis Thomas.[77]

The deep-seated divisions over access and use of original creative works is reflected in the language that both sides use to describe their intent and activities: theft versus creative borrowing, knock-off versus rip-off versus homage. But increasingly the idea that access trumps ownership is beginning to pervade both popular culture and certain intellectual milieus. The "copyleft" movement argues that works should be kept accessible and in as wide a circulation as possible, and that copyright can all too easily throttle creative expression and the free circulation of creative works.

Resistance to the idea that copyright is necessary, and support for free and open access, is becoming increasingly prevalent. Such a normative shift can be a powerful driver of change, compelling creative industries to rethink their approach to content production and delivery, and creators to reimagine their relationship to their audiences and peers.

4.12 Potential Repercussions of Propertization on the Public Domain

Creative industries generally consider propertization an important means of optimizing rent extraction. Even in historically low-IP regimes, such as fashion and cuisine, strong advocates of propertization argue that maximizing rights in creative work increases the value and protection of creative content.[78] But

75 David Kravets, Associated Press Settles Copyright Lawsuit Against Obama "Hope" Artist, *Wired* (Jan. 12, 2011), available at www.wired.com/2011/01/hope-image-flap/.

76 Andrew R. Chow, Copyright Case Over Richard Prince Instagram Show to Go Forward, *N.Y. Times* (Jul. 20, 2017), available at www.nytimes.com/2017/07/20/arts/design/richard-prince-instagram-copyright-lawsuit.html.

77 Chris McGreal, Plagiarism or Remixing? South African Photographer Accuses Artist of Theft, *The Guardian* (Sept. 13, 2018), available at www.theguardian.com/artanddesign/2018/sep/13/graeme-williams-hank-willis-thomas-photograph.

78 See, Brittany West, A New Look for the Fashion Industry: Redesigning Copyright Law with the Innovative Design Protection and Piracy Protection Act (IDPPPA), 5 *J. Bus.*

what may be overlooked is that over-propertization can be problematic. Some concerns are administrative, such as the increased transaction and administrative costs that property rights typically involve. Other issues that arise in competitive markets, including licensing, rights clearing, and the prospect of increased litigiousness among rightsholders, can also undermine the efficiency of creative ecosystems.

Other concerns that do not seem to directly affect creative firms may be less evident but equally impactful. Creative industries may not realize how much they rely on industry norms of openness in sharing of information, resources, training, and skillsets. All of these practices have developed organically and over time, and they work best when embedded in systems that are not heavily propertized from the outset.

Another consideration is the effect on the public domain. To some content companies, "the public domain" means works that are not subject to property rights and that therefore cannot be obviously or easily monetized. On first glance, then, the public domain is likely to seem unimportant to profit-oriented companies, and only of passing importance to creative industries.[79] Creators may worry that if their works pass into the public domain they will not be able to make a living, while still wanting other creators' works to be widely available. But members of creative industries may not consider the public domain beyond these immediate concerns.

Creative industries should recognize, however, that creators draw from the wellspring of the public domain for inspiration, ideas, and source materials. In industries that are highly propertized, such as music and publishing, works that have entered the public domain over time continue to inspire artists and to be foundational to their efforts. This is why copyright law limits the grant of exclusive rights, after all—so that artistic archives can be accessed, used, and enjoyed.

In creative fields that have historically been propertized, the balance between property rights and access is often contested and patrolled by both sides of the issue, whether advocates of property rights or advocates of broad access. In fields that have not traditionally been highly propertized, the impetus to impose or expand property rights can be more challenging, raising the prospect of sweeping changes that could remove entire areas of work from the public domain. It is hard to tell how much the growth of the public domain would be affected by granting IP rights in currently non-protected creations. But if propertization were increased, the public domain would only be

---

Entrepreneurship & L. Iss. 1 (2011). available at https://digitalcommons.pepperdine.edu/cgi/viewcontent.cgi?article=1071&context=jbel. See also Brandon Scruggs, Should Fashion Design Be Copyrightable?, 6 *Nw. J. Tech. & Intell. Prop.* 122 (2007). available at https://scholarlycommons.law.northwestern.edu/cgi/viewcontent.cgi?article=1061&context=njtip.

79 This is not universally true: in classical music, for example, multiple recordings of works can be lucrative.

meaningfully enlarged if some creators who would otherwise keep their works secret would consent to publishing them in return for copyright protection. The default would alter from a regime that begins with open access to one in which access is granted by a few generous parties. This seems likely to lead to more restrictions being placed on content, which may hinder creators who seek both to contribute to and to draw from the creative marketplace.

4.13 Possible Negative Effects on Creative Content

Making creative work copyrightable may have an effect on the nature of the content itself. Several prominent commentators, including Neil Weinstock Netanel,[80] Dotan Oliar and Christopher Sprigman,[81] and Michael Smith and Rahul Telang,[82] argue that while conventional wisdom sees IP protection as mainly affecting how much creative work is produced, it may also affect the nature and kind of content produced.[83] Oliar and Sprigman point to stand-up comedy to illustrate some of the effects that changes in the environment might have on creative material.[84] They trace an evolution in the culture and economics of stand-up comedy that tracks a corresponding evolution in the norms of stand-up comics: away from a regime that treated jokes as a commons and toward property rules that limit appropriation.

In the comedy world as it has evolved to the present day, a comic is lauded by his peers as well as audiences for the unique nature of his creative material, such as jokes and stand-up routines. His reputation is critical to his being hired for various engagements or gigs, and it is therefore the coin of his realm. A comic's routine must be fresh, unique, and topical to retain the interest of audiences and gain the approval of peers. This means that comics today are incentivized to invest in new, original, and personal content, and to develop unique stage personas.

While paying attention to one another's creative material, comics are discouraged from borrowing jokes or routines without due attribution. Appropriation is prohibited not by externally imposed rules, but rather by internalized norms that render copying an unforgivable transgression against fellow comics. Comics who flout the norms and appropriate creative work may be sanctioned by

80 See Neil Weinstock Netanel, *Copyright's Paradox*, 135–6 (Oxford University Press, New York, NY, 2010).

81 Dotan Oliar & Christopher Jon Sprigman, There's No Free Laugh (Anymore): The Emergence of Intellectual Property Norms and the Transformation of Stand-Up Comedy, 94 *U. Va. L. Rev.* 1787 (2008).

82 Michael D. Smith & Rahul Telang, *Streaming, Sharing, Stealing: Big Data and the Future of Entertainment* (MIT Press, Cambridge, MA, 2016).

83 *See generally* Dotan Oliar & Christopher Jon Sprigman, There's No Free Laugh (Anymore): The Emergence of Intellectual Property Norms and the Transformation of Stand-Up Comedy, 94 *U. Va. L. Rev.* 1787 (2008).

84 Id.

overt criticism, shunning, and other social penalties that may have a negative impact on a comic's employment prospects and standing.

Comic creativity, and unwarranted appropriation of comic creativity, are regulated by an informal norms-based system. The substance of the creative work—the one-liners, delivery style, and other expressive elements of a comic's stock-in-trade—is protected against encroachment and theft. Such protection may not be perfect, but the norms of the community do raise the cost of appropriation, which a prospective copyist may be unwilling to assume.

By raising the cost of appropriating creative comic work, the norms of stand-up comedy incentivize comics to invest more in innovative creative output. Comics today tend to invest in new, original, and personal content, which tends to be observational in nature and point-of-view driven, rather than generalized. Oliar and Sprigman trace the rise of the personalization of comedy in recent years. They argue that comics today invest less in developing the performative aspects of their work, such as sight gags, slapstick, and physical humor, as once occurred in such classic comedic settings as vaudeville. Comics now invest more in original stand-up, such as the routines of Jerry Seinfeld, Sarah Silverman, Wanda Sykes, Louis C.K., and Dave Chappelle. Following the rise of norms, comics do not simply invest in creating more of the same kinds of material as before; rather, they have changed the content of their material and diversified the types of comedy on offer.

Changes in stand-up comedy over time suggest that the benefits of normative self-governing include increasing the amount and value of original material. Norms can therefore enhance the economic prospects of the creative industry. And self-governance may also be self-reinforcing: the more original the humor, the easier it may be to detect appropriation. This may lower the costs associated with policing comic output and sanctioning violations.

The emergence of a particular kind of humor in stand-up comedy—one that relies more on the delivery of personal observations, original observations and witticisms, and self-reflective commentary—supports the idea that creative industries can have real effects on the work of their creators. The structural choices that creative industries make, including deciding what kind of IP-regime will prevail, will also have effects on creative work. Some of these choices involve deciding what communal norms will be supported. These decisions may help shape creative work, and so should remain an important consideration for creative industries as they strategize and move forward.

5 What Doesn't Work

Focusing Exclusively on Business- or IP-Based Solutions

5.1 What Can Changing the Business Model Do?

5.1.1 Changing the Business Model Can Promote Certain Key Behaviors Generally Agreed on as Being Optimal for the Growth and Development of Private Enterprise

Creative firms, like most businesses, reach first for private ordering strategies and solutions—contracts, private arrangements, licensing and cross-licensing agreements, and mutually agreed upon commons—when seeking to respond to new business challenges.[1] These challenges can involve disruptive technologies such as digitization, but also changes to logistics systems, data compilation, and data mining.[2]

Business-based solutions give private enterprises the freedom to pick and choose exactly what suits them without requiring cumbersome governance mechanisms, burdensome administrative and other transaction costs.[3] They may have government oversight, but the rules of that oversight are usually foreseeable and relatively clear-cut.

Private ordering solutions allow both emerging and mature industries to adapt to technological and other kinds of disruptive innovation by rewarding positive innovative choices and behavior and weeding out regressive choices and behavior. In creative sectors, as in most business communities, market-based solutions are also preferred because they tend to be more fast-paced than policy-oriented and legislative fixes.

1 William M. Landes & Richard A. Posner, *Indefinitely Renewable Copyright* (John M. Olin L. & Econ. Working Paper No. 154, 2002), available at www.law.upenn.edu/fac/pwagner/ip/2003sp/downloads/landes-posner_indefinite.pdf.

2 Mark A. Lemley, Is the Sky Falling on the Content Industries? 9 *J. Telecomm. & High Tech. L.* 125, 133 (2011).

3 Jennifer E. Rothman, Copyright's Private Ordering and the "Next Great Copyright Act," 29 *Berkeley tech. L.J.* 1595, 1598 (2014). ("In some instances, the best option is for [copyright] law to get out of the way and leave room for a variety of private approaches to flourish.").

Business model changes may also promote relationships between firms, and motivate them to enter into transactions, licensing deals, cross-subsidization, and other arrangements that maximize value for multiple entities. In fostering both competitive and cooperative relations, a strategic repositioning may benefit not just industries but also entire regions of work, often creating spillover effects and enabling the capture of positive externalities.

In changing times, businesses can turn to their users to crowd-source ideas, funding, or other resources, which may drive innovation faster, as a greater number of participants can generate an overall increase in creativity. It can provide clarity and convenience to users, mainly through transparency of the business plan and what it offers to consumers. By signaling what is available in the market, it gives consumers free choice in goods and services. And it can build brand loyalty by making consumers feel integral to business success.

Changing the business model can help to correct static, broken, or intractable industries from within, particularly when they have been rendered obsolete. It can support industries that can flourish without the need for significant layers of IP protection. And in some cases, it can help creative industries learn and draw from the successful business models of no-IP or low-IP regimes.

Creative industries that develop good business models can reduce their transaction costs, such as those involving IP rights management. Economies of scale can help lead to even larger savings. Taken as a whole, these factors contribute to the idea that changing business models has an edge over changing IP-based allocations as the most efficient first-order solutions to commercial challenges.

5.1.2 Changing the Business Model Can Facilitate Interoperability

Negotiated agreements enable companies to secure their market position in an industry, giving content-rich companies the ability to compete in new, or newly contested, markets. When technological innovation brings elemental changes to an industry, companies have to vie for a foothold. For instance, a new technology may give rise to new venues for content dissemination, and content providers will then be compelled to seek out and secure channels for distribution of their content.

In music, the development of portable music players—beginning with boom-boxes, tape players, the Sony Walkman, and evolving to the iPod and other handheld devices—required music producers to ensure that each successive new device would accommodate their product. While each development made it easier for audiences to carry and listen to their preferred music, each time the technology improved also made it critical for music producers to make their works available on the latest portable product.

In the era of the Internet, however, technology companies are raising the bar of exclusivity in the portable music market. Contemporary electronics manufacturers are able to limit interoperability by restricting their software to prevent content from being carried on competing devices. By curtailing compatibility among devices, these electronics companies can lock consumers into their universe, and can compel content providers to release their product via exclusive, proprietary pipelines.

While digital music may be released in a standard format, such as the MP3, it may not necessarily be able to be released via multiple devices without prior negotiation among the content providers and each specific electronic delivery system. The lack of compatibility, or interoperability, demands a level of negotiation that is far more complicated than occurred when simpler, more generic electronics were commonplace. But consumers can press creative firms into creating delivery channels that satisfy their needs, driving interoperability through demand.

Today, content companies must look to business strategies that optimize the release and delivery of creative products on multiple devices under multiple negotiated agreements. One area in which music is improving is the growth of online streaming services, which enable music to be streamed on a wide variety of devices and via a range of providers. There is growing competition among streaming services, however, and whether rights can be cleared across those services remains to be seen.

5.1.3 Changing the Business Model Can Draw From the Business Model of Low-IP and/or No-IP Regimes

Industries that are built on low-IP or no-IP frameworks can offer a useful blueprint for companies that want to build business plans flexible and resilient enough to adapt to disruptive innovation. Mature creative industries that are structured to promote product and innovation flows without substantial property rights and protections have evolved the means to protect core competencies. They also tend to be flexible, enabling them to capitalize on trends, tastes, and built-in obsolescence. Many low-IP creative industries have developed the ability to capitalize on creative performance, rather than merely on creative product. And they have the vision to allow copying to drive creativity, indirectly leading to increased profitability for the original creative individual or entity.

In creative industries with high turnover, protecting core competencies can mean turning out original productions at a high rate. In the fashion industry, original designers must constantly create new designs that feed consumers' insatiable appetite for new and trendy apparel and accessories, a turnover known as industry churn.[4] Fashion design is not copyright protected, but the need for copyright can be lessened when the value of goods has a short duration and when initial high volumes of sales are made.

4 See generally James Surowieki, The Piracy Paradox, *New Yorker* (Sept. 24, 2007), available at www.newyorker.com/magazine/2007/09/24/the-piracy-paradox.

In fashion, some profits may be lost due to knock-offs. But top haute couture designers rely on the appeal of their original and exclusive works to protect the profitability at the top of the fashion pyramid. They also use haute couture to secure their reputations and bolster their trademarks, which they exploit to generate profitable licensing streams. Trademarks, therefore, are by far the main IP protection they rely on, but the trademarks are based on, and take value from, the creative work that fashion designers produce at the beginning of the fashion cycle. Equally important, the originality of creative fashion designers creates an imprimatur that is in a sense captured by trademark, but which speaks to the creativity and authorship that creators value and use to secure their distinction in the field.[5]

Other industries, such as architecture and technological and industrial design, similarly have core competencies that are not easily replicable, which can help protect the efforts and output of their skilled workforce (although these industries do enjoy varying, and in some cases significant, degrees of IP protection). In architecture, for instance, design protection is limited, but the originality of star architects is prized, and their distinctive design is strikingly identifiable and readily associated with the architects and the firms that they establish.[6] Lower tier architects find it hard to replicate their work, and may face some degree of censure within the industry if they borrow too heavily, or imitate too closely, the recognizable work of industry leaders.

Computer software is another case in point, although slightly different than creative fields: the software product may ultimately be IP-protected, both by copyright and by patent. But many software designers and programmers value contributions to open-source software, which is not subject to IP protection.[7] In part, this is due to the value attributed to creative prowess in the computer design world. Working on open-source software enables professionals in the computer field to demonstrate their mastery of software design, while still protecting their own skills, work, and the value of their creative production.

Comedy is a creative industry that is moving toward commodified performances and away from commodified creative products.[8] In comedy, the

5 As one prominent commentator on fashion and copyright notes, "the rhetoric of authenticity performs much the same social function as property ownership, placing the claimant group in a position superior to all others with respect to the item in question." Susan Scafidi, Who Owns Culture? *Appropriation and Authenticity in American Law* 54 (Rutgers University Press, New Brunswick, NJ, 2005). On authenticity and authorship, see Martha Woodmansee and Peter Jaszi, The Construction of Authorship: Textual Appropriation in Law and Literature (Post-Contemporary Interventions) (Duke University Press, Charlotte, NC, 1994).

6 Edwin Heathcote, Age of the "Starchitect," *The Financial Times* (Jan. 26, 2017), available at www.ft.com/content/d064d57c-df01-11e6-86ac-f253db7791c6.

7 See generally Steven Weber, *The Success of Open Source* (Harvard University Press, Cambridge, MA, 2004).

8 Christopher Buccafusco, A Theory of Copyright Authorship, 43 *Virginia Law Review* (2016).

stand-up comedy routine as performed by a talented comedian can be more valued than the jokes and/or actions, such as sight gags, that make up the act. Recordings of stand-up routines, whether broadcast or televised, enable professional comics to capitalize on performance rights as well. But fresh routines and live acts remain the coin of the realm in the contemporary comedy circuit.[9]

Analogously, in cuisine, the recipes of famous chefs may only occasionally generate revenues when compiled in cookbooks. More significant are the performances of chefs, such as cooking shows, lessons, demonstrations, and of course the meals that they produce in restaurants, which are not typically copyrighted. Even when famous chefs are involved, recipes are not generally deemed valuable in the culinary realm. Many recipes are freely shared and circulated, for instance via such websites as epicurious.com, marthastewart.com, and so on. These recipes are viewed as loss promotional items, intended to drive cooking audiences to purchase products such as the sale of magazine subscriptions, such as *Bon Appetit*, *Gourmet*, and *Cooks Illustrated*, or to follow the ventures of famous chefs, such as Gordon Ramsey, Nigella Lawson, and Ina Garten.[10]

5.1.4 *Changing the Business Model Can Help With Contracting Into Optimal Arrangements*

Creative firms are typical commercial firms that use contracts to set the terms of their relationships, whether within the industry or with respect to end users, or both. Where it is optimal to contract around IP entitlements, or in some cases even to contract them away, creative firms can find that contractual arrangements are a superior means of striking an optimal balance of ownership and access.[11]

Contracting can be particularly effective when IP rights have been inefficiently allocated in a given sector, or when judges, legislators, or administrators create systemic inequities that cannot be easily rectified, appealed, or reversed. Contracting allows multi-party arrangements and complex licensing schemes to be secured in the case of large, complicated creative endeavors, many of which will span multiple genres, locales, domestic and international venues for release, and long-term payouts.

In creative industries that involve a number of interrelated rights, business models need to be structurally sound yet versatile, allowing for multiple rights

9 Daniel Smith, Self-Heckle: Russell Kane's Stand-up Comedy as an Example of "Comedic Sociology," 15 *Ephemera: Theory & Politics in Organization* 516 (2015).

10 See Hell's Kitchen (Fox 2005-Present); Simply Nigella (BBC Two 2015-Present); Barefoot Contessa (Food Network 2002-Present).

11 See generally Robert Merges, Contracting into Liability Rules: Intellectual Property Rights and Collective Rights Organizations, 84 *Cal. L. Rev.* 1293 (1996); Mark Lemley, Contracting Around Liability Rules, 100 *Cal. L. Rev.* 463 (2012).

that must be cleared and new rights that may be valuable to add on as new opportunities arise. In the film industry, examples of complex business models have long involved clearing rights for music, background, any historical resources, and other materials and resources that are copyright protected.[12] The emergence of motion picture franchises has increased the complexity of rights clearing due to several new profitable features: valuable characters that can play roles in multiple films (for example, DC, Marvel Comics, and action figures), product tie-ins, television and mini-series rights, video game rights, and a host of trademark, merchandising, product placement, and other related rights.[13]

5.2 What Does Changing the Business Model NOT Do?

Changing the business model can also be problematic. It can interfere with interactions among companies, or between companies and end users. It can curtail interoperability, restrict spillovers, or counter positive externalities. It can also lead to suboptimal outcomes due to imbalances of bargaining power among stakeholders. And changing the business model can potentially have a negative effect on non-commodified values, social interests, and democratic goals.

5.2.1 Changing the Business Model May Not Promote Interoperability

Business model changes may be made in pursuit of a supra-competitive advantage, such as one company establishing a dominant position that imposes a closed ecosystem on its users and thereby locking up the entire industry. Typically this closed system precludes interoperability with outside devices, products or systems, as its raison d'etre is to keep users dependent on one company's spectrum of products and services.

While this can work to the advantage of a single entity, it tends to be suboptimal for the industry and its community of end users. A closed system can lead to monopoly like pricing, as users who are compelled to purchase goods and services within a closed system can neither seek out compatible but less costly products nor engage in comparison price shopping. A tightly controlled ecosystem can force third-party vendors such as applications developers to

12 See Baseball (PBS Series, 1994); but see Margaret Hartman, Ken Burns Won't Have to Turn Over Central Park Five Footage to the City, *New York* (Feb. 20, 2013), available at http://nymag.com/intelligencer/2013/02/ken-burns-beats-citys-central-park-five-suit.html.

13 See, e.g., Cathy Jewell, From Script to Screen: What Role for Intellectual Property?, World Intellectual Property Organization (WIPO), available at www.wipo.int/pressroom/en/stories/ip_and_film.html.

conform to the dictates of the controlling company. Such dictates may include assurances that the third-party entities will not create products compatible with competitors' products, thereby reinforcing the dominant position of the initial company. And closed ecosystems that preclude interoperability can impede or divert innovation of a range of new devices, systems, or products.

Typically, a dominant company can constrain competitors or third-party vendors to innovate within its parameters or to risk being marginalized. Competitors that devise entirely new systems, even if such systems are superior in various aspects to the dominant ecosystem, run the risk of being shut out of the market, due to their inability to secure a position at the margins of industry production. Thus, innovation across the industry may be constricted by the inability of an industry to sustain parallel or multiple tracks of development among competitors, particularly in cases where a single company or cluster of companies can establish a prevailing industry standard.

5.2.2 Changing the Business Model May Not Promote Collective Solutions, and Other Communally Worthwhile Outcomes

Individual companies that change business models are typically acting competitively, which may or may not promote collective solutions. If it is in their rational self-interest to enter collaborative arrangements, companies will leave room for collaborating in their business plans. Illustrative are scientific research institutions, which often cooperate in building data-sharing resources such as genetic databases that make gene sequences available to researchers within the scope of the patent pool.[14] In these cases of rationally driven collaboration, institutions that are otherwise competitors agree to share access to data within the scientific community in order to promote advances in fundamental research and discovery. These collaborative arrangements foster promising scientific research, but also try to put into place mechanisms to avoid contentious claims and disputes that can arise when research ultimately yields significant breakthroughs, discoveries, and inventions.[15]

In highly propertized regimes, collaboration becomes useful when competitors require access to a common pool of data or resources and seek to avoid costly rights-clearing processes in advance of their efforts. In the latter situation, however, the commons that is created offers a collective solution to a potential early-stage roadblock, but it does not perforce promote collaboration in the research and discovery work itself. Valuing collaboration also entails a normative preference that might seem fairly common but that is, in fact, far from universal.

14 See Online Mendelian Inheritance in Man, *Omim* (last updated Mar. 1, 2019), available at www.omim.org.

15 But see, Adam Rogers & Eric Niler, A Patent Decision on CRISPR Gene Editing Favors MIT, *Wired* (Feb. 16, 2017), available at www.wired.com/2017/02/patent-decision-crispr-gene-editing-favors-mit/.

Many creative industries do seem to share the idea that collaborative, interdisciplinary, or team-driven work helps innovators to reach goals together that may not have been attainable individually, and that it should be seen as an intrinsically desirable social good. But when property rights give preference to individual creators, collaborative values may not seem so pressing as to be prioritized at the expense of a copyright owner's rights and rewards. When individual and communal rights and rewards do not align, business solutions may advance the former at the expense of the latter, absent specific choices that are designed to advance or protect the communal good.

5.2.3 Changing the Business Model May Not Promote Cumulative Innovation

Changing business models may promote cumulative innovation in creative industries, but it must be a goal that is pursued deliberately. In many industries that rely primarily on patent rights to thrive and grow, cumulative innovation is promoted not only by business models but also by a strategic use of patenting versus publication rights. Here, publication can be a strategic way to distribute or divide the bargaining surplus between the original inventor and cumulative improvers.[16]

Similarly, employee mobility and knowledge portability can serve to advance cumulative innovation within innovative industries.[17] Human resource strategies can be shaped by changing business models, such as, for instance, crafting non-competition agreements for employees at various levels, or promoting the exchange of ideas in some open-source endeavors; or they may be advanced by changing IP policies, such as extending publication rights to employees. Other possibilities include changing the baseline of ownership rights in employee work, and possibly moving from a default work for hire rule to more flexible rules that allow employees some ownership stake, or equity position, in their work.

In education, scholarship and research in scientific fields have often sought to promote cumulative innovation through a combination of business-related and IP-related strategies. Increasingly, instruction and coursework in education are becoming potential grounds for cumulative innovation, collaborative efforts, and useful idea exchange. But changing business models in education may not advance such causes, particularly as the increasing adjunctification of education does not particularly incentivize or reward collaborative work. If valued, cumulative innovation in education is likely to require both changing business models and adaptive IP entitlements to continue to occur.

16 See generally Oren Bar-Gill & Gideon Parchomovsky, The Value of Giving Away Secrets, 89 *University of Virginia Law Review* 1857 (2003).

17 See generally Oren Bar-Gill & Gideon Parchomovsky, *Intellectual Property Law and the Boundaries of the Firm* (Penn Law, Legal Scholarship Repository, Paper No. 65, 2004).

5.2.4 Changing the Business Model May Not Protect End-User Rights, the Public Domain, or Less-Powerful Stakeholders

Creative industries or firms customarily change their business models to protect their revenue-generating properties and processes. But these industrial priorities, however rationally self-interested, can run counter to the interests, rights, activities, and values of other stakeholders.

Changing business models may have a varied effect on consumers and end users. On the one hand, they can create economies of scale, cost efficiencies, or other positive effects that can get passed down to the consumer, such as through lowered prices. On the other hand, however, they may prove adverse to end users' interests. They may change previously accepted terms, such as reducing the scope of permissible activity (for instance, imposing new restrictions on "personal use," or curtailing rights of "fair use"). They may raise user fees for consumption or engagement with products. And they may redraw the lines of access to creative properties that can serve as building blocks for user-generated content or other creative activities. Changing business models may also fence in properties and activities that were previously considered part of a creative and cultural public domain. Not only end users but also the general public may be implicated in fencing off, which can detract from common welfare.

Changing business models can have an adverse effect on the rights and rewards of stakeholders that do not have a strong or competitive bargaining position. Stakeholders that have less leverage may be effectively forced into suboptimal positions with consonantly suboptimal results. This is likely to occur when a changing business environment causes companies to pursue new profit-maximizing strategies that favor well-positioned entities over emerging, independent, or newer entrants. The lack of leverage can prove even more costly when new entrants stand alone, unsupported by supporters or lobbyists that can fight to protect their profit paradigm and market share.

In music, as in other areas of entertainment, end users can face extensive costs levied by changing business models.[18] They can include new restrictions on the use of content, as in the case of music or films that are purchased online and that can only be downloaded onto a limited number of devices.[19] In terms of personal use, the right to reproduce creative works—even those that have been duly purchased by the end user—may be limited or cut off by technological

18 Netflix and its ever-increasing pricing is a good example. Netflix needs to differentiate itself, so they make more content, which requires more money, so prices go up. See, available at www.cnn.com/2019/01/15/media/netflix-raising-prices/index.html. Another example is 2-D and the effect on Imax's ticket prices. See, Lauren A.E. Schuker and Ethan Smith, Higher Prices Make Box-Office Debut, *Wall Street Journal*, March 24, 2010, available at www.wsj.com/articles/SB10001424052748703312504575142143922186532.

19 Similarly, in the case of film, video and recorded television series, works that were previously available for multiple personal uses are similarly curtailed, such that an end user may only view the works on certain devices.

means (that is, anti-copying protections). This can lead to an odd imbalance, such as a user's ability to enjoy a wide range of personal uses of hard copies of creative works (for instance, the ability to copy movies onto hard drives) but her inability to extend these same personal uses to digitized versions of creative works (for instance, her inability to stream films on multiple devices).

The access that end users have to creative work, as well as their ability to use it in innovative, creative, or transformational ways, may be impeded or thwarted by changing business models. In music, established practices have historically allowed artists to borrow from one another and thereby to create new and transformative works, and even entirely new genres—the growth of much modern folk, rock, blues, and R&B music is predicated on such creative borrowing. Increasing emphasis on the propertization of music may be one approach that the music industry has taken to disallow creative borrowing without rights clearing and/or royalty payments being assessed.[20] This may be primarily an outcome of IP-based solutions that seek compensation for musical borrowing, even in cases where the new artist is not clearly appropriating the original work but may rather be trying to use it in an innovative and transformative manner.[21]

Some critics have argued that the music industry seems to have made a concerted business decision to repress creative borrowing that may entail even the slightest of inroads on propertized material. Thus, for instance, in the 1980s the industry brought its force to bear on the practice of music sampling, in which the creative practice called for mixing short portions or samples of recorded music to create a new, fresh, and original work.[22] As sampling grew in popularity, the music industry demanded that artists and/or DJs obtain clearance of copyrights of all the short samples used to comprise their works.[23] Clearing the copyright thickets proved challenging for all but the most successful musicians and DJs, which led to a number of musicians encountering legal difficulties with respect to their use of uncredited samples.[24] As a result, the innovative practice of music sampling was largely thwarted, and many of its creative practitioners were forced to abandon their efforts in order to steer clear of the sampling stalemate.

20 See generally Michael W. Carroll, The Struggle for Music Copyright, 57 *Fla. L. Rev.* 907 (2005).

21 Olufunmilayo Arewa, *YouTube*, UGC, and Digital Music: Competing Business and Cultural Models in the Internet Age, 104 *NW. U. L. Rev.* 431 (2010); Urs Gasser, iTunes: How Copyright, Contract, and Technology Shape the Business of Digital Media - A Case Study (Berkman Center for Internet & Society at Harvard Law School Research Publication No. 2004-07, June 2004), available at http://ssrn.com/abstract=556802.

22 See Chris Richards, The Court Case That Changed Hip-Hop—From Public Enemy to Kanye—Forever, *Wash. Post* (Jul. 6, 2012), available at www.washingtonpost.com/opinions/the-court-case-that-changed-hip-hop--from-public-enemy-to-kanye--forever/2012/07/06/gJQAVWr0RW_story.html.

23 Id.

24 Id.

5.2.5 Changing the Business Model May Not Maximize Spillover and Network Effects

Spillover and network effects are positive externalities that frequently arise in locales that are rife with creative and innovative industries (for example, Silicon Valley, Boston, and the Research Triangle in North Carolina). In these areas, innovation by a firm may spill over to others in its orbit, fostering the productivity of other firms without the need for recourse to exogenous incentives, such as direct governmental intervention.

Spillover effects cause the area in which they occur to become more active, fertile, and ultimately desirable, drawing more talented people and generating more dynamic activity. When productivity is concentrated in a vibrant locale, it accelerates the pace of growth and development, leading to positive network effects—that is, the products and services that are generated gain additional value as more people use and contribute to them.

In these conditions, the social returns to overall innovation, and to the creative and innovative ecosystem, are likely to exceed the private returns to any given entity. In part, this is because the benefits of innovation may spill over to other firms in ways that cannot be fully internalized by any one firm or even cluster of firms.[25] The level of these spillovers varies by industry and by the degree of industry and knowledge concentration in the area. Further, sector-specific productivity is directly related to the level of spillover.

The inherent "leakiness" of practices and propertization can have a positive effect on innovation in some industries. In general, spillover effects and network effects are not driven by any single corporate entity. When a single entity changes business models, it is usually making a strategic choice that is intended to maximize its market position and its revenue: it is engaging in a competitive strategy that is self-interested, and not aimed at enhancing spillover and network effects. But when entire industries grow and benefit from the cumulative impact of changing business strategies, they may realize spillover and network effects that percolate throughout their ecosystem.

5.3 What Are the Relative Advantages and Disadvantages to Changing the Business Model *versus* Changing the IP Model?

5.3.1 Business Model Advantages

Business solutions typically offer more granular solutions that can be structured to fit the needs of a company, a class of companies, or a given industry. They can be more specific than the "one size fits all" model of IP entitlements,

25 Hart, Oliver, Thinking About the Firm: A Review of Daniel Spulber's the Theory of the Firm, 49 *Journal of Economic Literature* (2011); Coase, Ronald H., The Nature of the Firm, 4 *Economica* 386–405 (1937).

which are usually so broadly written and construed as to span many industries under one paradigm, such as the relatively monolithic grant of copyright, rather than being shaped to fit the contours of any particular industry. Business model changes tend to be more flexible than alternatives, and can be adjusted and readjusted as environments fluctuate, without requiring external approvals from legislatures, governing bodies, administrators, and industry stakeholders.

The basis for industrial private ordering is generally rational self-interest on the part of industry actors. Private ordering is a negotiated decision intended to obtain the best possible results for all of the interested parties. While policymakers may strive for such a utilitarian outcome, they may be hampered by information asymmetries, a lack of deep understanding of the industry, or the need to strike a compromise with outside stakeholders who may bring their own interests to the table. While these are not always negative considerations, they may not seem to business interests to be cost-effective or frictionless means of change.

5.3.2 IP Advantages

Changing IP entitlements in a creative industry involves across-the-board measures that are not privately ordered, open to negotiation ex post (that is, after IP measures have been put in place), or granular at a company-specific level. When disruptive innovation occurs, creative firms rush to devise counter-attacks that will secure their profitability. These efforts have the advantages of speed, customization, and responsiveness to immediate challenges. In contrast, changing IP entitlements can entail a laborious and painstaking process of negotiating rights among stakeholders, persuading legislators and policymakers, establishing new practices and norms under the newly enacted system, and hammering out the details once the new rules are in place.

Yet when disruptive innovation threatens, and market failure is imminent or at hand, industries sometimes clamor for changing IP entitlement allocations as a sure-fire solution. They calculate that changing IP will increase the overall returns flowing from the exploitation of content owned by copyright holders. Most industry stakeholders call for increased IP protection. Some argue that more protection plus technological lock-ups such as DRM are required to stave off incursions from Internet-enabled activities that negatively affect revenues, such as widespread copying, dissemination, and resales. Despite the lack of granularity, changing IP entitlements as an industrial strategy can be seen as an important weapon in the arsenal of many creative industry participants.

Creative industries that call for changes in IP policy and practice may have good reasons for seeking recourse in legal solutions. While the call to change IP may be based in rational self-interest on the part of individual industry members, it may also appeal to a broader group of stakeholders than a changed business model might, as it is more likely to distribute its benefits and costs more equitably across the industry spectrum. As a policy decision that affects broad swathes of constituents, changing IP is likely to require ex ante negotiations that involve multiple parties, including groups that may otherwise be underrepresented, such as creators and/or inventors, startup or emerging ventures, and end users.

Broadly implemented IP systems may comprise entire licensing systems, such as rights-clearing organizations, which can protect the rights of creators and at the same time allow access to their works. In some cases, this may prove more widely beneficial than a changed business model that puts all creative work behind impenetrable or costly layers of copyright.

Collective rights organizations (CROs) can be built on lines of transparency, with membership rights that include the ability to structure the CRO in ways that are fair and even-handed. If IP rights are expanded, CROs can ensure that the royalties that are expected will be distributed to its members without privileging larger, more powerful firms over smaller enterprises or individuals. And CROs may be subject to oversight—legislative, judicial, or industry initiated—offering greater accountability than privately ordered arrangements.

IP systems may be established or expanded (for instance, by adding new layers of copyright protection to a product that has previously been unpropertized or protected only by patent or trademark) as an alternative to imposing technological protections on creative output. More layers of IP protection may reduce the need for enhanced technological protection on some works. The caveat here, however, is that an industry may instead choose to pair heightened IP with strengthened technological safeguards, thereby fencing in products behind multiple barriers to access and increasing the points at which products can be metered, controlled, and monetized.

Changing IP systems may make allowance for openness of access and use, such as maintaining fair use exceptions to protections, re-affirming the right to personal use of copyrighted works, or expanding the grounds for transformative work. These allowances may be more likely to arise when stakeholders other than copyright holders, such as follow-on creators, consumers, and social or political activists are able to represent the rights of end users and other parties that may not always be represented when legislation is lobbied for, agreed upon, and enacted.

Addressing levels of IP protection in creative fields can bring users and other members of creative ecosystems that do not hold or benefit from copyrights into active roles that help shape the system and put into place its priorities and rights. That promise alone can be attractive to non-copyright holders, who often feel that their interests are not represented when creative businesses act alone or even when they engage in collective action.

Changing IP systems can have positive effects on creative users who are actively engaged in creation, such that the lines between creators and users may blur. Changing IP can also have major effects on consumers in cases where "secondary" production, such as knock-offs, generics, and discounted products, give consumers access to products that they might not otherwise be able to afford. This can vary considerably from field to field, but in many cases will offer a certain openness to follow-on creators that may want to address the needs of non-mainstream parts of the market.

Changing IP can help to maximize spillover and network effects. As suggested by various studies on spillovers, positive externalities can be created in some industries when innovation by one firm leaks out to other firms, naturally subsidizing their productivity without external intervention.[26] Spillovers in the creative context tend to be positive, due to the nature of creativity that almost invariably involves borrowing, sharing, exchanging, and inspiring among generations of creators. In creative industries, there is also the potential for cumulative innovation, which can contribute to and advance industry-wide productivity. Changing IP can have a significant impact on such cumulative innovation, particularly when it enhances employee mobility and knowledge portability.

Changing IP can contribute to important societal interests, needs and goals. Ensuring that creators are compensated for their work can increase creative output and encourage artistic professionalism. Encouraging robust online participation, production, and user-based input serves to enrich democracy and advance the free speech of public citizens through open and equal exchange in the "marketplace of ideas."

Changing IP can also mean opening up creative works and resources, whether by voluntarily contributing works to the public or expanding allowable protected uses of work under doctrines such as fair use. These practices can increase the availability of cultural and intellectual resources, such as news and information, arts, books, and media and entertainment. Moreover, improving access to education and knowledge by offering open-source courses, as well as enhancing open access scholarship and publication, can serve to educate and inform the citizenry. These goals may seem too lofty to be achieved simply through changing IP entitlements. But by shaping IP in the creative industries with measures that protect creators and copyright holders, yet at the same time keep in mind the need to advance greater social aims, IP allocations can have a profound effect on the well-being of creative stakeholders, consumers, and the public.

5.4 What Can IP Do?

5.4.1 IP Can Help Create Markets

A fundamental rationale for copyright is that it offers a solution to market failures in creative industries that are threatened by disruptive innovation.

26 See, e.g., Brett M. Frischmann & Mark A. Lemley, Spillovers, 107 *Colum. L. Rev.* 257, 278–9 (2007). The market also is likely to skew toward production of consumption information goods rather than productive information goods because of the problem of valuing positive spillovers. See, e.g., Brett M. Frischmann & Mark A. Lemley, Spillovers, 107 *Colum. L. Rev.* 257, 278–9 (2007).

An argument for increasing IP entitlements is that when new technologies threaten to diminish the value of industrial output, extending or expanding copyright protection in creative works may create, reinvigorate, or reinforce the market in those works. Creators and copyright holders can benefit from expanded protection by securing their revenue streams, and by feeling incentivized to generate new output secure in the knowledge that they will be compensated for their creations.[27]

5.4.2 IP Can Help Manage Rights Metering via Collective Rights Organizations

In a changing environment, IP rights and rewards need to be managed so that creative businesses continue to receive vital revenue streams, including royalties, licensing fees, and other payments for the use of copyrighted works. Rights-clearing institutions such as collective rights organizations (CROs) and performing rights organizations (PROs) centralize the management and administration of licenses, whether individual or collective, and ensure that rights flows are streamlined and transparent. They also strive to attain a degree of fairness and parity among disparate participants and users of the system (for instance, individual creative artists versus larger entities, copyright holders versus users, and so on).

As in the case of some music rights, compulsory licensing via clearing houses or PROs can regulate the flow of copyright-protected work.[28] Compulsory licensing ensures that royalties get paid to copyright holders whenever a work is accessed or used. At the same time, it makes creative work available to follow-on creators or artists for access or use. In the case of music "covers," for instance, an original artist may have copyright in her work, which gives her the rights to record and perform her work.[29] But a secondary artist may also record or perform her copyrighted work, contingent upon paying royalties to the primary artist for such access and use.

In a digitized economy, the very real possibility of "slippage"—that is, access and/or use of creative works that are not accounted for, metered, or compensated—can challenge an artist's livelihood or an industry's vitality. Metering via PROs can offer a pragmatic solution enabling copyright holders to register each occurrence of access and use of a work and to levy fees accordingly. Such metering works best when mechanisms, often technological in nature, can be positioned at the point of interaction between user and device, and thereby count and charge for each discrete transaction.

27 See Wendy J. Gordon, Fair Use as Market Failure: A Structural and Economic Analysis of the *Betamax* Case and its Predecesors, 82 *Colum. L. Rev.* 1600 (1982).

28 See, Compulsory License for Making and Distributing Phonorecords, U.S. Copyright Office, available at https://www.copyright.gov/circs/circ73.pdf.

29 Often the representative record label with which she has signed may actually retain the copyright, but the principle and the outcome remain the same.

Metering may benefit the creative industries, but even to copyright holders and their representatives it may become more convoluted. Music in the digital age offers a good illustration. Digital music is disseminated via three main sources: peer-to-peer file-sharing networks, such as BitTorrent; online music stores, such as the Apple iTunes Store, Amazon, and Google Music; and online music streaming services, such as Spotify and Apple Music.

All three avenues for music sharing follow a basic model of disaggregating and disseminating single digital music tracks—that is, discrete songs rather than compiled albums. There, however, the resemblance ends. In the first case, music is shared directly among users, and disaggregation of the online music files renders metering functionally impossible. Even if certain occurrences of file sharing are licit via this method as, in a parallel drawn from earlier practices, sharing a mixed tape for personal use among friends might once have constituted licit sharing, they cannot be metered. Online file sharing by design bypasses compensation to the copyright holder altogether.

Online music stores simply sell or license digital music tracks to listeners. While there is some debate over whether the songs are sold or licensed—and increasing consensus that they are indeed merely licensed—the works are paid for and remain in the possession of the listener, whether stored on a personal device or in the cloud. As in the case of traditional music sales, royalties flow from the purchase of each digital track.

Increasingly, digital music listeners are flocking to streaming services. Here, music is streamed directly to the listener via an online service that is closely analogous to broadcast radio. The metering of streamed music follows the model of traditional radio, and licensing is paid by the broadcaster to compensate the copyright holder. Although the mandated compensation schemes of radio and streaming remain very different and highly contested, they still function in much the same way.[30]

In the digital music universe, not only the choices for music delivery systems are changing, but the choices for music distribution to those delivery systems are changing as well. Creative artists are beginning to use digitization to bring their works directly to audiences, and in some instances choosing to bypass traditional middlemen such as record labels and agents. PROs can assume an important role in this regard. Musicians and composers can take advantage of PROs to ensure that they are duly compensated for their work.

Clearing-houses do not require the input of record labels or agents to function, and therefore are likely to prove a valuable and cost-effective mechanism to artists seeking remuneration for their creative work. Moreover, the largest music PROs, BMI, and ASCAP, are expanding the range of benefits they offer artists, such as informational workshops on copyright, rights management services, and so on, which can contribute to securing artists' rights and royalties.

30 Bill Rosenblatt, Here Are the Loopholes Closed by the Music Modernization Act, *Forbes* (Oct. 11, 2018), available at www.forbes.com/sites/billrosenblatt/2018/10/11/music-modernization-act-now-law-leaves-one-copyright-loophole-unclosed/#1147ba3e7.

However, PROs may become less critical with respect to sound recording rights and more important with respect to live performance rights if digitization effectively reduces revenue streams in online music and compels artists to look to live performance for a greater share of royalties. As these kinds of shifts occur, middlemen such as record labels and agents may become newly deputized to manage performance rights, related royalties and licensing fees, and to oversee the metering that PROs offer the individual artist who is increasingly making her living from live concert performances. Thus, rather than rendering the middleman obsolete, the PROs may come to reinforce their centrality to copyright clearing processes and returns.

Digital music is likely to require mechanisms that uphold artists' rights and returns in the face of swift, widespread, and detrimental copying. To defend artists' rights and rewards, PROs will be required to continue to offer a consistent, transparent, efficient, and relatively straightforward mechanism for the continued clearing of rights. This may prove useful when new sources of revenue open up via newer technologies, such as online music streaming, video streaming (with music as a part of the video), and other as-yet unforeseeable uses of music on the Internet and related technologies and devices.

5.5 What Can More IP Do?

5.5.1 More IP Can Help Increase Revenues Extracted From Copyrighted Material

Some copyright holders contend that they lose out on rents when certain unremunerated uses are permitted by copyright. The law may allow copying material for some uses, such as making individual copies of a music CD to use on personal devices. In the digital era, however, some copyright holders can see even individual acts of copying as problematic. They argue that any digitally recorded content can be all too easily used for potentially illicit purposes, such as widespread dissemination through peer-to-peer file sharing. In other words, there is a slippery slope between licit and illicit uses of content that is facilitated by new technologies.

Copyright holders concerned about loss of earned but uncollected rents sometimes argue that even if the copying is licit, the user may make copies for multiple uses to an extent that deprives the copyright holder of significant returns. This argument may contravene the first sale doctrine, but attempts have been made to reconcile it with the doctrine among creative content producers and copyright holders.[31] Increased copyright, therefore, might entail requiring payment for each and every occasion on which an individual gains access to, uses, or copies a copyrighted creative work.

31 See Jessica Litman, Lawful Personal Use, 85 *Tex. L. Rev.* 1871 (2007).

5.5.2 *More IP Can Increase Revenues by Allowing Creative Works in Low-IP or No-IP Regimes to Be Copyrighted, and Protect Emerging Creators in Those Fields*

Some proponents of expanding copyright argue that it should be extended to certain creative industries that historically have been extended limited IP protection. They argue that in a world of extensive, inexpensive, and increasing copying, original works may need more protection than they did in the past, and expanding IP will help protect and sustain their value. Further, they argue that emerging creators are most vulnerable to protection, and least able to afford to defend themselves. With respect to these emerging owners, expanded IP protection is argued to offer increased rights and defenses, helping them to be competitive in the nascent stages of their careers. Broadly, proponents of expanded IP contend that a formalized system of IP rights and licensing is better suited to a freewheeling digital world, and will protect against new forms of copying and appropriation that informal systems cannot adequately address.

5.6 What's Wrong With Just More IP?

5.6.1 *More IP Can Change the Balance of IP and Public Domain; More IP Can Change the Balance of Rights Between Copyright Holder and Consumer*

Advocates of strong nonpropertized space, as expansive as the public domain or as constructed as a commons, argue that historically a balance has been struck between IP and non-IP spaces. They have a valid point: entire areas remain unbounded by copyright policy, such as "personal use,"[32] while other areas are explicitly carved out by copyright law, such as the fair use exception. Moreover, the original grant of rights in the Constitution explicitly limits the time of protection, albeit not to a given term. Most scholars agree that this helps ensure that works will eventually fall in the public domain to enrich the social good once copyright has fairly compensated creators and owners.

Advocates of restricted copyright, or copyright "minimalists," further argue that when IP protections are expanded—whether in length of time, scope, or other measures—the balance struck by copyright law and policy is effectively reneged upon. They contend that these measures are often pushed through by copyright holders without fair representation and the buy-in of those stakeholders, including users, emerging creators, and the general public, who can be underrepresented by lobbyists and legislators.

Some critics of expansive copyright agree with Jessica Litman's argument that personal use has been left out of the discourse of copyright law deliberately and perniciously: "We are in danger of obliterating lawful personal use

32 See generally Litman, supra 29, at 1909.

because we've been pretending that it isn't there."[33] Advocates have targeted personal use as one such area of compromise, but it is only one aspect of the important bundle of rights that many legal scholars consider to comprise "users' rights" as a whole. As legal scholar Glynn Lunney states:"[w]ith the development and dissemination of digital technology, the importance of private copying and its legal status, whether fair or unfair under copyright law, has only increased."[34] Advocates of users' rights argue that expansions in IP in the creative content industries are significantly disruptive of balances of rights between those who own and those who use copyrighted works, and that copyright maximalists fail to recognize or make allowances for the blurring of lines between these parties.

It should be noted that not all legal scholars are such strong advocates of users' rights. One prominent opponent is legal scholar Jane Ginsburg, who argues that "people who read, watch movies, and otherwise use copyrighted materials are merely 'consumptive users' and not active or creative participants and thus don't merit special attention by copyright law or policy."[35] Professor Ginsburg also argues that users encroach upon authors with their claims to rights, and thereby challenge creative production, observing that "the perspective of user rights, albeit important, should remain secondary. Without authors, there are no works to use."[36]

But advocates of users' rights, including Professor Litman, argue that users' rights comprise a broad range of freedoms that users are meant to have in creative works, including "creative and imaginative behaviors such as reading, listening, watching, and playing [which] further copyright's goals."[37] These rights inhere in the array of copyrightable works, including those that are more recently emerging through digital creativity. As Professor Litman puts it,

> [t]he tendency to see music listeners, art viewers, television watchers, or video-game players as less deserving of copyright's solicitude than book readers, though, strikes me as misguided. We've made the choice to give authors of music, art, television and video parity with writers of books in the rights conferred by the copyright system. If we believe that these works merit copyright protection, it should follow that we value opportunities to experience and enjoy those works enough to assure the reasonable freedom to take advantage of them.[38]

33 See Id. at 1903.

34 Glynn S. Lunney, Jr., Fair Use and Market Failure: Sony Revisited, 82 *B.U. L. Rev.* 975, 977 (2002).

35 See Jane C. Ginsburg, Authors and Users in Copyright, 45 *J. Copyright Soc'y U.S.A.* 1, 15 (1997).

36 See Jane C. Ginsburg, Putting Cars on the "Information Superhighway": Authors, Exploiters, and Copyright in Cyberspace, 95 *Colum. L. Rev.* 1466, 1468 (1995).

37 Jessica Litman, Readers' Copyright, 58 *J. Copyright Soc'y U.S.A.* 325, 331, 22 (2011).

38 Id.

These uses and their related rights are deeply culturally embedded, necessitating the freedom for users to engage with culture or, as legal scholar Julie Cohen, puts it, they should afford users the freedom to be involved in processes of "working through culture" that are "irreducibly contingent" and ever-changing. Professor Cohen describes the relational interplay between users and creative works in the cultural landscape:

> [T]he cultural activities of situated users take place within a web of semantic and material entailments. One cannot simply step out of or around the resources, values, and absences within her own culture, but must negotiate one's way through them, following the pathways or 'links' that connect one resource to the next. This process, which I will call 'working through culture,' is irreducibly contingent. It moves in patterns that are both (and sometimes simultaneously) recursive and opportunistic, and supports an understanding of creativity as relational at its core.[39]

These scholars' views on users' rights align with those who believe that expansions of copyright are liable to occur at the expense of vital user freedoms, and risk upending copyright's balancing act by neglecting to recognize the user altogether. As Professor Cohen describes the condition: "Copyright doctrine, however, is characterized by the absence of the user . . . [This] absence produces a domino effect that ripples through the structure of copyright law, shaping both its unquestioned rules and its thorniest dilemmas."[40]

When seen from the viewpoints of legal scholars Jessica Litman, Rebecca Tushnet, Julie Cohen, and Larry Lessig, the expansion of IP in creative content industries appears poised to threaten, or at least drastically affect, the relational interplay between users and creative works. This has particular force when the user is actively engaged with such works in ways that can themselves contribute to the creativity that lies at the heart of copyright law and policy.

> Users play two important roles within the copyright system: receive copyrighted works, and some users become authors. . . . [one such role is] the situated user who engages cultural goods found within the context of her culture through a variety of activities ranging from consumption to creative play, and whose activities are the vehicle through which copyright's collective project is advanced.[41]

39 Julie Cohen, Creativity and Culture in Copyright Theory, 40 *U.C. Davis L. Rev.* 1151, 1179 (2007).

40 Julie E. Cohen, The Place of the User in Copyright Law, 74 *Fordham L. Rev.* 347, 347–8 (2005).

41 Id. at 348–9.

In this respect, the situated user "should be left untrammeled by unduly expansive copyright restrictions, which perhaps (or seemingly) paradoxically will serve to further copyright's goal of encouraging creative production."[42]

These user activities include "creative remixing," which is merely one point on a spectrum of uses of creative work that are encroached upon and threatened by expansions in copyright. Professor Litman elaborates on the new complexity of creating in the digital space: "As digital tools enable audience members to interact with works of authorship in different and interesting ways, any sharp distinction between passive consumption and creative remixing dissolves into a spectrum of different ways of enjoying works."[43] Professor Lessig points out that this is undeniably a trend toward "remix" culture: "it is no surprise that other forms of 'creating' [such as remixing] are becoming an increasingly dominant form of 'writing.' "[44] He concludes, "[c]reators here and everywhere are always and at all times building upon the creativity that went before and that surrounds them now. . . . No society, free or controlled, has ever demanded that every use be paid for."[45] Professor Lessig goes on to point out that other forms of creative interplay between the user and creative materials are also able to thrive when copyright is kept suitably at bay. He maintains that they are best able to flourish in a "hybrid economy" that leaves ample room for spontaneous user generation of creative materials that may be inspired by, or draw from, earlier cultural output.[46]

Some legal scholars sympathetic to copyright minimalism contend that expanding copyright leads to increasing the metering of creative works. Increased metering, on this view, is liable to encroach upon historically established freedoms of users to enjoy such works with broad liberties and without undue payment requirements. For instance, Lawrence Lessig, an advocate of users' rights, argues that the interplay of creativity and users has always been liberally granted and largely accepted as free and unfettered.[47]

On this line of argument, as articulated by legal scholar Joseph Liu, the fundamental nature of copyright law is distorted by overly expansive IP: "[a]fter all, the overall purpose of the Copyright Act is not to reward authors for authors' sake, but to reward authors to benefit consumers and society more generally."[48] The strongest claim on this view, as expressed by legal scholar Glynn Lunney, is that a broad array of uses should be permissible to users so

42 Id.
43 Litman, supra note 35, at 350.
44 Lawrence Lessig, *Remix: Making Art and Commerce Thrive in the Hybrid Economy* 69 (2008).
45 Id. at 29.
46 Id. 69.
47 Id. 29.
48 Joseph P. Liu, Copyright Law's Theory of the Consumer, 44 *Bos. Coll. L. Rev.* 397, 398 (2003).

that their rights and liberties can be preserved without intrusive or burdensome expansions of rights in creative works. Lunney argues that only when users undermine creative production should copyright step in and curtail or meter their activities. Or as Professor Lunney contends, "unauthorized copying, again unlike theft, becomes socially undesirable only when it goes so far as to threaten the public's interest in an adequate supply of creative works."[49]

Some users' rights supporters argue that recalibrating the balance between creators and users by expanding or tweaking copyright may have an unwarranted, and possibly unwanted, effect on the actual nature of works that are generated in various creative content industries. One leading scholar, Neil Netanel, argues that that "an expansive copyright law will tend to diminish the creation and dissemination of additional works and lead to a clustering in already popular genres."[50]

Users' rights advocates often ally with those who argue that creative content industries have moved from a predominantly sales-based model to a licensing-based model, and that consumers are being moved from ownership rights to licensing rights in the creative goods they consume. Generally, licensing creative works implies a diminution of rights for users—they do not own the works in perpetuity, and they do not retain the rights that owners enjoy as a matter of course. Users' rights argue that the change in the fundamental rights conferred in the digital space is itself a critical change that has been made unilaterally and without the informed consent of the customer.

Moreover, users' rights advocates argue that the shift toward licensing rights has real implications with respect to the consumer's interaction with, and control over, the creative content she has selected and paid for. The right and ability of licensees to copy, share, sell, or repurpose licensed material is significantly different—and more limited—than those held by purchasers. And when licensed material is further restricted by technological lockup, the rights of the user may be further constrained or withheld. Thus, users of encrypted works may find that they cannot make copies of the creative work they have paid for, or they can only use that work in certain ways or contexts that are delineated by the vendor. This again changes the balance of rights between the copyright holder and the end user, yet only the rights holder wields the unilateral power to initiate such a reconfiguration.

Many copyright minimalists argue that new kinds of creativity, such as performance arts and multimedia works, often rely upon access to a broad swath of works to build layered, collage-like pieces that offer a kind of cultural tapestry of many contributions, inspirations, and artifacts. They argue that overly restrictive copyright can hinder complex work, as well as the access that creative multimedia artists are afforded to their baseline materials. This may eventually have broad repercussions on the kind of work being produced. It is

49 Lunney, supra note 32, at 983.
50 Neil Weinstock Netanel, *Copyright's Paradox* 135–6 (2010).

possible that an expansive reading of fair use may protect some of these works. But fair use has historically proven to be a tricky point of repose for creative endeavors, and may not prove adequate in the face of challenges by copyright holders in creative works.

More IP Can Lock Up Too Much So That Follow-On Innovation May Be Choked Off

Adding or reinforcing IP in creative industries can risk incentivizing companies to create locked, segregated ecosystems that thwart follow-on innovation or interoperability with external products, devices, or systems. In a competitive market, this risk can arise when companies change their business models to respond to a changing environment by exploiting a competitive advantage to effectively corner market share and thwart encroaching challengers. But changing business models are continually subject to competitive pressure arising from industry innovations. Even in cases where a company seems to enjoy a quasi-monopolistic position, their dominance may not be sustainable.[51]

In contrast, adding or reinforcing IP can institute systemic changes that operate across a broad swathe of the sector (for instance, affecting an entire class of creative producers and/or copyright holders within an industry). Adding IP may be additionally fortified by technological lock-ups, such as DRM protections. And adding IP typically requires regulatory change, resulting in relatively fixed solutions that may be less susceptible to external competitive pressures than individual firm-driven changes.

In an innovation-driven industry such as computer software, propertization of products has a marked effect. In the U.S., giant firms like Microsoft, Google, Oracle, and IBM regularly propertize software to secure their competitive advantage. The proprietary nature of software is reinforced by statute, as software is expressly included under the protection of the DMCA (which criminalizes the illicit evasion of copy protection in those properties in its purview).[52] As in the case of other copyrightable products, copyright for computer programs prohibits not only literal copying, but also copying of "non-literal elements," such as a program's structure, sequence, and organization.[53]

An array of protections allows commercial developers of proprietary software to safeguard their products against competitive inroads, and to protect against practices such as reverse engineering software in order to reproduce and appropriate its essential source code. At the same time, however, these

51 E.g., Microsoft is a leading company whose operating system dominated the market for several decades, but whose hegemony has arguably diminished considerably in recent years (although some argue this is due in part to antitrust lawsuits and other exogenous factors).

52 See DMCA § 1201, available at www.law.cornell.edu/uscode/text/17/1201.

53 See generally Copyright Registration for Computer Programs, U.S. Copyright Office, available at www.copyright.gov/circs/circ61.pdf.

measures allow software companies to create closed software systems that compete against one another and that may not be interoperable without expressly designed cross-licensing arrangements.

Particularly for new entrants, the complexity involved in negotiating such arrangements may not be cost-effective, particularly in markets that are fast-changing, with little certainty as to which operating system or software products will rise to the top. Further, there is little incentive to promote interoperability, as creating a proprietary software system that dominates the market may lead to supra-competitive rewards, thereby incentivizing competition at the expense of potential collaboration.

The negative ramifications of proprietary software were recognized early on by innovative software developers, and gave rise to the "free software movement" arising as early as 1983, under whose auspices the GNU General Public License (GNU GPL) was developed.[54] In 1998, the open-source movement broke off from the free software movement, but at the heart of both movements lies the basic principle that software developed openly, and free of proprietary constraints, promotes innovation, sharing and cooperation, and increases digital and social freedoms.[55]

The free and open-source software movements represent a compelling pushback against certain restrictions and conditions that proprietary software has imposed on its products, consumers, and follow-on innovators. They have been criticized by some copyright critics as being restrictive,[56] but their primary goal is to promote follow-on innovation not just by market leaders but also by new innovators and entrants.

5.6.2 More IP Can Undermine a Constructed Commons

Increasing IP entitlements can expand the rights and revenues in a propertized system that regulates the flow of creative work. However, expanding IP rights can displace or overturn tacitly agreed-upon arrangements that underlie a constructed commons. In the classic case of commons delineated by Elinor Ostrom and Robert Ellickson, negotiated rights are struck among parties who share a common resource, such as a grazing land or a pool of water, and the behaviors and norms of the parties are mutually agreed upon and adhered to without resort to externally imposed and administered mechanisms.[57] In creative spaces, constructed commons can be as formal as agreements struck

54 See The History of the GPL, *Free-Soft*, available at www.free-soft.org/gpl_history.

55 See Richard Stallman, Why Open Source Misses the Point of Free Software, *Gnu Operating Sys.*, available at www.gnu.org/philosophy/open-source-misses-the-point.html.

56 Id.

57 See Elinor Ostrom, *Governing the Commons: The Evolution of Institutions for Collective Action* (Cambridge University Press, Cambridge, UK, 1990); see also Robert Ellickson, *Order Without Law: How Neighbors Settle Disputes* (Harvard University Press, Cambridge, MA, 1991).

among industry players, or as informal as a set of practices and norms that govern a creative industry and eventually establish its shape and structure. A commons could be an agreement to share and exchange creative works in a collaborative shared space, such a workshop or a news collective. Another commons could be an institution that brings together creators who work independently but enjoy and benefit from each other's work, such as a university or a think tank.

Imposing an IP regime upon a constructed commons may seem at first glance merely an act of reinforcement, adding a level of protection that offers "belt and suspenders" coverage to defend against disruptive innovation. But it may not be a neutral addition. Expanding IP can run counter to the agreements that have been struck and that sustain the operations of a group of actors or an entire industry; or it can weaken long-standing but unspoken shared practices that can be overwritten once propertization takes over. Formal IP rights can also displace intangible benefits that are useful and normatively powerful but that do not confer immediate and measurable rewards.

Consider what might follow if the culinary arts opted to expand IP rights by allowing property rights in recipes, rather than only in cookbooks that annotate and elaborate on recipes. Chefs might well be motivated to pursue the more lucrative course of chasing after recipe rights than the more intangible benefits of teaching and mentoring young talent. Rather than teaching apprentices how to master an individual cooking style and set of recipes, a chef might choose to assert copyright in his instruction and recipes, despite the possibility that such a substitution could undermine the system of apprenticeship and homage on which the commons of haute cuisine has been constructed.

Expanded property rights can dissuade creators from generously sharing the fruits of their labor, rather incentivizing them to seek to maximize monetary rewards in exchange for such work. It is not that reputational benefits, sharing and collaboration, and a rewards-based system cannot exist side-by-side with a propertization-based regime. It is rather that in certain important cases property rights may demand exclusivity, and prioritize rent-seeking behaviors. In turn, this may close off the rights of follow-on creators (such as former apprentices) to share in the creative efforts of the professional creators who instructed them and who gave them the building blocks on which they hope to forge their own creative work.

5.6.3 More IP Can Change the Balance Between Propertization and Disclosure

Expanding or reinforcing IP rights can change the weight given to propertization versus disclosure in creative ecosystems. Suboptimal changes can emphasize the rewards that property rights offer at the expense of the value that disclosure confers. This is particularly problematic in creative industries that value disclosure as a vital part of free knowledge flow and enrichment of the public good.

The case of academic patenting versus publication is a useful illustration. In academic work, publication is considered a critical feature of scientific research, serving as a means of sharing scientific research and discovery, and enhancing scholarly reputations. It also helps advance diverse institutional aims such as attracting top students and research assistants, attracting external funding, and building research and discovery (R&D) centers. But publishing and scholarship can conflict with interests in propertizing scientific R&D, notably when the outcome is likely to be profitable to institutions and their allies.[58]

Some commentators argue that while there is an inherent tension between the goals of patenting and publication, academia has still been able to strike a compromise between patenting activity and publishing activity, and that patenting and fundamental research can even be sustained as complementary activities. Ajay Agrawal and Rebecca Henderson, two leading scholars in the field, have studied patenting and publication activity at the Departments of Mechanical Engineering and Electrical Engineering at the Massachusetts Institute of Technology. Their findings are generally positive:

> (i) Patenting as a minority activity: a majority of faculty in the sample never patent, and publication rates far outstrip patenting rates; and (ii) Patenting is not representative of the patterns of knowledge generation and transfer from MIT: patent volume does not predict publication volume, and those firms that cite MIT papers are in general not the same firms as those that cite MIT patents. However, patent volume is positively correlated with paper citations, suggesting that patent counts could be reasonable measures of research impact.[59]

They conclude that the implications of their findings are likewise positive: "Our results offer some evidence that, at least at these two departments at MIT, patenting is not substituting for more fundamental research, and that it might even be a complementary activity."[60]

In contrast, other commentators, such as legal scholars Rebecca Eisenberg and Arti Rai, have argued that an increasing reliance on propertization has become increasingly prevalent in academia, placing essential values at risk.[61]

58 When propertization takes the form of patenting, the process of filing a patent does indeed entail disclosure. However, this is late-stage disclosure, and occurs long after the run-up to patentability. In that period of run-up, the knowledge gained and the advances made may not be available to others. Perhaps the better distinction to draw is between the end-game disclosure of patenting versus the lifetime of disclosure of publication. But this seems to erase the importance of early-stage and fundamental research disclosure, which is what gives rise to the distinction used here between patenting and publication.

59 Ajay Agrawal & Rebecca Henderson, Putting Patents in Context: Exploring Knowledge Transfer from MIT, Vol. 48 *Mgmt. Sci.* 44, 44–6 (2002).

60 Id. at 59.

61 See Rebecca S. Eisenberg, Proprietary Rights and the Norms of Science in Biotechnology Research, 97 *Yale L.J.* 177 (1987); Arti K. Rai & Rebecca S. Eisenberg, Bayh-Dole Reform and the Progress of Biomedicine, 66 *L. & Contemporary Problems* 289 (2003).

In both cases, it is recognized that IP can place basic scholarly aims and publication rights at risk, and that increasing propertization only serves to heighten that risk and threaten the balance that academia strives to maintain.

5.7 What About Eliminating IP?

5.7.1 Why It May Not Be Feasible to Eliminate IP

Some proponents of keeping creative work nonproprietary argue that some fields would be better off curtailing IP, such as keeping only trademark protection; or eliminating IP protection altogether, such as moving to wholly open-source production. Proposals point to examples of low-IP regimes, such as fashion, comedy, and cuisine; various kinds of open-source production, such as Wikipedia, some blogs, and some free software; and open copyright-based systems, such as the Creative Commons.[62]

Advocates of nonproprietary systems argue that effectively eliminating IP tends to work best in conjunction with changing business models to draw substantial revenue from nonpropertized sources, such as live performance (music, teaching, or lecturing in front of live audiences), advertisement-based models and subscription-based models, and cross-subsidization of creative work that is supported primarily by the sale of technological devices and services (electronic devices, platforms, applications, and support systems).

One might argue that it is possible to change business models while at the same time continuing to protect revenue from core propertized sources. But some copyright minimalists argue that even closely cabined property rights are inherently liable to overreach, threatening areas that should remain accessible or imposing unnecessary barriers and payment schemes on creative work. These objections raise the question of whether it is feasible to eliminate IP, and what ramifications that might involve.

The overarching objection to reducing or eliminating IP is grounded in the underlying rationale for IP: the concern that copyright's incentive structure is required to ensure that creators can invest in the act of creation knowing that they will be able to secure a livelihood and have a professional career. It is difficult to imagine how creators will be able to make a living from their creative labor without the right to receive revenue from their work.[63] The recent losses faced by creators in industries whose IP has come under attack due to technological disruptions seems to confirm the centrality of IP to the profitability calculus that is integral to the professional creator's life.

Another concern is that while the overall quantity of content may have increased, the quality of some content may be compromised. Reducing or eliminating IP may serve to reduce or eliminate the role of intermediaries

62 See Software: Free and Open Source Code, Creative Commons, available at https://creativecommons.org/about/program-areas/software/.

63 Government subsidies might be an alternative, but seem unrealistic in the current sociopolitical environment in the U.S.

who traditionally served an important role in developing, authenticating, and reviewing creative work. Doing away with these intermediaries can compromise the high standards of production that were once ensured by industry professionals.

Some proprietary systems have been essentially underwritten by advertising. Broadcast radio, for instance, has historically been free to listeners, but audiences have paid for consumption by being compelled to listen to periodically broadcast advertisements. Advertising is equally available to entities that disseminate creative content online. However, music broadcasters pay licensing fees to music copyright holders, thereby enabling the content to be duly compensated for online performances. Advertisers recognize this licensing scheme, and support the music broadcasting system in order to reach audiences that are listening and consuming its content.

The absence of a proprietary scheme may not completely drive advertisers away from sites or services that disseminate creative content, for if nonpropertized content reaches a critical mass of viewers or listeners, reaching such an audience may still prove attractive enough to warrant advertisers' investments. But proprietary systems are the sole means of ensuring that creators are remunerated for their production of content. Thus, while advertisers may be somewhat indifferent to the context of delivery, they may prefer to support sites that promote proprietary content in order to attract the best creative talent and thereby to attract and capture audiences' attention.

Many mature proprietary IP systems are predicated upon licensing schemes that manage rights, administer compensation and enable the circulation of creative content. Simply removing IP entitlements would strike at the heart of the terms of production and compensation that are integral to the industry and its creators. The efficacy of an entrenched licensing scheme would be replaced with a nonproprietary system that would be required to generate a new set of practices, norms, rights, and means of compensation. While this might prove possible in the long run, it would create a great deal of instability in the short run, which might well prove particularly devastating to an industry already undercut by technological disruption.

Often ventures that involve nonproprietary work, including open-source ventures, are effectively subsidized by free and/or volunteer labor, or by institutional support that indirectly compensates creative or innovative work. In open-source software development, a collaborative community of software program producers and developers contribute their efforts and ideas to improve computing source code and then to share and circulate it within the community.[64]

The input of the open-source community is typically made on a voluntary basis, and is generally unremunerated. As the software world shows, open

64 See generally Steven Weber, *The Success of Open Source* (Harvard University Press, Cambridge, MA, 2004).

source may not begin with ownership rights: the source code is developed and made available via an open license in the product's design or blueprint. Further, open source usually bars ownership rights in the improved source code subsequent to modification of its original design.[65]

Open-source project participants may be motivated by different ambitions. Some are interested in problem-solving for its own sake, some pursue the reputational benefits of prestige and renown that accompany innovative work within a knowledgeable community that highly values innovation, and some are interested in learning as much as in imparting knowledge and know-how. Entrepreneurial businesses or individual software developers may also participate in open-source projects in order to solve a particular problem. They may choose to open some of their proprietary work product to an open-source community, seeking to benefit from the insights and improvements that the collaborative community efforts can contribute to the original work.

By communalizing the process of development, entrepreneurial producers can distribute the costs of innovation. They can even make reasonable allowance for free riders to benefit without undermining the creative process or the value of the project. Even in these cases, the work of contributors to the open-source part of the effort is effectively subsidized. Often, contributors are likely to hold remunerated positions of employment, and are engaged in the open-source work as a side project undertaken primarily for interest.

At the same time, entrepreneurs understand that their work may contribute to the productivity of members of the open-source community, either directly as the basis for some licensed follow-on innovation or indirectly as the source of inspiration for follow-on entrepreneurs. Certain open-source developers may eventually stake proprietary claims in some portion of their work, creating companies that are based in open-source code but that monetize its application in a concrete, profitable, and acceptable way.

Whether springing from proprietary rights or developing from open-source processes, the product of creative work is likely to have value. It may be donated by creators to the public, but that is a choice that the intellectual property system makes possible but does not mandate. Asking creators to give up their valuable work product ex ante necessarily means asking them to forfeit the basis of their professionalism. Some creators may be able to substitute for the returns they would make from their work by other means, such as private incomes, patronage, government grants, prizes, and rewards, or salaries from other work. But requiring that substitution strikes at the heart of IP by decoupling the incentive to create from the fruits of creation. It is hard to imagine how this division could "promote the progress of science and useful arts."[66]

65 In some cases, individuals may avail themselves of Creative Commons licenses, with varying levels of restriction, for their work. See, available at https://creativecommons.org/.

66 U.S. Const., Art. 1, Section 8, clause 8, available at www.law.cornell.edu/constitution/articlei#section8.

6 What Does Work

Tailoring

6.1 Introduction to the Tailoring Framework

Creative industries contending with disruption are almost always acting under pressure and are bound by constraints. They have a limited number of strategies and finite resources to meet the challenges that beset them. They are subject to time pressures and threats from competitors, and contend with the need to remain profitable while adapting to change. They face systemic changes driven by major shifts in the technology sector, including the rise of Big Tech, that are hugely consequential yet largely unpredictable and unstable. And they have to meet the needs of their constituents and the demands of their audience. These vexing concerns mean that creative industries need to have a plan for survival. Managing comprehensive change entails creating a framework for action, identifying the salient factors that are critical to address, breaking down the steps that need to be taken, and ensuring that the right balance is struck between rights and access.

Each creative industry will have its own challenges, calling for specific strategies and tailored solutions.[1] The chapters that follow suggest a course of

1 My theory of tailoring draws upon the framework for tailoring elucidated by Michael Carroll in two seminal works: Michael W. Carroll, One Size Does Not Fit All: A Framework for Tailoring Intellectual Property Rights, 70 *Ohio St. l.j.* 1361 (2009); and Michael W. Carroll One for All: The Problem of Uniformity Cost in Intellectual Property Law, 15 *Am. U.L. Rev.* 845 (2006). 16 I begin with accepting the premise underlying patent and copyright law—that creators or innovators must be able to exclude others in order to extract benefits from them to compensate for the costs of creation or innovation. *See* Mark A. Lemley, The Economics of Improvement in Intellectual Property Law, 75 *Tex. l. Rev.* 989, 994 (1997) ("In a private market economy, individuals will not invest in invention or creation unless . . . they can reasonably expect to make a profit from the endeavor."). I do not go so far as to assert, like some commentators, that pecuniary motivation is the sole, or even primary, motivation to create. *See, e.g.*, Tyler Cowen, in praise of commercial culture 18 (2000). I believe that innovative activity many have many overdetermined motivations; and a rational, selfish actor may innovate without receiving entitlements, and may still confer the benefits of her creativity on society. *See, e.g.*, Teresa M. Amabile, *The Social Psychology of Creativity* 14–15 (1983); Teresa M. Amabile, *Creativity in Context: Update to the Social Psychology of Creativity* 153–77 (1996); Bruno S. Frey & Reto Jegan, Motivation

action that can be pursued by all creative industries, beginning with a series of questions that industry decision-makers will want to ask when considering the array of options that await its selection. These questions are followed by illustrations of how various industries can shape their plans to their own specifications, and tailor solutions that best fit their contours.

6.2 The Four-Factors Test: Weighing Legal, Business, Technological, and Behavioral/Normative Factors

There are four major factors that creative industries can address when changing their game plan and building their road map to success: (1) business models and strategies, (2) IP policies and practices, (3) technological measures, and (4) behavioral and normative approaches. These factors are interrelated to such an extent that changing any one will have an effect on all the others. This ripple effect is not necessarily problematic—it may well have a positive impact by revealing new paths to innovation and commercial viability—but it does mean that no factor can be considered in isolation, or without attention to the repercussions and follow-on effects that change will incur.

The four-factors test is flexible in allowing creative industries the ability to change one or more factors, and further in affording several kinds of changes to each factor. The following four chapters will lay out each of these factors in depth, starting with the questions that creative industries must ask themselves and moving to the choices that they make and how those choices play out in the real world. Asking these questions systematically and comprehensively helps creative industries devise a critical framework for action. While they are a starting point for inquiry, they are not meant to be definitive or comprehensive. Rather, they set the stage for strategizing and structural choices. And they are not novel: creative industries have always engaged in asking and responding to these questions, although not always in a systematic way.

Crowding Theory, 15 *J. Econ. Surv.* 589 (2001) (reviewing evidence that intrinsic motivation can be reduced by prospect of external reward). *See also* Julie E. Cohen, Creativity and Culture in Copyright Theory, 40 *U.C. Davis L. Rev.* 1151, 1198–1204 (2007) (examining creative processes and proposing a decentered model of creativity). As in the case of "economies of prestige," certain non-pecuniary rewards may also offer sufficient motivation for creative production, even absent formal entitlements. See, e.g., Dan L. Burk & Mark A. Lemley, Policy Levers in Patent Law, 89 *Va. L. Rev.* 1575, 1586 (2003) (describing alternative incentives to innovate). Business strategies and motivations may also suffice, as in the case of publication used as a loss leader to increase future income streams, such as speaker's fees, improved professional status, and so on. *See, e.g.*, William M. Landes & Richard A. Posner, An Economic Analysis of Copyright Law, 18 *J. legal Stud.* 325, 333 (1989) (describing forms of non-pecuniary income authors derive from publication). And competitive motivations may also prove sufficient stimulus to create and innovate, in order to differentiate their products and services from their competitors, whether or not exclusive rights ensue. *See, e.g.*, Jonathan B. Baker, Beyond Schumpeter vs. Arrow: How Antitrust Fosters Innovation, 74 *Antitrust L.J.* 575, 590–92 (2007).

The first factor considers how creative firms can change their business models, strategies, and solutions. Business questions focus on the strategies that individual firms and entire industries use to build models that are stronger on several fronts: revenues and prices, content licensing or ownership, the use of supporting intermediaries, and the remuneration of labor. Some other options include rolling out innovative sales and marketing practices, changing the nature and mix of their products, or leveraging new online platforms for growth.

The second factor considers how creative firms can calibrate their IP rights and protections. The legal inquiry begins by demarcating creative industries and the relative level of IP that prevails in various sectors. Where IP is a dominant force, maximizing protection and enforcement may move to the fore. In low-IP sectors, or "negative spaces" where IP does not currently seem to operate extensively, choosing to increase protection may be weighed against alternative measures or maintaining the status quo. In hybrid-IP sectors, which may offer multiple layers of protection such as extending some measure of copyright, trademark or trade secret protection, a strategy that balances IP rights may be needed to preserve the particular features that keep the industry robust and active.

The third factor considers how creative firms can incorporate technological protections or barriers to infringement in their goods and services, such as building in digital rights management, encryption, or other anti-circumvention features. Technological questions look at higher order concerns, including the effectiveness of technological protections, their effects on interoperability, and their impact on positive externalities.

The fourth factor considers cultural and normative questions, beginning with the features of creative industries that do important work or offer important benefits, whether alongside or in lieu of IP protections. Some creative cultures share structural features with constructed commons, guilds, or guild-like spaces. These features can confer considerable benefits, such as boosts to reputation, and room for homage and attribution. They can also sustain communal norms, such as shared condemnation of copying and plagiarism, which help to protect against the theft of creative work. Importantly, good creative cultures can also keep ample space available for both access and production in the user community, whether by encouraging collaboration, promoting open-source production, or enabling user-generated content. A strong cultural foundation can also foster spillover and network effects by building and scaling interactive creator and user communities.

Creative cultures also embed normative questions that implicate both creators and users. Creative industries should ask whether users recognize, accept, and appreciate the values that creative communities have to offer. They should further ask whether user appreciation extends to recognizing the value of creative work not just as an intangible value but also as a commodifiable good. Do users agree that creative work is valuable and therefore worth paying for? And do users understand that if their work is not paid for, professional artists will not be able to continue to create in a serious and sustained way? In crafting their responses to these vital questions, creative firms can devise strategies that will enable them to engage consumers and grow their user base through consumer-friendly practices such as educating and persuading users of the value of creative content, building consumer loyalty through direct outreach, and actively recruiting users in product launches and creative ventures.

Each of these factors is complicated enough on its own. But it is the interplay between factors that is hardest to assess when devising a well-tailored tactical plan. Recalibrating various factors, such as adjusting business models or recalibrating IP entitlements, will involve a number of risks, including posing challenges to long-standing supports that have kept creative industries well-functioning and maintained a healthy balance between property rights in, and access to, creative works.

The risks that creative industries face, and the choices that risk-taking may compel, are also liable to come in conflict with each other. Improving competitive advantages and increasing profitability can come at the expense of important cultural values and norms, such as leaving room for work that is valuable but may not be readily captured by property rights. Building technological impediments to copying, theft, and other detrimental activities can hinder interoperability and user freedom. And creating barriers to ease the use of protected work, such as making licensing expensive or onerous, can hamper creative collaboration, sharing, user-generated content, and open-source production. The interconnectedness of these risks also means that they are hard to address systematically, and harder still to manage in a way that makes sense for a particular industry with its own needs, objectives, output, and community.

It is evident that the best approach for creative industries to take would be to tailor their strategies in the ways that they consider best suited to meet their challenges and needs. In the best of cases, tailoring allows a creative industry to determine how to balance ownership and access in a way that enhances its prospects for sustainable growth while preserving its core values and norms. With that balance in place, a creative industry can optimize its business for the current climate, while still remaining open and adaptable to changes that may lie ahead.

But even a tailored approach is not risk-free, and each set of tailored choices comes with costs as well as benefits. Understanding the tradeoffs—knowing which advantages can be preserved, and which may have to be compromised or sacrificed when a tailored solution is chosen—is critical to making a successful choice. Only knowing the values involved will enable creative industries to make informed and judicious cost-benefit analyses when choosing the strategies and solutions that will chart their course to long-term sustainability.

It is important to look at how creative industries have addressed these inquiries and where they have and have not succeeded. Each of the four factors presented is illustrated with real world examples of creative industries that have wrestled with the respective questions raised and have constructed strategic approaches and solutions to fit their immediate objectives and long-term ambitions. Not all of these choices have resulted in success, and not all have reached a definitive conclusion; indeed, many are in flux and subject to revision. But they all vividly depict the multi-faceted approaches that creative industries have been taking to meet disruptive innovation head-on. And they offer instructive lessons in how creative industries can forge ahead.

One simple illustration of the applicability of the four-factor test arises in the academic research and scholarship, the creative work of education. When a scholar writes a journal article, it is standard practice that she cedes the article's copyright to the academic journal that publishes it. But the scholar retains important reputational benefits from her work. She may make some royalties from the work, but the more significant returns are likely to be her ability to secure a tenured position and to gain status in her field. And at the same time her scholarship may confer reputational benefits on her home institution.

But what would happen if academic institutions were to jettison the tenure system and to downplay the importance of scholarship and research as significant factors in tenure decisions? Scholars might then lobby for the right to retain copyright in their works so that they can carry their work with them in an increasingly mobile and insecure academic employment market. They also need copyright to earn royalties from their published works. The argument for their retaining copyright can be argued to follow from a change in the traditional tradeoff that once existed, and can seem to offer a fair compensation for the lack of stability and affiliation that once prevailed among traditional academic institutions.

On the other hand, what would happen if concerted efforts were to effect a change in the allocation of copyright within academia, conferring the rights on the original author? This might advantage productive scholars by increasing their direct royalties. But it might also make scholarship less valuable as part of an institution's reputation. And while it may enhance a scholar's professional mobility, it could at the same time undermine the idea that scholars should be affiliated with an institution for their scholarly career—in other words, help to further undermine the idea of tenure. Ultimately, it may also reduce the value of scholarship altogether, increasing an emphasis on teaching and knowledge portability but decreasing the utility of sustained research and publication.

In this example, changing IP practices is liable to cast ripples throughout academic ecosystems, changing business models that have prioritized stability and the exchange of creative labor (scholarly publication) for intangible rewards (reputation), and generating new business models that prioritize creative mobility (teaching and knowledge portability) and monetization of academic work (royalties) above all else.

It may not be obvious which set of choices is preferable in the long run. But it is clear that changing one factor, IP rights, has profound effects on other factors, not just business models but also normative values. Academia is on the verge of changing its practices, and may choose to jettison these values while privileging copyright in academic work that can be used, marketed, and sold.

In so doing, it may give rise to fluid but nonpermanent exchanges that more closely resemble commercial transactions rather than traditional academic collaboration: teachers that move from one institution to another, courses that are taught with materials that are replicated and used multiple times, publications that serve more practical than reputational purposes, and output that is bought, sold, or licensed in competitive markets. As a creative industry, academia has the potential to transform itself from the ground up. Still, the academic world will need to weigh the changes and their likely repercussions before doing so. Working through a tailoring framework can help clarify these choices and their consequences.

7 Tailoring Business Models and Strategies

7.1 Introduction to Business Issues

Creative industries should begin by assessing the business plans and practices that they have mapped out. These questions work at both structural and operational levels—that is, they address how the industry is configured and how firms in the industry carry out their functions. When considered together, they offer a business paradigm that can be used as a template for creative industries and firms that are at various stages of development and success, whether startups or established ventures, and whether situated in stable, disrupted, or rapidly innovating environments.

7.2 How Resilient and Adaptable Is Your Business Model?

Most creative industries have well-established business models that predominate across firms and practices. Assessing how a business model works will give rise to several interconnected questions. These questions cluster into a set of inquiries that flesh out business operations and their receptiveness to change.

The first set of questions asks, how high are industry production and capital costs? Relatedly, how fixed are industry production costs? Ancillary to that question, can the industry harness technological innovations and changes to its benefit by reducing production costs? Various industries may have differing answers to these questions. The music and entertainment industries can reduce costs of using agents and representing new artists by searching for musical talent on YouTube and other online sources. The education industry can use cheaper and larger online courses to supplement their regular courses, teach more students for more revenues, or use third-party educators to add to course catalogs. The fashion industry can use social media to disseminate patterns, websites like etsy.com to sell lower-end but unique designs, or bloggers to move merchandise rather than expensive print magazines.

Many creative industries, such as film, television, entertainment, and video games are understood to have high fixed costs. Making a movie, for instance, typically requires initial capital infusions to cover large up-front production costs, including casts and labor, location, filming, and rights clearing, as well as extensive distribution costs, including theatrical releases, recording and shipping, and licensing to cable or online streaming. Some of those costs may be fixed but may be reduced by technological innovation, such as recording or storing copies. Other costs are likely to be variable and to remain high, such as labor and licensing.[1]

This leads to the related question, where do recoupment costs need to be built into the business model? Does the investment have to be profitable early on in its life cycle, or can its expenditures (including up-front costs or startup costs) be amortized over time, subsumed into other larger capital outlays, or otherwise absorbed? In industries with high up-front costs, a sound business model will need to show clearly that initial investments can be offset by adequate returns, whether realized immediately or over the long term. Where those costs are fixed and predictable, there may be more room for amortizing them over time. But when initial costs are high and variable, the margin for absorbing risk becomes harder to accommodate, and investors are likely to demand substantial early returns to demonstrate that their investment will pay off. Higher education offers a good example. In universities, some institutional costs can be deemed part of an annual operating budget, and can be offset by various funds, such as endowment, grants, outside funding, or funds raised by lucrative activities at the school, such as licensing of major sports games or university-branded merchandise.[2]

Creative industries are rife with firms that are not well established, even though some will have passed the startup or venture capital phase. Those firms' ventures are risky propositions by definition. But many established creative firms engage in work that is itself high-risk, such as making movies or television series that are costly to produce and whose success is uncertain to predict. In both cases, initial investments tend to be high, which means that the risk-benefit analysis will be critical to clear and will require being able to make assurances to investors that costs are recuperable and profits can be made over time, possibly with some margin for long-term returns in foreign markets or secondary licensing streams.

Secure IP rights can go a long way in assuring investors and creditors that creative works will retain their value and will not be subject to copying, piracy, or otherwise illicit activities. For creative industries that are predicated on high production and distribution costs, secure rights also help to ensure that creative works are underwritten by investors and, where needed, supported by outside credit. IP protections ensure that copyright owners block potential infringers and retain the right to pursue actual infringers in legal action.

1 Anatomy of a Blockbuster, *The Guardian* (Jun. 10, 2004), available at www.theguardian.com/film/2004/jun/11/3.

2 See Business Models for Online Higher Education, *Hanover Res. Rep.* (Sept. 2013), available at www.hanoverresearch.com/insights/business-models-for-online-higher-education/?i=non-profit-organizations.

These send a powerful signal throughout creative industries that their work will retain its market value over its lifetime.

There are a host of questions that arise early on in the life cycle of creative works and that can enhance the value of creative efforts. One question is whether competitive firms in creative industries can secure first-mover advantage and capitalize on their standing within the industry. First-mover advantage means that when a firm secures a strong market position early on it is able to capitalize on potential network effects, building strong user bases that can grow rapidly and extensively to achieve a dominant market share. This is often referred to as the "Facebook effect," which effectively secures users in a given universe and raises their costs of moving to another, competing universe, a barrier that is often reason enough for users to remain captive and committed to the space in which they consume and interact with creative content.[3]

Creative firms that are able to secure a first-mover advantage also achieve economies of scale that help them grow efficiently and economically, minimizing costs that may otherwise hamper them or that may need to be assumed by their competitors. First-mover advantage is a tricky proposition in a highly changing environment, and disruptive innovation can undermine its benefits or confer them on a competitor. Prior to the dominance of Facebook, MySpace appeared to have secured first-mover advantage, only to see its dominance eroded and eventually superseded by the Facebook platform.[4] Clearly, even a second-mover or latecomer can secure a dominant market position and arrogate the advantages that come with capturing a market, securing economies of scale, and enjoying network effects. Creative firms can position themselves accordingly, but few are able to keep their positions secure. Nonetheless, some established creative firms, such as The Walt Disney Company, show that it can be done.

IP rights can help situate first movers into a dominant market position by locking up rights in underlying software and hardware, securing the ownership of artists and back catalogues of earlier artists' works, or corralling an entire universe of creative properties, as in the case of Marvel and DC Comics. They can also help close off a universe to interoperability with competitors, compelling them to enter into lucrative licensing arrangements that can be restricted, made exclusive, or otherwise controlled by the owner of the creative properties. They can also secure secondary or ancillary rights, including rights in international markets, translated works, and re-releases. And they can secure rights in lucrative merchandise that is tied in to popular creative works, which can involve products, such as toys and apparel; services, such as priority ticket sales and special events; and related forms of entertainment, such as books, comic books, and video games.

3 See generally David Kirkpatrick, *The Facebook Effect* (Simon & Schuster, New York, NY 2005).
4 Id.

Content industries should realistically assess their production costs and values. They should harness technology on all points of the value chain, from creation through production through marketing and distribution and sales. They should also consider new ways of using technology to garner more profits out of their properties wherever possible. If feasible, content industries should consider forfeiting short-term payoffs in order to secure market position (possibly using loss leaders as a strategic tool) and to seek a long-term payoff.

In education, the elite institutions and some spin-offs, such as edX, MIT Open CourseWare,[5] and Coursera, are sacrificing immediate payoffs in the search for market position and ultimate profitability. Coursera has shown that ensuring first-mover advantage has significant benefits, as it has been able to corner the MOOC market among elite institutions, virtually compelling many schools to join its ecosystem and thereby reinforcing its lockup.[6] Much like technology companies that are able to corner the market and compel consumers to work within their ecosystem—even at the price of interoperability—the ability of content industry participants to corner a market may be the single most important step in ensuring their competitive viability over the long haul.

Creative industry participants should consider the extent to which they want to invest in trying to secure market position by the business strategies outlined here. They may then choose to add layers of IP to ensure protection of their revenue-generating properties while still covering other goals, such as retaining maximum flexibility, gaining buy-in from labor, and ensuring that they are not locked into a single system until the market leaders have been established.

Most commercial industries producing highly finished content are likely to factor high production costs as a major expense, such as entertainment, journalism, and print publishing. Other more individualized industries may have slightly lower costs, such as comedy, yoga, magic, and exercise.[7] Some content industries may be able to harness technology to increase the value that their properties offer. For instance, the publishing industry should try to profit

5 See EDX, available at www.edx.org; MIT Open Courseware, available at https://ocw.mit.edu/index.htm.

6 See generally Michael Horn, The Intrigue of Coursera, *Forbes* (Dec. 19, 2013), available at www.forbes.com/sites/michaelhorn/2013/12/19/the-intrigue-of-coursera/.

7 See Christopher J. Sprigman & Dotan Oliar, There's No Free Laugh (Anymore): The Emergence of Intellectual Property Norms and the Transformation of Stand-Up Comedy, 94 *Va. L. Rev.* 1789 (2008) (discussing comedy); Kristen McCallion & Sara O'Coin, Yoga, Exercise or Dance, *Intell. Prop. Mag.*, Mar. 2013, at 28, available at www.fr.com/files/Uploads/Documents/McCallion,OCoin.IPMagazine.YogaExerciseDance.March2013.pdf (discussing Yoga and exercise); Jacob Loshin, Secrets Revealed: How Magicians Protect Intellectual Property without Law, in *Law and Magic: A Collection of Essays* (Christine Corcos, ed., 2010) (discussing magic). There may be a caveat here: creating new exercise classes, such as cycling or spinning, step aerobics, weights classes, or pole dancing classes may require some investment in creating and perfecting the equipment and training. But these creative endeavors generally involve a single performer, minimal props, and relatively low production costs.

from licensing rights in extracts or abstracts of works that can be widely made available through electronic devices, as the music industry has done with ringtones. Google Search already makes short snippets available, but has secured a ruling that they fall under the fair use exemption to copyright protection.[8] However, longer extracts and abstracts may still be fair game, and may be sufficiently valuable that they can be monetized, albeit perhaps modestly.

Publishing, as well as entertainment and media companies such as the film industry, should also experiment with a "windows" model of new product releases, in which staggered releases maximize the profitability of new works when they are first revealed and at the height of their popularity with most audiences.[9] The film industry is leading the way on this charge, and the music industry is beginning to explore its options to follow suit, but there are further expansions of staggered release models, as well as changed models of simultaneous release, often with multiple or varied products, that are beginning to come into play. The music industry is also researching ways to inform its consumer base of compensation models to artists and creators in order to justify their revenue models and pacify consumers, particularly with respect to growing markets in online music streaming.[10] Using windows of release, pay gates, subscription plans, and tiered pricing are solutions that are being proposed for adoption.[11] These are potentially powerful tools to use in conjunction with these new revenue-generating plans.

Many of the content industries will need to lengthen their timelines to profitability in order to explore, shape, and fine-tune these new business models. Journalism, publishing, and other content providers with high production costs may need to resort to cross-subsidization within their parent companies, where possible, to defray the immediate costs of such exploration

8 See generally, Google's Publication of Electronic "Snippets" as Part of Plans to Digitise Books Is "Fair Use" Says US Judge, *Out-Law* (Nov. 15, 2013), available at www.outlaw.com/en/articles/2013/november/googles-publication-of-electronic-snippets-as-part-of-plans-to-digitise-books-is-fair-use-says-us-judge/; Marvin Ammori, Copyright Misunderstandings and the Google Competition Inquiry (May 8, 2012), available at http://ammori.org/2012/05/08/copyright-misunderstandings-and-the-google-competition-inquiry/.

9 See, e.g., Reel Time: The Incredible Shrinking Window for Movie Releases, *Knowledge@Wharton* (Nov. 24, 2009), available at http://knowledge.wharton.upenn.edu/article/reel-time-the-incredible-shrinking-window-for-movie-releases/; see also Helienne Lindvall, Staggered Releases—Everyone's a Loser, *The Guardian* (Nov. 27, 2008), available at www.theguardian.com/music/musicblog/2008/nov/27/staggered-releases; see also Greg Sandoval, Spotify: Staggering Music Releases (Like Movies) Won't Work, *CNET* (Feb. 29, 2012), available at www.cnet.com/news/spotify-staggering-music-releases-like-movies-wont-work/.

10 See Sam Wolfson, "We've Got More Money Swirling Around": How Streaming Saved the Music Industry, *The Guardian* (Apr. 24, 2018), available at www.theguardian.com/music/2018/apr/24/weve-got-more-money-swirling-around-how-streaming-saved-the-music-industry.

11 See How to Fix Music Streaming in One Word, "Windows" . . . two more "Pay Gates," *The Trichordist* (Nov. 11, 2014), available at https://thetrichordist.com/2014/11/11/how-to-fix-music-streaming-in-one-word-windows-two-more-pay-gates/.

and expansion.[12] Adhering to long-term strategies is especially necessary in a quickly changing environment, where many complex forces can rapidly change the direction of growth, the domination of the market by industry leaders, the system or entity that emerges as a powerhouse driving the market, and the shape that products, devices, and outcomes will take.

The examples of cellular telephones (the dominance and decline of Nokia),[13] television recording devices (the triumph of VHS over BetaMax),[14] computer hardware (the declining market share of once-powerful entities such as IBM, Hewlett-Packard, and Dell),[15] and computer software (the relative decline of Microsoft versus the rise of Apple)[16] all provide ample evidence that markets change extremely swiftly as technology evolves at lightning pace, and the advantages of consumer lock-in and a self-contained ecosystem may be offset, or even erased, by the disadvantages that lack of interoperability generates when the market turns to new systems, devices, and controlling forces. For entertainment and media industries, this appears to be a challenging proposition: they have traditionally been driven by the need to realize immediate returns on their products. However, the long-tail of entertainment—for instance, the realization of longer-term profits in international markets in the film industry—has begun to spark a recognition that long-term payoffs may be the best path to long-term vitality.[17] As technology continues to force these recognitions, content industries should continue to pursue longer term, and possibly riskier, solutions to their business endeavors.

To maximize the value of their content, some creative industries should consider unbundling their offerings and attempt to profit from sales or licensing of individuated works. This may prove to be a challenge. In the case of journalism, for instance, the customary product is an entire newspaper or magazine. However, many publications are discovering that a subscription model for a publication—traditionally the practice for retaining readers and thereby retaining the viewership for the advertising supporting the publication—only works online when an audience is willing to pay for the entire product. The *Wall Street Journal* and *The New York Times* have

12 See generally Joe Moran, The Role of Multimedia Conglomerates in American Trade Book Publishing, 19 *Media Culture Soc'y* 441 (1997).

13 See Roger Cheng, Farewell Nokia: The Rise and Fall of a Mobile Pioneer, *CNET* (Apr. 25, 2014), available at www.cnet.com/news/farewell-nokia-the-rise-and-fall-of-a-mobile-pioneer/.

14 See generally Michael A. Cusumano, Yiorgos Mylonadis, & Richard S. Rosenbloom, Strategic Maneuvering and Mass-Market Dynamics: The Triumph of VHS over Beta, 66 *Buss. History Rev.* 51 (1992).

15 See Steve Denning, Why IBM Is in Decline? *Forbes* (May 30, 2014), available at www.forbes.com/sites/stevedenning/2014/05/30/why-ibm-is-in-decline/.

16 See Kurt Eichenwald, Microsoft's Lost Decade, *Vanity Fair* (Aug. 2012), available at www.vanityfair.com/news/business/2012/08/microsoft-lost-mojo-steve-ballmer.

17 See, e.g., The Television and Movie Industry Explained: Where Does All the Money Go? *Strategy Analytics*, available at www.strategyanalytics.com/reports/vg5d52vcWt/single.htm.

succeeded in this practice,[18] but others, such as the *Times* (London), have been unable to follow suit.[19]

Some stand-alone products may not be desirable enough that a readership is willing to pay for them: initially the *New York Times* experimented with an online business model that placed editorial content, such as op-ed and opinion pieces, behind a firewall, and made it available only on a subscription basis.[20] This effort resulted in almost immediate losses. In the end, the experiment of placing editorial content behind a paywall was abandoned due to an apparent lack of interest among its readership in paying for editorial content.[21] But it was also doomed in part by the ready availability of such content through workarounds that do not require payment: for instance, the same content offered via various services (Lexis and Westlaw), or linked by third parties and thereby made available through generally available blogs, websites, and other online resources.[22] Eventually, the *New York Times* decided to rebuild its subscription-based readership with the more traditional approach of promoting its investigative reporting, selling subscriptions to the entire paper, and awaiting long-term readership growth. Its efforts succeeded, but its model proved a cautionary tale.

Even in the case of new revenue initiatives, such as offering versions of news publications on tablets, handheld readers and other devices, the results have been decidedly mixed, and have run into many of the same issues that basic online services have faced.[23] Nonetheless, the verdict is still out on paywalls, and major journalism sources are still striving to make them revenue-positive

18 See generally, The Media's Risky Paywall Experiment: A Timeline, *Week* (Jul. 30, 2010), available at http://theweek.com/articles/492336/medias-risky-paywall-experiment-timeline, But see Jeff Bercovici, Whoa! WSJ.com Quietly Makes Big Traffic Strides, *Upstart Bus. J.* (Apr. 11, 2008), available at http://upstart.bizjournals.com/companies/media/2008/04/11/whoah-wsjcom-quietly-makes-big-traffic-strides.html ("No wonder Rupert Murdoch's in no hurry to do away with *The Wall Street Journal*'s online paywall. Even with it still in place around large sections of the site, traffic is still growing at a most impressive rate.").

19 See, e.g., Gilligan Reagan & Lauren Hatch, Five Failed Paywalls and What We Can Learn from Them, *Bus. Insider* (Apr. 28, 2010), available at www.businessinsider.com/failed-paywalls-2010-4; Erick Shonfeld, The Times UK Lost 4 Million Readers to its Paywall Experiment, *Tech Crunch* (Nov. 2, 2010), available at http://techcrunch.com/2010/11/02/times-paywall-4-million-readers/.

20 See Reagan & Hatch, Id.

21 The *New York Times* itself is now behind a partial paywall. That is, it offers free access to a limited number of articles per month (10 articles per month as of this writing). However, the success of its current model remains mixed at best. See Id.

22 See, We Take You Beyond the Paywall . . . to Deliver More Relevant Results, *LexisNexis*, available at www.lexisnexis.de/whitepaper/beyond-paywalls-whitepaper.pdf.

23 See, e.g., John Reinan, Can Paywalls and Tablets Save Newspaper, *Minn. Post* (Nov. 7, 2011), available at www.minnpost.com/business/2011/11/can-paywalls-and-tablets-save-newspapers.

in new and emerging media.[24] Newspapers can continue to experiment with various blends of paywalls, subscription services, or metering-per-pay models, and it is possible that they will eventually find a successfully balanced solution. But there remains little doubt that new media will continue to push journalism to identify its most valuable properties—those for which its readership will pay—and that the proliferation of diverse sources, free content, and freely available links will continue to pose significant challenges to traditional journalism's long-term success.

These roadblocks reveal that the disaggregation of content on the Internet is a challenging proposition: if journalism cannot be fully protected behind a paywall and is widely available for free or competing with free resources, it is very unlikely to be a source of revenue, and it is unlikely to be a reliable source of viewership for supporting advertisers. On the other hand, in the case of more protected properties, such as e-books in the publishing industry, content may be more readily monetized.[25] While offering some of their works through lending libraries, the publishing industry may prove successful in keeping their e-book properties profitable by imposing similar restrictions on them to those imposed on digital tracks by the music industry. Further, if abstracts, excerpts, or other kinds of properties become desirable to consumers—perhaps enhanced by products such as Google Books[26]—publishers may find new revenue sources in the sale or licensing of portions of written works.

7.3 Can You Change Your Profitability Paradigm?

Creative industries should ask whether they are taking advantage of the broadest possible range of commercial opportunities that they find available, some of which may have been opened by disruptive innovation. A profitable business model may be attained by examining not just the most obvious strategies, such as price adjustments and growth of advertising and product placement, but also by taking into account more subtle calculations, such as separating revenue-generating content from content that can be used as promotional material to build and secure audiences, or for other important but indirect purposes.

Questions relating to pricing of creative properties should begin by asking how important price signaling is to the industry. Typically, price signals convey information to industry participants as to production needs, consumer

24 See, e.g., Roy Greenslade, Soft Paywalls Retain More Users than Hard Paywalls—by a Big Margin, *The Guardian* (Nov. 7, 2014), available at www.theguardian.com/media/greenslade/2014/nov/07/paywalls-charging-for-content; Paul Osgerby, Paywalls and the Future of Online Journalism, *Daily Iowan* (Jan. 23, 2015), available at www.dailyiowan.com/2015/02/23/Opinions/41046.html.

25 See, eBook Sales Growth—Where It's Really Coming From (an Analysis of Author Earnings), *Pub. Tech.* (Feb. 14, 2014), available at www.publishingtechnology.com/2014/02/ebook-sales-growth-where-its-really-coming-from-an-analysis-of-author-earnings/.

26 *Google Books*, available at https://books.google.com.

demand, and the value of products circulating in creative markets. For creative producers, price signals can be essential tools to determine how they can optimize the development, marketing, and sales of their output. But to some extent price signals are tied into, if not contingent upon, both consumer demand and perception. Related questions, then, are do consumers rely upon clear, transparent, and readily available pricing information (as for instance in the case of commodities), or do consumers accept or embrace price opacity?

Pricing strategy is important for creative producers to determine supply and demand, but it is also a powerful tool that can be deployed strategically to build or secure financial success. How creative industries can wield pricing is, therefore, a critical inquiry giving rise to a host of queries with the object of maximizing returns on copyrighted properties. Can they increase revenues from properties that they already own via exploitation of related rights? Can they adjust, differentiate, or otherwise tweak pricing to maximize their returns in rent-producing properties? Can they create business synergies with other content industry players or complementary enterprises?

The approach to pricing and price signaling may vary considerably among creative industries. In music, pricing of music is generally clear, but the allocation of revenues among industry participants may not be available to outside audiences. In fashion, arguably, price opacity is accepted and even embraced by consumers, some of whom enjoy the "hunt for the bargain," sales, and other common industry practices. In education, pricing is somewhat clear, as the sticker price of schools is readily available. However, "discounts" given in the form of scholarships, grants, loans, and other aid can have a considerable effect on sticker price. Some of these may also be negotiable, variable, and highly unstandardized. Therefore, opacity goes hand-in-hand with tuition pricing at traditional schools. However, in the case of single course units, there may be less variation between the price that is stated and that which is actually paid. The difference between just these industries makes it clear that creative industries must pay close attention to the role that prices play in their practices and policies and the customs that are accepted by their customer base.

Creative industries should tackle pricing plans that both maximize their immediate returns from properties and capitalize on the potential for future returns, which may be enhanced by the emergence of new technologies and venues. In the publishing industry, the explosive growth of e-books should compel publishers to undertake new approaches to pricing of product licensing and sales.[27] As distribution is facilitated by the Internet, publishers should be able to deliver e-books to various audiences both efficiently and at cost points that are calibrated to different market sectors. Technological tools, algorithms, and other strategies should be harnessed to put into place refined

27 See Brady Dale, "Despite What You Heard, the E-Book Market Never Stopped Growing," *The Observer*, Jan. 18, 2017, available at https://observer.com/2017/01/author-earnings-overdrive-amazon-kindle-overdrive-digital-book-world/.

pricing schemes, allowing publishers to derive the best returns possible from their e-books, e-readers, and related materials.

While there may be pushback from distributors, retailers, and third-party participants, publishers should be in a position to control the initial pricing and terms governing the dissemination of their product.[28] Some publishers should also consider tying in marketing, promotion, and possibly retailing in their arsenal. Vertical integration offers a means of freeing the publisher from the distributor, and thereby enhances the autonomy of the publisher over the pricing of both hard copy books and e-books. In relation to pricing plans, creative content industries, including publishing, should also appropriate rent-maximizing pricing strategies and schemes devised by other industries.[29]

Illustrative are the film, television, and entertainment industries' differentiated pricing plans that serve important strategic goals in targeting consumer markets, cross-pollinating viewership, and taking advantage of a property's maximum value at its peak commercial moments, typically upon first release or run. The cable television industry achieves these goals by offering bundled packages of channels that viewers must subscribe to in order to have access to their preferred programming.[30] In this way, viewership of a popular channel, such as HBO, can effectively subsidize viewership of other, more niche channels, such as TMC, TLC, and others. These packages of channels are also priced variously, so that viewers may choose how many to purchase and have available. At the same time, "on demand" offerings make immediate viewership of standalone shows both immediately accessible and profitable on an individuated basis.[31] The film industry similarly engages in tiered pricing, in part by offering movies at different prices based on the popularity of venues and the time of release (first-run or second-run shows).[32] The film industry

28 One caveat is that publishers must steer clear of behaviors that may trigger antitrust concerns, such as making concerted efforts to control pricing and delivery terms, or other such potentially cartel-like behavior. The case of the retail and distributor giant Amazon versus the publisher Hachette, as well as the conglomerate Time Warner, are illustrative. See generally, e.g., Jim Milliot, BEA 2014: Can Anyone Compete with Amazon? *Publishers Weekly* (May 28, 2014), available at www.publishersweekly.com/pw/by-topic/industry-news/bea/article/62520-bea-2014-can-anyone-compete-with-amazon.html; see also David Streitfeld, Hachette and Amazon Dig in for a Long Fight over Contract Terms, *N.Y. Times* (May 28, 2014), available at www.nytimes.com/2014/05/29/technology/amazon-hachette-book-publisher-dispute.html?_r=2; David Streitfeld, Amazon Stops Taking Advance Orders for "Lego" and Other Warner Videos, *N.Y. Times* (Jun. 10, 2014), available at http://bits.blogs.nytimes.com/2014/06/10/amazon-stops-taking-advance-orders-for-lego-other-warner-videos/.

29 See Moran, supra note 12, at 441–55.

30 See generally Gregory S. Crawford & Joseph Cullen, Bundling, Product Choice, and Efficiency: Should Cable Television Networks Be Offered a la Carte? 19 *Info. Econ. & Pol'y* 379 (2009).

31 See generally Ronald J. Rizzuto & Michael O. Wirth, The Economics of Video on Demand: A Simulation Analysis, 15 *J. Media Econ.* 209 (2009).

32 See Reel Time, supra note 9.

also engages in tiered releases of its output through a series of "windows," beginning with the most lucrative first-run window in which the movie is priced for maximum returns, followed by windows of release on cable and DVD, Netflix, streaming, and eventually second-run releases, television screenings, online streaming, and so forth.[33] This also enables the film industry to time international releases in ways that will maximize their popularity and returns in multiple international markets.

Other creative industries should consider these models of release and determine whether they are appropriate. The publishing industry has traditionally incorporated the windows scheme of release, first releasing books in hardcover, followed by paperback, trade paperback, and similarly lower-priced versions.[34] In the case of e-books, it should consider first releasing digital copies at a premium price, without distribution to libraries and lending sources, followed by less expensive releases to e-readers and eventually online. Similarly, the music industry should consider releasing digital tracks in various windows, with differentiated pricing that reflects the time of release, popularity of the work, and other key factors. Particularly in the case of music streaming, this option offers the industry the opportunity to release the work to large audiences without undermining their revenue models. In some cases, such as the subscription-based models of Rdio, Spotify, and others, the windows model is already proving effective, and thus should be further pursued to capture new markets without sacrificing immediate or long-term returns.[35]

Another tool to improve profitability is increasing revenues from advertising, sales, marketing, which have all been traditional supports for most creative sectors. Creative industries should ask what they can do to strengthen their position vis-à-vis advertisers. Can they improve advertising-related returns? How dependent are they on advertising revenues? Do they have the ability to move beyond advertising-supported models? Can they improve their exploitation of the digital realm? And can they leverage their digital presence to pursue new markets and opportunities?

Photography offers several interesting examples of the ways in which advertising plays into creative industries' business models. Traditional photographers can find that the Internet poses a threat to their livelihoods, particularly when infringers post their works online without permission, licensing, or

33 See Id.

34 See also Evil Wylie, Staggered Digital Release Dates Worry Music Industry—Are Books Next? *Digital Reader* (Oct. 8, 2010), available at http://the-digital-reader.com/2010/10/08/staggered-digital-release-dates-worry-music-industry-are-books-next/ (noting that some publishers stagger the release dates for e-books "in a move intended to artificially inflate demand for print books").

35 This has been presented as an alternative to the kind of release, and the concerns, recently raised by the dispute between Taylor Swift, an enormously popular artist, and the online streaming site Spotify. See Kaitlyn Tiffany, A History of Taylor Swift's Odd, Conflicting Stances on Streaming Services, *The Verge* (Jun. 9, 2017), available at www.theverge.com/2017/6/9/15767986/taylor-swift-apple-music-spotify-statements-timeline.

attribution, and often with the intent to make money from the appropriated work. In photojournalism, for instance, the unauthorized use of photographs has become a rampant practice that many seasoned photojournalists have come to deplore.[36]

The reproduction of photojournalists' work deprives them of the right to publish their works in newspapers, magazines, and online venues that depend on advertising dollars for support. It also enriches infringers by diverting advertising dollars to the places where they post the appropriated works, which adds insult to injury. The threat of appropriation in photojournalism is so serious that it has given rise to a veritable cottage industry in litigation over copyright infringement of photojournalists' work.[37] In this case, litigation appears to be emerging as the primary solution that photojournalists resort to when trying to thwart copyright infringement and when seeking to reap the benefits of their work that should be derived from placing their work in advertising-supported venues and sites.

The battles over photojournalists' work represent one venue in which ad-supported revenue plays out to the disadvantage of creators when works are easily replicable on the Internet. In other sectors, the battle lines are drawn rather differently, and the results are mixed but in some respects promising. In celebrity photography, tabloid news and celebrity-gossip websites such as TMZ drive audience views that advertisers are keen to garner. These sites thus earn the bulk of their considerable revenues from advertisers.[38] TMZ stands alone as a tabloid site that often gets breaking news from its own photographers and paparazzi,[39] whereas most of its major rivals rely upon stock photos that are less original but easier to license and obtain.[40] Due to its size and power, TMZ has the means to litigate potentially infringing behavior that threatens its output. Its advertising-based revenue is therefore relatively stable and secure.

While TMZ remains a fairly traditional tabloid site, it has given rise to competitors that are notable for their entrepreneurial and more freewheeling nature. Perez Hilton, for instance, is a singular tabloid blogger who has

36 For an alleged case of such infringement, see Tyler Falk, Photojournalist Sues NPR Over Copyright Infringement, *Current*, May 12, 2017, available at https://current.org/2017/05/photojournalist-sues-npr-over-copyright-infringement/.

37 Justin Peters, Why Every Media Company Fears Richard Liebowitz, *Slate* (May 24, 2018), available at https://slate.com/news-and-politics/2018/05/richard-liebowitz-why-media-companies-fear-and-photographers-love-this-guy.html.

38 See Scott Goodson, The 30 Most Popular Celebrity Gossip Sites and Why Big Brands Love Them, *Forbes* (May 24, 2013), available at www.forbes.com/sites/marketshare/2013/05/24/the-30-most-popular-celebrity-gossip-sites-and-why-big-brands-love-them/#49b16fa55264.

39 See Anne Helen Petersen, The Down and Dirty History of TMZ, *Buzzfeed* (Jul. 24, 2014), available at www.buzzfeed.com/annehelenpetersen/the-down-and-dirty-history-of-tmz.

40 TMZ is a tabloid news website that was developed as a collaboration between AOL-Time Warner and Telepictures Productions, a division of Warner Brothers. See, available at www.tmz.com.

made a career from posting celebrity gossip, photographs, and commentary.[41] Hilton's primary revenues also derive from his ability to drive audience views, attracting sizeable advertising support. But rather than suffering losses at the hands of infringers, Hilton has engaged in a number of activities that have sparked copyright infringement lawsuits against his blog. These activities include posting various previously copyrighted works, including recordings of pop artist Britney Spears,[42] images of actor Jennifer Aniston from unreleased movie footage,[43] and paparazzi photographs from the celebrity photography agency X17Online.[44]

While the allegedly infringing practices of Perez Hilton are certainly regrettable, they do not entirely overshadow the individual entrepreneurship that has driven the blogger to build a commercially successful website that conveys tabloid gossip, photographs, and commentary to very large audiences, and that derives significant income from related advertising revenues. Perez Hilton is only one of a number of celebrity photographers (paparazzi), bloggers, and social media influencers who have carved a lucrative profession in the journalism sector. Many celebrity photographers now take photographs for agencies, which then license out the content. Licensing fees are considerable, and supplement the revenues that come from directly posting the photographs on advertising-supported sites.

Interestingly, in some of these cases the paparazzi photographers not only claim copyright in the celebrities' photos, but will also sue celebrities who then try to repost the photos on their own initiative and for their own promotional purposes. In two pending cases against the celebrity figures Gigi and Bella Hadid,[45] as well as Khloe Kardashian,[46] the photographers who claim copyright in the original works are suing the celebrities who then tried to post the photos on their personal media feeds. If nothing else, these suits make it clear that copyright in celebrity photographs is a growing and increasingly profitable niche in the creative industries, and will continue to be supported by licensing fees, advertising revenues, and other copyright-driven returns.

41 See generally Perez Hilton blog, available at www.perezhilton.com.

42 See Perez Hilton Sued Over Britney Spears Songs, *Huffington Post* (Updated May 25, 2011), available at www.huffingtonpost.com/2007/10/11/perez-hilton-sued-over-br_n_68132.html.

43 See Judy Faber, Blogger Sued Over Topless Aniston Pic, *CBS News* (Feb. 21, 2007), available at www.cbsnews.com/news/blogger-sued-over-topless-aniston-pic/.

44 See 7Online Sues PerezHilton.com for Copyright Infringement, *Business Wire* (Nov. 30, 2006), available at www.businesswire.com/news/home/20061130006074/en/X17Online-Sues-PerezHilton.com-Copyright-Infringement.

45 See Gigi Hadid, IMG Models Slapped with Copyright Infringement Lawsuit Over Instagram Post, *The Fashion Law* (Sept. 11, 2017), available at www.thefashionlaw.com/home/gigi-hadid-img-models-slapped-with-copyright-infringement-lawsuit-over-instagram-post; available at www.teenvogue.com/story/gigi-hadid-sued-paparazzi-instagram-post.

46 See Erika Harwood, Why Celebrities Are Getting Sued for Posting Photos of Themselves, *Vanity Fair* (Apr. 27, 2017), available at www.vanityfair.com/style/2017/04/khloe-kardashian-instagram-photo-lawsuit.

Countless examples are also arising in fashion and beauty and other creative industries in which individuals can create online media presences that are monetized through a combination of advertising based on audience views, sales of merchandise, and relationships with major brands that afford these "influencers" sway over product lines and page views alike. Two examples suffice to illustrate the close connections that entrepreneurs can build through the savvy manipulation of social media and online marketing to create synergies between their brands, audiences, advertisers, and products. Fashion blogger Chiara Ferragni (known online as "The Blonde Salad"), began launching her empire with a popular blog, created and promoted her own line of high fashion shoes,[47] and moved into mainstream influence.[48] Similarly, Huda Kattan[49] began a beauty blog with makeup tutorials, created and promoted her own line of premium false eyelashes, and leveraged that success into a beauty line that is currently valued at a billion dollars.[50] It is entirely possible that these entrepreneurs' creative output will be threatened by potentially infringing imitators, appropriators, or illicit actors. But their unique combination of commentary and advice, proprietary products, and influencer status positions them well to stave off such challenges and to keep advertisers supportive of their business model and their creative output.

New technologies can increase potential revenues in already-existing content and products. Creative industries should assess whether they are able to increase revenues from properties that they own and/or to which they have proprietary rights, including but not limited to performance rights, ancillary and subsidiary rights,[51] related merchandising rights,[52] and digital rights.[53] They should critically assess the extent to which they can change or adjust pricing, create pricing tiers to serve differentiated market segments, and/or price discriminate as a means to maximizing returns in rent-producing properties.

47 See Clare O'Connor, Forbes Top Influencers: Instagram "It" Girl Chiara Ferragni on Building a Fashion Empire, *Forbes* (Sep. 26, 2017), available at www.forbes.com/sites/clareoconnor/2017/09/26/forbes-top-influencers-instagram-it-girl-chiara-ferragni-on-building-a-fashion-empire/#302531ad3001.

48 See Lauren Cochrane, Chiara Ferragni—How A "Crazy Blogger" Turned Her Life into a Shop Window, *The Guardian* (Nov. 29, 2016), available at www.theguardian.com/fashion/2016/nov/29/chiara-farragni-blogger-the-blonde-salad-socia-media-style-posts-multi-million-pound-business.

49 See Shelia McClear, Why Huda Kattan Is One of Beauty's Most Influential Women, *Allure* (Jun. 28, 2017), available at www.allure.com/story/huda-kattan-profile.

50 See Chloe Sorvino, How Huda Kattan Built A Billion-Dollar Cosmetics Brand With 26 Million Followers, *Forbes* (Jul. 11, 2018), available at www.forbes.com/sites/chloesorvino/2018/07/11/huda-kattan-huda-beauty-billion-influencer/#6e7adc6a6120.

51 See generally Gregory Goodell, *Independent Feature Film Production* 252 (1982).

52 See, e.g., Alan Bryman, *The Disneyization of Society* 79 (2004); Opinion: On Ringtones and Copyrights, *Macworld* (Sept. 20, 2007), Available at www.macworld.com/article/1060142/ringtones.html.

53 See, e.g., William Coates et al., Streaming into the Future: Music and Video Online, 20 *Loy. L.A. Ent. L. Rev.* 285 (2000).

7.4 Do You Still Rely on Intermediaries?

Creative industries are not made up of content producers alone: they also comprise enterprises and individuals who facilitate the processes that bring works to consumers and the public. Intermediaries, including artistic agents and editors, IP rights managers, curators and critics are essential participants in creative work, and like content producers they are increasingly confronted by disruptive innovation. Industry-wide disruptions are changing their roles, business models, and practices, and are imposing new risks that threaten their viability.

Some critics of intermediaries may see these challenges as healthy, compelling intermediaries to reform their structures and strengthen their approaches to producing and delivering content and rewarding creators.[54] But intermediaries still have an important role in creative ecosystems, taking many critical but time-consuming functions—such as content selection and preparation, sales and marketing, and rights management—out of the hands of creators, facilitating more time and focus in true creative work that cannot be delegated. Creative industries should recognize that tailoring good policies should include grappling with the role of creative intermediaries, determining how they are to be improved but also ensuring that they are supported and sustained.

The term "intermediary" covers a broad range of roles. Some intermediaries serve as agent and talent scout services that identify, select, and cull artistic talent, which may include connecting artists with content companies and nurturing artists throughout their career. Others engage in editorial services that help prepare, refine, and finish creative works, including polishing content, checking accuracy, finessing production values, and preparing works for commercial rollout. Some intermediaries serve important critical functions. They engage in curating, recognizing, and reviewing works, as well as rewarding exceptional work with praise, prizes, or other reputational boosts to deserving creators. Many intermediaries are involved in the business side of creative work, including sales and marketing services, product distribution services, and the management of IP-based rights and rewards, including collective rights management. And some intermediaries are involved in work that goes on behind the scenes, such as archival and storage services, and database and resource-based services.

Challenges within the creative industries raise important questions about the role and utility of intermediaries in creative sectors. Are there still roles that are irreplaceable by digital technologies, or are there newly emerging roles for intermediaries to undertake in order to facilitate production, commercialization, and other aspects of creative content generation that cannot be substituted by disintermediated processes? Which intermediary roles should

54 See, e.g., Raymond Shih Ray Ku, The Creative Destruction of Copyright: Napster and the New Economics of Digital Technology, 69 *U. Chi. L. Rev.* 263 (2002).

survive in the digital age, and how should they be supported? What are the costs entailed in automating intermediation, not just to human labor but also to human capital? If intermediaries are valuable, and if retaining them is critical to the health of creative industries, are they valuable enough, and valued enough, that they will continue to receive remuneration—in other words, will they get paid, and how will they get paid?[55]

New competitors among creative industry intermediaries are bringing new questions to the fore. What is the nature and role of these competitors, and do they have an impact on the delivery of content and the labor required to facilitate content delivery? Is the labor compensated directly, as has traditionally been the case with intermediaries, or does labor become contributory, contractual, underpaid, or free? Can digitally intermediated work reach audiences without intermediaries, such as agents or editors or critics? Does the rise of amateur creators, producers, and facilitators begin to render the role of traditional intermediaries obsolete?

In the online sphere, the emergence of blogs, online magazines, scholarly resources and databases of articles,[56] digitally maintained and peer-reviewed journals, and other sites, demonstrates the willingness of interested parties to contribute their labor toward the production of content and related materials. In many of these cases, the labor of contributors is donated voluntarily, often without compensation.[57] Moreover, the fruits of their labor, such as websites, databases, blogs, magazines, and so on, are released via the Internet directly to the reader, thus throwing into question the relevance and role of intermediaries.

The rise of online intermediation should be a wake-up call to creative industries and creative industry intermediaries alike. The long history of industry enrichment by intermediaries can illustrate the benefits they confer. In the music industry, traditional intermediaries have proven invaluable at talent identification and support, music production, marketing, and other functions. Moreover, music criticism, promotion, and "evangelism"—that is, praise of musical talent that critics can spread to build audience recognition and appreciation—has proven equally indispensable to the music industry's vitality. Notwithstanding the ability of amateurs to adopt some of these roles via the Internet, they have yet to demonstrate a commensurate capacity to the professionals who still fulfill these vital roles.

55 For a general discussion of iTunes's role as an intermediary, see W. Jonathan Cardi, Über-Middleman: Reshaping the Broken Landscape of Music Copyright, 92 *Iowa L. Rev.* 835, 852–3, 859 (2007).

56 See Frequently Asked Questions, *Soc. Sci. Res. Network*, available at www.ssrn.com/en/index.cfm/ssrn-faq/.

57 An early example is the Huff Post, formerly Huffington Post, which only recently announced that it would change its policy of not paying contributing writers. See, available at www.cjr.org/analysis/so-now-huffpost-decides-to-pay-writers-its-effect-on-the-industry-still-lingers.php.

Creative industries should support and sustain the frameworks, institutions, mechanisms, and inputs that are critical to keeping intermediaries operational, effective, and secure. In the case of agents and talent scouts, for instance, creative industries should support their efforts to cull talent from both digital sites and real space locales. In the case of credentializing and authenticating critics, reviewers, and curators, creative industries should recognize the many layers of value that they add to content dissemination, consumer appreciation, and other aspects of content generation.

Creative industries should also ensure that audiences are aware of the valuable role that critics and other intermediaries play. They should also continue to vest such critical participants with authority in their given field. This is not to suggest that critics do not have an obligation to defend themselves and to demonstrate their enduring importance. But at the same time, content industries have not typically ceded critics their due, nor have they communicated faith in critical faculties to their audiences. Creative industries should recognize the integral role that intermediaries play in serving as a bridge between creators, producers, and audiences.

Recognition of the value that intermediaries confer should be tangibly expressed. One means of such expression is to remunerate critics, reviewers, curators, and others; another is to continue to turn to and rely upon them for a host of activities, such as supporting artistic and cultural competitions and prizes, underwriting critical publications and reviews, sustaining institutions that promote creative talent, and so on. At the same time, creative industries can and should pursue critical figures that emerge through less traditional venues, including those enabled by the Internet. By bringing these outsiders into the mainstream, content industries can strengthen their position in the digital realm, while at the same time reinforcing the sense among their audience that critical intermediaries remain informative and valuable.

For their part, intermediaries must prove their continuing utility to content industries.[58] Intermediaries involved in creative production should strive to distinguish their products and services from amateur productions by adding value and retaining high quality standards and objectivity. In the case of music intermediaries, such as record labels, this should include keeping high quality of audio, recording, and sound editing. In the case of fashion intermediaries, such as fashion retailers, this should include maintaining both quality and exclusivity of curation, and the skillful review and promotion of designers. In education, this should include accreditation institutions and bodies, which subject educational institutions and programs to a process of peer review as a basis for measuring and authenticating institutional quality.[59]

58 See generally Derek Slater et al., *Content and Control: Assessing the Impact of Policy Choices on Potential Online Business Models in the Music and Film Industries* 11–15 (2005).

59 Among these recognized bodies are regional accrediting agencies, such as the New England Association of Schools and Colleges, national accreditors, such as the Accrediting Council for Independent Schools and Colleges, programmatic accreditors, such as the

Creative industry intermediaries should work to distinguish their product from those produced by nonprofessionals and to demonstrate that their labor cannot be readily displaced by advanced technologies alone. In music, personal computers can now easily be loaded with relatively sophisticated sound recording, mixing, and editing software programs, thus enabling talented amateur musicians to create and record digital tracks with remarkably polished finishes. Nevertheless, there remains a distinction between even competently produced amateur efforts and professionally produced tracks for commercial release. It behooves music intermediaries to bring this distinction to the fore, and to make clear that they are adding value by bringing music production to a professional level.

Intermediaries such as critics and curators should pursue online roles that play to their strengths, such as contributing to websites and blogs that highlight their knowledge, experience, and critical prowess. They should consider banding together to create high-value sites that may be attractive to interested audiences. At the same time, they should strive to monetize their offerings in creative ways, using a combination of advertising support, subscription-based offers and services, and where possible strategic alliances with content companies that can help underwrite their work. These activities can include joining online websites, group blogs, joint databases, scholarly resources, and other collaborative efforts that highlight the strengths of professional critics and reviewers while creating new opportunities for emerging talent, whether professional or amateur.

Intermediaries involved in authentication and authorization should increase their efforts to serve providers that digitally disseminate products and services. In education, online educational providers are increasingly offering authentication and authorization services to students for a variety of reasons, including allaying privacy concerns, securing the identity of students, thwarting attempts at plagiarism, and ensuring that students receive recognition and credentialization for their work.

7.5 How Do You Remunerate Your Labor?

Creative industries rely on valued creators and gifted artists as well as skilled workers, trained editors, researchers and technicians, and hard-working producers to conceive, generate, develop, and deliver rich content. Creative industries should recognize the centrality of these workers to their enterprises, and should ensure that their remuneration enables them to make a livelihood and to create in the best circumstances possible. Indeed, the central premise

---

Accreditation Council for Business Schools and Programs, and specialized accreditors, such as the American Bar Association. Other intermediaries in education that facilitate quality control are entities that review universities, such as *U.S. News and World Report*'s annual ranking of schools and programs, as well as other trusted reviewers that help applicants differentiate among educational products and services.

of IP law—that creators are incentivized to create when their work is rewarded and recognized—can find expression in the compensation structure of creative industries.

Creative industries should examine the structure of labor rights and rewards, the terms and conditions of labor, and the environment in which workers create and operate. The first set of questions to ask relates primarily to knowledge workers in creative industries such as education, scientific research, and other types of scholarly and academic work. What is the status of these workers? Are they primarily full-time employees, in which case the employer typically retains and owns rights pursuant to the work-for-hire doctrine, or are they independent contractors, in which case the employee may retain rights, depending on contractual agreements?[60] Do these workers have professional status, and are they well-compensated for their creative or innovative output, whether or not they retain IP ownership rights? Some indications of professional status include autonomy in the work that they undertake, and rights such as academic freedom. Are these workers compensated for their creative or innovative work by non-tangible rewards, such as authorship and publication rights, reputational benefits, awards and prizes, credit for work, and other resume-enhancing rights? Do they have job mobility and knowledge portability? Are they limited in their knowledge portability by non-competition agreements that prevail in their field? Are these workers eventually able to bring their know-how, expertise, and knowledge to their new employment?

The second set of questions relates primarily to working artists in creative industries such as music, fashion, entertainment and media, journalism, comedy, cuisine, or yoga. Are working artists independent, and do they have copyright ownership in their work? Or do they work with middlemen that traditionally retain ownership rights? Do working artists typically create without retaining a full roster of ownership rights, but are they otherwise compensated by other means such as returns from live performances, revenues from sales of merchandise, or reputational benefits that boost their earnings potential? How are working artists compensated with respect to licensing rights? Are they compensated by standard contractual licensing agreements that give them a percentage of royalties, or are they remunerated on a flat fee basis? Do working artists have the ability to assert other IP rights, such as trademark rights, in some aspects of their work? How are their rights managed and how are their compensation streams obtained? And what recourse do they have if their work is infringed, stolen, or otherwise used or taken illicitly? Do they have access to representation? Are there resources that can help them offset or compensate for their losses in the case of infringement, plagiarism, appropriation, or other harm?

Creative industries should consider business and IP-related solutions contiguously, as the status of industry workers will be inextricably linked to their

60 490 U.S. 730 (1989).

IP rights, and may in fact determine their IP rights. On the one hand, creative industries whose workers are long-standing employees, with tenure rights or rights comparable to tenure, such as full-time employment, retention rights, or partnership rights, should realize that their workers are professionals who may not retain IP rights in their output subject to the work-for-hire doctrine. Nonetheless, these professionals may be compensated by more than just salary and benefits. In the educational sector, they generally tend to have rights such as academic freedom, publication rights, peer recognition, and eligibility for outside funding, prizes, and awards. In these cases, IP rights may not be paramount for securing the rewards of creativity and innovation. Creative industries should understand that while professional workers may forfeit some of the purely financial rewards of IP rights, such as royalty streams or payouts from commercialized properties, they may be making a tradeoff—and arguably a fair and balanced tradeoff—for other compensations, rights, privileges, and rewards.

On the other hand, creative industries whose workers are short-term are differently situated. Workers who are subject to dismissal, have little professional autonomy or rights such as academic freedom, and are not particularly rewarded for creative work, tend to function more like independent contractors. Their employment may not hinge upon long-term prospects or payoffs. In education, such workers are often adjunct or non-tenure track professors, and graduate students. These workers are not likely to have the option to balance the various rewards that established professional employees in a tenure or partnership-type track position enjoy. In these cases, industries should consider whether their employees should be deemed independent contractors and granted IP rights in their output, or whether other forms of compensation should be extended in order to keep them remunerated and motivated.

Creative industries should also take into account their workers' job portability and knowledge mobility. In cases where workers are highly mobile and can bring their skills to bear on a number of desirable positions in their industry, creative industries can argue that perceived shortfalls in their immediate contract terms are counterweighted by the freedom to leverage their work to secure a stronger position in the future. This justifies giving content industries flexibility in setting the terms of employment of their workers, and should assist them in cases where they intend to retain the bulk of IP rights in creative properties. At the same time, highly skilled workers may be desirable throughout the field and therefore may be both valuable and mobile. This should indicate that worker salaries are likely to be elevated by competition, and in these cases creative industries should be aware that they may have to keep salaries at a highly competitive level to retain their best workers.

Creative industries should consider the standard in their field regarding the retention of IP rights as part of an employee's portfolio, rather than as part of the employer's holdings. In some industries, IP rights may travel with the employee, particularly if the employee is able to create or self-fund independent ventures, such as startups or spin-offs. For example, in startups, high-tech entrepreneurs often bring key IP rights to the table. In such cases, creative industries should realize that their ability as employers to retain IP rights may be limited by convention, competition, or self-sufficiency on the part of the employee. All of these factors must be taken into consideration when creative industries consider the balance of compensation, rights, and rewards in their labor pool.

Creative industries should recognize that some working artists may prefer some of the conditions of long-term employment to the retention of IP rights in their work. Not only should they acknowledge this tradeoff, but they should also recognize that the balance of power initially favors the industry in this case because artists who are making this choice may not yet be secure, and may not yet have leverage to call the terms of their employment. Creative industries should recognize that the terms of such contracts are liable to shift if and when the artists they are fostering develop reputational markers such as widespread recognition and the ability to draw and keep large audiences, as well as the ability to move products such as recordings and to sell branded merchandise.

The computer software industry illustrates one way in which division between the retention of IP rights and compensation, as well as related rights and rewards, may operate. In the software industry, long-term employees are deemed skilled professionals who are well-compensated with salary, benefits, and often stock options,[61] but who do not typically retain IP rights in their professional output.[62] These employees also garner reputational benefits in the field, in part by being recognized for their work—for instance, the developer of a software program may be named, be eligible to receive awards, or earn bonuses—and in part by being sought-after among their competitors and peers. Due to the desirability and job mobility of such workers, software industry companies often try to condition their employment on agreements to stay with the company for a given period of time, or not to transport their work or know-how to a competitor.[63] However, these non-competition agree-

61 See, Software Developer: Salary, *US News*, available at http://money.usnews.com/careers/best-jobs/software-developer/salary.

62 Employees may retain rights in work they have created on their own time and using their own equipment, but they must be scrupulous in segregating such efforts, and may face contentious claims if their work leads to IP-protected properties and success. The allocation of IP rights to the employer, which is the norm in the computer industry, is typically made pursuant to standard work-for-hire doctrine. See, e.g., Chris Shiplett, "Who Owns the Code?," Association of Software Professionals (2008), available at https://asp-software.org/www/misv_resources/business-articles/who-owns-the-code/

63 See Orly Lobel, *Talent Wants to Be Free: Why We Should Learn to Love Leaks, Raids and Free Riding* (Yale University Press, New Haven, CT, 2013). See also Dane Stangler, Noncompete Agreements: The Good, the Bad, and the Ugly, *Xconomy* (Aug. 14, 2014), available at www.xconomy.com/national/2014/08/14/non-compete-agreements-the-good-the-bad-and-the-ugly/; Bob Weinstein, What You Should Know Before You Sign a Noncompete Agreement, *TechRepublic* (Dec. 13, 2010), available at www.techrepublic.com/article/what-you-should-know-before-you-sign-a-noncompete-agreement/.

ments may be difficult to enforce, limited in scope and strength, and subject to lengthy and expensive dispute in the courts.[64] Moreover, many skilled software development workers consider non-competes to run counter to the balance of rights and rewards that are standard in the field.[65] Industry participants may on occasion give little deference to non-competition agreements when luring a worker away from a competitor. These are among the reasons that job mobility and knowledge portability remain at a premium in the software development industry.

In certain creative industries, such as film, entertainment, and music, established artists may resemble skilled and talented software developers in some respects. They may have job mobility and portability, they may not be bound for long periods of time by the equivalent of non-competition agreements, and they may enjoy reputational benefits from being associated with well-established industry representatives such as agents and promoters. While they typically do not retain IP rights in their output, some of these artists may in fact carve out certain rights that they choose to retain.[66]

In creative industries such as music, film, journalism, and publishing, the difference between established artists and emerging artists may be starker and more consequential than in fields like software development. Emerging artists typically do not retain ownership in their underlying properties. They do earn royalties in their work, but some of these rewards may be sacrificed for placement and visibility goals: for instance, releasing works online may gain audience share, but is not likely to be immediately monetizable. Further, initial contracts governing emerging artists often cede IP rights and the lion's share of profits to the companies that represent the artists rather than to the emerging artists themselves.

In the music industry, initial recording contracts often require artists to cede a large percentage of up-front earnings to the record label, only yielding returns to the artists after a large number of recordings have been sold.[67] Similarly, in the film industry, initial signing contracts often require artists to agree to a flat-fee payment for their performance in a new release, thereby forfeiting rights in royalties that will accrue over the lifetime of the film if it is successful.[68]

64 See Weinstein, supra note 64 (noting that many non-competes are not enforceable).

65 See Scott Kirsner, Time to Get Rid of "Noncompete" Agreements, *Boston Globe* (Apr. 19, 2014), available at www.bostonglobe.com/business/2014/04/19/time-get-rid-non compete-agreements/VcIjVuaAcOopLZOvwqSMtK/story.html.

66 For instance, they may also benefit from ancillary relationships based in product branding and brand promotion.

67 See generally M. William Krasilovsky, *The Business of Music: The Definitive Guide to the Business and Legal Issues of the Music Industry*, 10th ed. (Watson-Guptill, New York, NY, 2007); see also Mitchell Einhorn, Gorillas in Our Midst: Searching for King Kong in the Music Jungle, 55 *J. Copyright Soc'y U.S.A.* 145, 146–8 (2008).

68 See Mark Litwak, *Contracts in the Television and Film Industry*, ch.4 (Silman-James Press, Beverly Hills, CA, 2010).

Arguably, the differential in terms and returns between star artists versus emerging artists can largely be explained by the respective difference in bargaining power and leverage that they can wield. Still, creative industries should be aware of the discrepancy, and should recognize that in some fields, such as entertainment, publishing, and journalism, emerging artists may be particularly disadvantaged by not having up-front rights unless and until they achieve long-term success.

These differences may prove discouraging to emerging artists, but they may also provide an incentive for them to move from traditional contracting arrangements to more innovative and more favorable arrangements where nascent technologies make them possible. In music, some emerging recording artists are now retaining or re-obtaining rights in their work, releasing works directly on the Internet and thereby bypassing traditional intermediaries such as talent scouts, agents, and record labels.[69] In film, some emerging actors are requesting up-front payments coupled with the right to take a percentage of future royalties and secondary rights.[70] In publishing, some emerging authors are releasing works directly on the Internet, self-publishing via online publishers or e-book purveyors such as Amazon, and retaining rights in royalties and secondary rights.[71] And in journalism, some emerging authors are retaining rights to publish their articles in multiple venues, thereby retaining the ability to gain multiple streams of royalties in a given work or body of work.[72]

69 For example, singer-songwriter Ingrid Michaelson financed and released her first hits. See Jim Farber, It All Adds Up for Ingrid Michaelson, *N.Y. Daily News* (Jun. 19, 2008), available at www.nydailynews.com/entertainment/music-arts/ads-ingrid-michaelson-article-1.296269. The band Metallica re-obtained its rights and opened its own record label. See Randall Roberts, Metallica Leaves Warner Music with Its Masters, Forms Blackened Records, *L.A. Times* (Nov. 30, 2012), available at http://articles.latimes.com/2012/nov/30/entertainment/la-et-ms-metallica-leaves-label-forms-blackened-records-20121130.

70 See Dina Appleton & Daniel Yankelvits, *Hollywood Dealmaking: Negotiating Talent Agreements for Film, Tv, and New Media* ch.7, § 4 (2010).

71 See Ronald H. Balson, Bestseller Success Stories that Start Published Books, *Huff. Post* (Oct. 8, 2013), available at www.huffingtonpost.com/ronald-h-balson/bestseller-success-storie_b_4064574.html (detailing the stories of now-famous authors who started by self-publishing); Emma Barnett & Richard Alleyne, Self Publishing Writer Becomes Million Seller, *Telegraph* (Jun. 21, 2011), available at www.telegraph.co.uk/culture/books/booknews/8589963/Self-publishing-writer-becomes-million-seller.html (discussing John Locke's success publishing and promoting its own works); Ed Pilkington and Amanda Hocking, The Writer Who Made Millions by Self-Publishing Online, *The Guardian* (Jan. 12, 2012), available at www.theguardian.com/books/2012/jan/12/amanda-hocking-self-publishing (discussing how Amanda Hocking sold over 1.5 million books on Kindle); Lizzie Skurnick, '50 Shades of Grey,' a Self-Published Book, Is the Future of Publishing, *Daily Beast* (Mar. 17, 2012), available at www.thedailybeast.com/articles/2012/03/17/50-shades-of-grey-a-self-published-e-book-is-the-future-of-publishing.html.

72 See generally Allena Tapia, Know Your Publishing Rights, *About*, available at http://freelancewrite.about.com/od/legalissues/a/rights.htm.

Creative industries that derive significant revenues from performance rights should be aware that some artists may focus on live performance fees, merchandising revenues, and related returns.[73] In some creative fields, such as comedy, cuisine, yoga, or sports instruction, artists often find that creative content, brand, and value are integrally tied to the persona and performance of the artists themselves: their expertise and know-how, recognizable brand or identity, delivery of a performance, and signature characteristics.[74] Here, creative industries should recognize that some of the value that performing artists offer may inhere as much in their brand and performance as in their recorded output.

In comedy, performers often see major revenues in live routines performed on the comedy circuit. While some comics may earn revenues in recorded performances, the market for recordings may be modest or more intermittent, particularly for lesser-known acts. In cuisine, many chefs make substantial revenues in live performances, such as appearing in their restaurants, offering courses to aspiring cooks, and making other public and private appearances. While chefs do realize returns on specialized cookbooks that trade on their identity and brand, these are closer in nature and size of returns to merchandise and other brand-related products. In yoga and sports-related fields, many instructors can realize substantial revenues in instruction, workshops, and lectures. While they may earn revenues on related materials, such as instructional manuals, CDs, or DVDs, many sports instructors may find that these generate modest proceeds that supplement their performance-related returns.

Creative industries should recognize that artists in performance-based practices may be empowered in negotiations over IP rights and returns by the strength of their creative identity and position. For some creative figures, they themselves can become a product that is not only valuable but also non-fungible; and the value of their product can inhere in their very identities and identity-based performances. While such artists may not need to retain ownership rights in their recordings—although some might, especially if they have the leverage to be able to negotiate such ownership—they may have a powerful argument for garnering significant rights and returns in their performances.

As in any situation, of course, established artists are more likely than emerging artists to have and wield real bargaining power. But creative industries should recognize that in certain creative fields, performing rights and returns may be a critical point of contention and control. Some performing artists may be able to seek out or develop new, and possibly disintermediated, means of content delivery. They may, for instance, perform live to online audiences via streaming services. They may also seek to retain all rights in their performances. Alternatively, they may seek to enter broad contracts, such as the "360

73 There are some exceptions, as in the case of comedy recordings made by famous comics, which peaked in the 1950s–80s with the works of Mel Brooks, Richard Pryor, Bill Cosby, and Bob Newhart.

74 Rights of publicity may also apply, which are outside the scope of this book.

degree" contract in music,[75] which spells out their share of rights, including important performance rights. In all of these cases, creative industries should consider suitable means of granting artists a combination of rewards, services, and other value-adds in order to retain a talented and successful artist pool.

By adjusting their business models and legal strategies to accommodate changes in labor relations, creative industries should be able to secure fair terms for their companies and artists, so that both established and emerging creators feel secure and supported. This may mean that creative industries will have to contemplate granting a greater share of rights and long-term returns, broadly predicated upon success, to both established and emerging artists. It may also mean that the retention of ownership rights in promising IP properties becomes an increasingly contested issue in creative industries—and artists may have greater leverage than they once had, owing primarily to their ability to bring works directly to their audience via new digital technologies. But this need not be a cause for alarm among the creative industries. Rather, it should be a cause for reconsideration, and possibly recalibration, of the relationship between creative industry stakeholders.

75 See, e.g., Lee Marshall, "The 360 Deal and the 'New' Music Industry," *European Journal of Cultural Studies* (2012), available at https://journals.sagepub.com/doi/pdf/10.1177/1367549412457478.

8 Tailoring Legal Policies and Practices

8.1 Introduction to Legal Issues

Creative industries flourish when private ordering arrangements abound. In the U.S., private ordering is generally considered preferable to externally imposed arrangements, such as publicly or governmentally mandated solutions.[1] Many creative industry firms prefer private ordering solutions because they are more flexible, industry-specific, and entity-specific. They also entail fewer transaction costs, and can be readjusted, renegotiated, and renewed. They can be made privately, or even secretly, among private entities. Although they may entail some transaction costs, they do not ordinarily require exogenous costs, such as the need to lobby for government regulation or oversight.

Copyright, and to a somewhat lesser extent trademark, are the baseline protections of many creative industries. By design, they are closely intertwined with creative generation and production, to such an extent that both their presence and their absence can shape the way that works are brought to fruition and delivered to markets.

The main objective when considering legal issues in creative industries is to construct a framework that fits legal choices into an integrated course of action. The inquiry begins with questions regarding the nature of creative industries: are they generally considered IP-rich industries[2], such as music, film, publishing, and video games, which can have different layers and levels of rights, and often have layers of licensing as well? Alternatively, are they

1 Jennifer E. Rothman, Copyright's Private Ordering and the "Next Great Copyright Act," 29 *Berkeley Tech. L.J.* 1595, 1598 (2014). ("In some instances, the best option is for [copyright] law to get out of the way and leave room for a variety of private approaches to flourish.").

2 See, e.g., "Copyright Permissions: Understanding Layers of Rights," Copyrightlaws.com, available at www.copyrightlaws.com/copyright-permissions-layers-of-rights/; Brian Casillas, Attack of the Clones: Copyright Protection for Video Game Developers, 33 *Loy. L.A. Ent. L. Rev.* 137 (2013), available at https://digitalcommons.lmu.edu/cgi/viewcontent.cgi?referer=www.google.com/&httpsredir=1&article=1580&context=elr.

considered IP-limited industries[3], such as fashion, which is primarily protected by trademark and, to a more restricted extent, trade dress? Or are they low-IP industries, also known as "negative spaces,"[4] such as comedy, cuisine, yoga, magic tricks, typefaces, wikis, jambands, hip-hop mixtapes, or even roller derby pseudonyms,[5] that thrive without significant IP protection?

Identifying a creative industry's place in this taxonomy helps address the key question: is it properly calibrated to give the right amount of IP protection that will yield the optimal amount of returns in creative work? On initial consideration, reaching optimality may appear to mean using the maximum levels of IP protection available. Paradoxically, though, maximizing IP may not be the best solution for all creative industries. In many creative industries, particularly those that have historically restricted their IP protection, adding new layers of coverage may involve imposing significant transaction costs on a thriving industry, while not obviously helping emerging creators who are most vulnerable to copying or appropriation.

Optimizing IP requires tailoring protections to fit the architecture and contours of a creative industry ecosystem. Whether protected by relatively high or low levels of IP, creative industries should begin by thinking about what kind of model best suits their practices and needs. High-IP creative industries should ask: How can we maximize protection without sacrificing productivity or consumer satisfaction? Creative industries that are low-IP or negative spaces should ask: Would enhanced IP be advantageous for our industry? Is a certain amount of room for appropriation or copying beneficial? Is a hybridized model, in which some IP is counterbalanced with a certain amount of leeway for copying, most appropriate for the challenges we face?

3 See, Francesca Montalvo Witzburg, Protecting Fashion: A Comparative Analysis of Fashion Design Copyright Protection in the U.S. and Europe, *Cardozo Arts & Ent. L.J.* Blog (Sept. 19, 2014), available at http://www.cardozoaelj.com/ 2016/12/01/protecting-fashion-comparative-analysis-fashion-design-protection-united-states-europe/;Trade Dress Law, *The Fashion Law* (Sept. 19, 2016), available at www.thefashionlaw.com/learn/trade-dress.

4 See Elizabeth L. Rosenblatt, Intellectual Property's Negative Space: Beyond the Utilitarian, 40 *Fla. St. U. L. Rev.* 441 (2013), available at https://ir.law.fsu.edu/cgi/viewcontent.cgi?article=1000&context=lr.

5 See, e.g., Emmanuelle Fauchart & Eric von Hippel, Norms-Based Intellectual Property Systems: The Case of French Chefs, 19 *Org. Sci.* 187 (2008); Jacob Loshin, Secrets Revealed: Protecting Magicians' Intellectual Property Without Law, in *Law and Magic: Acollection of Essays* 123 (Christine A. Corcos ed., 2010); Blake Fry, Why Typefaces Proliferate Without Copyright Protection, 8 *J. Telecomm. & Hightech. L.* 425, 432–7 (2010); Jacqueline D. Lipton, To © or Not to ©? Copyright and Innovation in the Digital Typeface Industry, 43 *U.C. Davis L. Rev.* 143 (2009); Jon M. Garon, Wiki Authorship, Social Media, and the Curatorial Audience, 1 *Harvard J. Sports & Ent. L.* 95 (2010); Horace E. Anderson, Jr., "Criminal Minded?": Mixtape DJs, the Piracy Paradox, and Lessons for the Recording Industry, 76 *Tenn. L. Rev.* 111, 114, 140–53 (2008); David Fagundes, Talk Derby To Me: Intellectual Property Norms Governing Roller Derby Pseudonyms, 90 *Tex. L. Rev.* 1093 (2012).

8.2 How Do You Maximize Your IP Protection?

Creative firms should consider the role that IP rights play in their respective markets. In some industries IP rights help control transactions, stabilize and reinforce prices, and incentivize creativity. They also support rational price discrimination and help clarify pricing signals. Industry participants should consider amassing IP rights to be an important part of their strategic arsenal. Further, the accrual of IP rights should be wielded to strengthen the ability of content companies to dictate certain key terms in the market. When allied with good business models, a strong IP strategy may allow a company to price discriminate; set the terms of interoperability, meter rights and royalties; supplement anti-theft technologies; secure first-mover advantages; prevent the appropriability of key ideas, know-how, and work product; solidify a market position; reinforce and clarify price signals; and increase the amount that may be extracted from protected work.

Many commercial enterprises have portfolios of creative and innovative properties that they monetize for profit. Technology companies, biotech firms, the computer industry (both hardware and software), and the pharmaceutical industry offer a few major examples of IP-rich sectors that have a long history of building multilayered IP holdings and wielding them strategically.[6] In these sectors, IP rights are held for a variety of purposes, including bolstering cross-licensing potential that may be required for complex, multi-part works. They may help protect potential areas of development, such as basic research and discovery efforts that can lead to patentable, and eventually commercially valuable, results. IP rights can also enable firms to position themselves strategically against competitors. And individuals can benefit from holding IP rights that strengthen their strategic positioning, particularly when individually held IP rights contribute to incentivizing employee productivity.

Not only technical sectors but also creative industries value the propertization of output. The entertainment industry, including music, film, television, and cable broadcasting, ensure that their core creative portfolios are IP-protected. They too consider their ownership of IP properties central to their productivity and profit model.[7] Many creative industries likewise protect

6 See, e.g., Ralph Minderop et al., Key Issues in Building a Strong Life Sciences Patent Portfolio, *Intell. Asset Mgmt.* (Jul.–Aug. 2012), at 126, available at www.iam-media.com/Magazine/Issue/54/Management-report/Key-issues-in-building-a-strong-life-sciences-patent-portfolio; Julia Love, Apple's Growing Patent Portfolio Offers Clues about Future Products, *San Jose Mercury News* (Jan. 22, 2015), available at www.mercurynews.com/business/ci_27377473/apples-growing-patent-portfolio-offers-clues-about-future; Antonio Regalado, Google's Growing Patent Stockpile, *Tech. Rev.* (Nov. 29, 2013), available at www.technologyreview.com/news/521946/googles-growing-patent-stockpile/.

7 For examples of patent portfolios in the entertainment industry, see Gene Quinn, Apple Expands Patent Portfolio Relating to GarageBand, *IPWatchdog* (Oct. 27, 2009), available at www.ipwatchdog.com/2009/10/27/apple-expands-patent-portfolio-relating-to-garageband/id=6912/; Tribune Media Services Acquires Television Interactive

at least some of their properties and creations for various reasons, including providing incentives, protecting licensing and exploitation rights, and maintaining competitiveness in an increasingly global marketplace.[8]

Creative industries should ask which IP rights they rely on, and whether they benefit from having single or multiple layers of IP protection. An important facet of this question is whether, and how, a content industry uses IP strategically. IP may be used to protect an entire area of work, such as a set of commercial goods, processes, and output which may be vertically or horizontally integrated. IP may also be used to establish a balance between propertization and disclosure or publication.

Creative industries should regard IP as a strategic tool, whether used as a portfolio of copyright or patent rights that propertize an area of creative work, holdings, a single area of coverage such as the use of trademark to protect valuable brands, or a bargaining chip when transacting with competitors. Creative industries can also strategically hold back on granting IP rights to promote important features of production, including cumulative innovation, incremental development and improvement through a broad range of inputs and tweaks, and the ability to partner and cross-license.[9]

In many creative industries, increasing IP protection can give greater control over content that is especially vulnerable to infringing activities. In the video game industry, for instance, extending copyright and patent protection to the valuable software that underpins the production and delivery of video games ensures that games cannot be easily copied or played by unauthorized parties.[10]

Programming Guide Application and Patent Portfolio, *Media Daily News* (Jul. 30, 2003), available at https://www.mediapost.com/publications/article/15303/tribune-media-services-acquires-ipg-from-isurftv.html?edition= ; Press Release, GTT Announces Patent Portfolio Acquisition Opportunity Related to Video Game and Movie Animation (Aug. 2010), available at www.gttgrp.com/2010/09/16/gtt-patent-video-game-movie-animation/; Press Release, Soryn IP Group to Sell Patent Portfolio Related to Smart Home Technology (Nov. 15, 2013), available at http://sorynipgroup.com/2014/09/10/soryn-ip-group-to-sell-patent-portfolio-related-to-smart-home-technology/; Chris Ferrell, Comic Book Conundrum: Who Owns the Copyrights to the World's Most Valuable Entertainment, *L. Tech. & Arts Blog* (Nov. 17, 2014), available at https://wjlta.wordpress.com/2014/11/17/comic-book-conundrum-who-owns-the-copyrights-to-the-worlds-most-valuable-entertainment/.

8 See Sheldon E. Steinbach & Bruce T. Wieder, Protect Your Patent Portfolio, *Inside Higher Ed* (Apr. 24, 2008), available at www.insidehighered.com/views/2008/04/24/steinbach.

9 See generally John Palfrey, *Intellectual Property Strategy* (2011); William W. Fisher III & Felix Oberholzer-Gee, Strategic Management of Intellectual Property: An Integrated Approach, 55 *Cal. Mgmt. Rev.* 157 (2013), available at www.hbs.edu/faculty/Publication%20Files/CMR5504_10_Fisher_III_7bbf941f-fe1b-4069-a609-9c6cd9a8783b.pdf.

10 Video Games: A Growing Market and its Intellectual Property Needs, *J. Intell. Prop. & Ent. L.* (Apr. 4, 2018), available at https://blog.jipel.law.nyu.edu/2018/04/video-games-a-growing-market-and-its-intellectual-property-needs/.

Extending the term or scope of IP protection can keep creative properties under copyright throughout the period in which they are profitable.[11] Expanding IP can come at a cost to industry stakeholders: increasing the length of protection of popular entertainment characters, for instance, can increase licensing costs for companies seeking to incorporate these characters into new products and markets. The costs of licensing may be so prohibitive as to dissuade new entrants from licensing popular characters. But these drawbacks may have a positive effect if they challenge new ventures to create original content of their own.

Creative industries should ensure that they are fully exploiting their currently protected IP holdings. They should also take into consideration and adjust to any expansions in rights that have been recently granted by copyright policy and law. In the music industry, this may include exploitation of performance rights at a broad range of venues, such as restaurants, sports facilities, new forms of content delivery such as ringtones, and new devices or platforms that circulate content widely.[12] In the case of comedy, this may include recordings of live performances and staged readings.[13] In the case of cuisine, this may include performance rights, such as chefs doing demonstrations, lectures, television shows, and professional competitions such as Iron Chef.[14] In the case of yoga and certain sports activities, this may include teaching moves and poses, routines, programs such as Tabata and CrossFit, and football plays.[15]

The exploitation of IP-protected properties is the simplest example of maximizing IP. Other strategies such as cross-licensing, vertical integration, and expanding monetization of IP-protected properties in online venues also help to maximize IP. Content industries should ensure that they have strong governance methods for these ventures, and should work to secure industry-wide backing for favorable conditions for IP exploitation, such as strong clearinghouse institutions, and capable regulatory oversight.

Expanding IP-related rights occurs within and among content industries. The commercial exploitation of secondary and ancillary rights already exists in

11 Many commentators have argued that the Sonny Bono Copyright Term Extension Act was passed specifically to help Disney keep its valuable Mickey Mouse property out of the public domain. See, e.g., available at www.wired.com/story/congress-latest-move-to-extend-copyright-protection-is-misguided/.

12 See, e.g., Jennifer Mariano Porter, Comment, Compulsory Licensing and Cell Phone Ringtones: The Phone Is Ringing, a Court Needs to Answer, 80 *Temp. L. Rev.* 907 (2007); Ellen Rosner Feig, Do Cellular Ringtones Violate the Copyright Act? *Legalzoom* (Dec. 2009), available at www.legalzoom.com/articles/do-cellular-ringtones-violate-the-copyright-act.

13 See Michael J. Madison, Response, Of Coase and Comics, Or, the Comedy of Copyright, 95 *Va. L. Rev. 27* (2009).

14 See Malla Pollack, Intellectual Property Protection for the Creative Chef, or How to Copyright a Cake: A Modest Proposal, 12 *Cardozo L. Rev.* 1477 (1991).

15 See, e.g., Alexander Bussey, Stretching Copyright to Its Limit: Copyrightability of Yoga and Other Sports Movements in Light of the U.S. Copyright Office's Characterization of Compilations, 20 *Jeffrey S. Moorad Sports L. J.* 1 (2013).

many established content industries. In the entertainment and media industries, large-scale approaches to new media markets and opportunities abound. The entertainment industry continues to move aggressively to license works in international markets. Entertainment companies diversify their online offerings via strategic alliances with Netflix, Hulu, Amazon Prime, Apple TV and other venues for digital release. They also increase availability of their content on a host of personal electronic devices via relationships with Apple, Android, and other technology companies.[16] Further ancillary rights can and should be explored, such as the limited release of snippets, trailers, ringtones, and other individuated properties that are valuable to consumers. Likewise, expansion should occur with respect to merchandising rights such as merchandise tie-ins: for instance, film tie-ins tend to be hugely profitable, such as t-shirts, mugs, McDonald's Happy Meals, "action figures" based on heroic movie characters, and other branded products that rely heavily on the exploitation of trademarked properties.[17]

8.3 Do You Use IP Rights to Retain and Reward Your Employees?

Creative industries should consider the rights, responsibilities, and rewards of employees to determine how best to balance and allocate their IP rights. Employees should be afforded a good measure of job mobility and knowledge portability, both to support their position within a company and to ensure their standing in the market. While this may seem contrary to a firm's ability to retain its employees, in the long run having employees that are recognized and compensated by a healthy mix of rewards—possibly including returns in their original output—will strengthen a company's position and build an industry's competitiveness across the board.

Employees' rights should be valued, but not ceded at the expense of a firm's competitive advantage. Nor should their rights compromise trade secrets, come at the expense of investment in high-cost projects, or undercut costly

16 See, e.g., Ian Paul, Amazon Prime vs. Netflix: Video Streaming Feature Showdown, *Pc World* (Feb. 23, 2011), available at www.pcworld.com/article/220399/Amazon_Prime_vs_Netflix_Video_Streaming_ Feature_Showdown.html. Interestingly, nontraditional producers are moving in on this space, as Amazon itself is beginning to launch movies on Amazon Prime. See Amazon to Produce Original Movies for Theaters, Prime Instant Video (Jan. 19, 2015), available at www.businesswire.com/news/home/20150119005090/en/Amazon-Produce-Original-Movies-Theaters-Prime-Instant#.VPEa4oVQlsM. It will be interesting to see if this pushes movie producers to be more innovative, or if it will stiffen competition that crowds them out of the lucrative Amazon market.

17 See, e.g., Jeff Jensen, McDonald's Hungry for Disney Tie-Ins, *Advertising Age* (Apr. 17, 1995), available at http://adage.com/article/news/mcdonald-s-hungry-disney-tie-ins/81441/. This is analogous to the merchandise tie-ins that are proving so popular in music, such as concert and band t-shirts and other memorabilia.

build-outs. One instance of the high costs of up-front investments arises in the education sector. The costs associated with creating and supporting online education programs and support systems are considerable. An institution that needs to offset those costs may not be able to compromise its business model by giving full IP rights in courses to academic faculty. If faculty develop copyrighted courses and take them to competitor institutions, the initial investment may never be recovered. Institutions that plan on building out large online programs should evaluate the longer-term consequences that allocation of copyright in courses may bring about.

Creative industries constructed around the retention, and conversely the free flow, of highly skilled employees may want to consider ceding some IP rights and returns to their employees. This may include a nonexclusive license in creative output, which may be limited over time so that the firm can recoup its initial investment costs. Such a strategy may allow employees to exert fuller control over rights in their output over time. Further, room may be left to carve out certain rights and privileges, such as the right to make some derivative works. Alternatively, firms should consider offering employees the option of a Creative Commons-type license that is open and usable by all, but requires attribution and restricts access to output to strictly noncommercial uses and purposes.[18]

In some creative industries, offering the right to publish to key employees should be considered a strategic measure that will help build and sustain an optimal workforce. The competitive value of publication rights can be part of an IP-based arsenal. Publication rights can incentivize employee productivity and reward valuable discoveries not with propertization but with disclosure. Other vital interests may be served by publication including supporting scholarship, rewarding collaboration, conferring peer recognition for significant intellectual contributions to the field, rewarding creative and innovative output, encouraging originality, contributing to a rich scholarly and public domain, and reinforcing shared values and communal exchange.

The value of publication may need to be weighed against the value of amassing and wielding IP rights and garnering IP-based returns. However, a heavy-handed emphasis on IP properties can stifle innovation, throw up impediments to creative exchange, and reduce the reputational capital that may be integral to creative industries.[19] Creative industries should not only consider sharing their IP-based rights and/or rewards with productive employees, but should also consider when those rights and rewards should be restrained in order to further other equally important goals, such as promoting research and discovery and encouraging creative and intellectual exchange.

18 Creative Commons, available at http://creativecommons.org.

19 See Gavin Clarkson & David DeKorte, The Problem of Patent Thickets in Convergent Technologies, 1093 *Annals of the N.Y. Acad. of Sci.* 180, 188 (noting that IP law can be used to stifle innovation); Alex Tabarrok, Patent Thickets Reduce Innovation, *Marginal Revolution* (Apr. 2, 2013), available at http://marginalrevolution.com/marginalrevolution/2013/04/patent-thickets-reduce-innovation.html.

8.4 If You Are Seeking to Implement or Enhance Your IP Protection, How Much Transaction Costs Would Change Incur?

Creative industries contemplating restructuring their IP rights should carefully scrutinize the transaction costs involved. These are typically known as the costs associated with changing from one system to another, but more broadly read they can also comprise the costs of establishing and maintaining a new system. A clear example of how transaction costs can arise at more than one point can be found when creative industries put into place an overarching system to manage creative properties, such as establishing collective rights organizations that administer IP rights and rewards.

Even without organized administrative bodies, the negotiation of IP rights among interested parties in creative industries can involve multiple parties including employees, contributing users, third-party providers, and contractors. Complex multi-party negotiations increase the likelihood that transaction costs will be non-negligible. Some industry-wide solutions may also require legislative change and approval, the costs of which are likely to be passed on to industry stakeholders. The precise outcome of legislative processes is difficult to predict, and while some costs may be foreseeable, the uncertainty that typically accompanies legislative change and the implementation of new legal regimes may make them impossible to estimate or account for ex ante.

It may be hard to ascertain in advance whether entities will be winners or losers in a landscape that has new or altered IP rights and protections. Creative industry participants should consider their position vis-a-vis their competitors and other stakeholders before lobbying for significant change. And creative industries should recognize that interests are likely to differ among stakeholders precisely because there will be new competitive advantages and disadvantages that arise from newly imposed IP rights. The inevitable tensions are bound to make creating a coalition among stakeholders challenging and costly. It is imperative, therefore, that proposed IP solutions should be shown to be sufficiently rewarding to undertake at all.

8.5 How Important to You are Licensing Rights Vs. Ownership Rights?

While traditionally creative content ownership may have been the standard across creative industries, content licensing has been surging since the advent of the Internet. In industries like music and film, licensing practices have become increasingly dominant and may eventually displace ownership altogether.[20] Questions abound when the licensing vs. ownership debate arises, beginning with which strategic choice is likely to lead to secure revenue

20 See Aaron Perzanowski & Jason Schultz, *The End of Ownership: Personal Property in the Digital Economy* (MIT Press, Cambridge, MA, 2016).

streams with good growth prospects. There are consequences to adopting a model primarily based in licensing rather than sales.[21]

There are copyright-based consequences to opting for licensing-based returns over ownership-based returns. In some industries, the move to licensing may shift the battleground of rights: copyright may still be crucial to allocating rights and reaping revenues, but rights based in ownership may become less worth fighting over, and rights based in licensing may become paramount. In music, movies, and some video games, licensing rights are becoming increasingly dominant, particularly as an increasing number of music-related transactions are occurring online.[22] There are some exceptions, however, such as music rights in the ownership of valuable properties such as back catalogs of content, and classic music albums and recordings. These can be significant revenue sources over time, as reissues, revivals, and remastered albums are enduringly popular among music listeners and consumers.

Services based in licensing content may likewise become more valuable, yet often more contentious, when the model changes, in particular when technology allows consumption of licensed content to become more immediate, streamlined, and often transitory. In music, iTunes and similar music-playing services, and related music-playing devices, allow streaming and other temporal ways of consuming entertainment to become more dominant, pervasive, and negotiable among interested parties.

The central question for creative industries is should the industry adhere to a traditional ownership model, in which product is sold by the company and owned outright by the consumer, or should it move to a licensing model? Creative industries may choose a hybridized model, in which some products are sold—in the publishing industry, for instance, hard copies of books sold in traditional retail stores—and others are licensed—in publishing, e-books transmitted digitally. They may choose to retain an interest in other rights, such as performance rights, which also flow from their properties. If they find that consumer preferences move them in the direction of primarily license-based models, creative firms may entirely support licensing as a means of satisfying audiences while retaining control over their properties. This may eliminate some open questions, such as whether the initial sale of a property has an effect on later rights in the disposition of that property.[23]

In some creative fields, moving to a licensing model can make good commercial sense, aligning consumer preferences and trends with innovative means of conveying content, such as digital streaming. Film, entertainment, and music

21 Id.

22 See Michael Upshall, *Content Licensing: Buying and Selling Digital Resources* (Chandos Publishing, Oxford, UK, 2009).

23 E.g., the first sale doctrine may be relevant, although its disposition may change over time. See, e.g., John Villasenor, The 'First Sale Doctrine' and Its Impact on the Music Business, Brookings, May 3, 2013, available at www.brookings.edu/opinions/the-first-sale-doctrine-and-its-impact-on-the-music-business/.

are areas that are increasingly realizing major returns from licensing-based models, and most metrics suggest the trend is only likely to accelerate.[24]

But as in the music industry, licensing can come with its own set of concerns. Rate setting for the licensing of digital works in music is an area that is contentious due in large part to the marked disparity between rates levied upon streaming services versus terrestrial broadcast radio.[25] The disparity creates an unequal playing field that skews the competitive advantage in favor of traditional radio, or so digital platforms have long contended. While rate-setting may require legislative intervention to change or recalibrate, its effects may be felt across the music market in ways that would not be as manifest if ownership-based business models were still the prevailing norm. Moreover, the effects of licensing-based models may affect other participants in the music sector.

Consumers may feel the effects of licensing-based models in the subscription rates that they pay to listen to music digitally, as online music providers must clear their margins in accordance with the rates they have to pay. Consumers may also be affected in the array of musical offerings that are available to them, as digital providers must enter into licensing agreements for both current music and back catalogues. And while music delivery may become more varied online, with multiple digital providers and services on offer, competition for rights to streaming music may become more relentless, resulting in more fragmented and convoluted delivery systems. In the past, consumers have complained that bundled services compelled them to purchase access to content streams in which they were not interested. But in a universe of fragmented and competitive services, consumers may find they are compelled to subscribe to multiple providers in order to gain access to the full range of content that they want to consume and enjoy.

Creative industries that focus their energies on building out licensing of their properties should ensure that adequate support mechanisms are in place to facilitate the smooth flow of content to satisfy consumer demand. They should equalize and fully operationalize licensing-based services, such as online release of products and services via online streaming. Creative industries should also strive to promote interoperability among content providers, both among creative and technological allies, thereby allowing content licensing to occur on many platforms. This will further enable consumers to have as wide a range of choices as possible on which to have access to the content they license. Not only will this increase consumer satisfaction, but it will also likely increase consumers' willingness to pay for products that they can immediately use and enjoy. For some consumers, this may also be considered an acceptable

24 See Joshua P. Friedlander, News and Notes on 2017 RIAA Revenue Statistics, *RIAA Music*, available at www.riaa.com/wp-content/uploads/2018/03/RIAA-Year-End-2017-News-and-Notes.pdf.

25 See CRS Report R43984 (Jun. 7, 2018), available at www.everycrsreport.com/files/20180607_R43984_caf9b623f727ecb9b1b83a6a0ad773c4bb63556f.pdf.

tradeoff: that is, an increase in immediacy of goods and services may counterbalance any reduction in actual ownership and its associated rights. It may also counterbalance potential reductions in the actual rights consumers have in the use and enjoyment of their products.[26]

Creative industries should strengthen cloud-based services to afford consumers strong, stable, and adequate storage of their licensed content, as well as ready access to such content. Further, they should consider creating strategic alliances with companies that facilitate online payments, micropayments, data encryption, and other technological services and products needed to support online commerce.

Licensing of creative content is expanding in an array of industries. Examples abound, including streaming of films, television shows and series, e-books, and any other content that may be streamed online rather than outright purchased.

Technological innovations can help support and promote the availability of licensed content. These innovations may include the expansion of cloud computing and cloud-based software, improvements in streaming technology, increases in availability, speed, and efficiency of broadband, the management and oversight of Internet Service Providers (ISPs), the growth of data storage and security in personal computers and devices. These innovations may be furthered by the diversification and proliferation of electronic devices that enable consumers to obtain quick, easy, affordable, and typically temporary access to a range of creative content. This last factor is significant, as it appears to reflect a growing preference among users and producers in favor of licensing content.[27] Creative industries should recognize that building user satisfaction is the most direct and reliable inroad to creating a system in which licensing becomes the de facto practice, and which eventually becomes the prevalent and preferred mode of consumption of creative commercial content, goods, and related services.

Further, a possible compromise is building a hybrid model in which some goods are offered for sale and others are available through streaming or by other licensed means. Creative industries have already followed this model for some time. Movies are usually widely available for purchase in DVD, Bluray, or other formats designed for home ownership and use, and at the same time, they can be watched in movie theaters, streamed via online services, and rented through On-Demand channels. Analogously, the publishing industry

26 For instance, if Apple iTunes music consumers are only permitted to make 10 copies of their music on personal electronic devices, the fact that they can listen to the music on various devices may seem a kind of fair compensation or trade. See Manage Your Associated Devices in iTunes, available at https://support.apple.com/en-us/HT204074.

27 It may be, however, that the market is driving consumer preference by increasing its offerings of licensed content. But users do not seem to be resisting in any concerted way; and many users do seem satisfied to relinquish long-term ownership for more immediate but transitory availability.

makes books and magazines available for purchase in physical copies, e-books and e-zines, and in some cases serially available online. It may be that the physical world of content becomes limited to more niche markets, as some critics of digitization contend. But the persistence of bookstores and surprisingly robust book sales seem to indicate that the appetite for owning hard copies of creative works need not be displaced by digital formats but rather can, and indeed should, co-exist side-by-side.

8.6 Have You Implemented Collective Rights Management?

Creative industries that are considering expanding or adding new layers of IP to their works, such as proposed plans to bring copyright to the fashion industry, should consider whether centralizing the administration of copyright would be effective, transparent, and helpful in managing the orderly flow of rights and rewards. Just as the Copyright Office has proven absolutely critical in managing U.S. copyrights since its inception, so might a rights management organization that regulates the rights in a given creative industry enable artists to maximize the value of their works, help them to manage disputes that arise over those works, and assist those who seek access to creative works to discern their rights and responsibilities in accessing and using the creative materials concerned.

It is interesting to compare creative content concerns with the issue of transaction costs as it pertains to collaborators in patent-related work, particularly in areas such as scientific research. In the patent context, there is an acute concern with clearing multiple rights prior to engaging in cumulative innovation, on which much scientific research and patentable work is predicated. This is often referred to as the threat of "patent thickets," and is especially relevant where rights in underlying scientific materials, such as gene sequences, are concerned.[28] The fear of encountering patent thickets, or "a dense web of overlapping intellectual property rights that a company must hack its way through in order to actually [generate and] commercialize new technology" can be a major impediment to productivity.[29]

Clearing patent thickets, analogous to clearing copyright rights, is a vital step that must precede innovative and protectable activity and output.[30] In the case of scientific research, rights-clearing organizations—whether formally instigated, privately undertaken, or narrowly engaged—may serve to help overcome the impasse that overly complex rights regimes can present, thereby

28 See generally Intellectual Property and Genomics (National Human Genome Research Institute), available at www.genome.gov/19016590.

29 Carl Shapiro, Navigating the Patent Thicket: Cross Licenses, Patent Pools, and Standard-Setting, in 1 *Innovation Policy and the Economy* 119, 120–1 (Adam B. Jaffe et al. eds., 2000).

30 Id.

opening the path to collaboration and improving the prospect of rewarding scientific research and development in the greater scientific community.

Content industries that depend upon multiple properties, complex contractual and licensing arrangements, products that may require an array of rights to be cleared such as tie-ins and other forms of brand-based marketing, are well-advised to consider instituting centralized rights-clearing organizations. The film industry, for instance, shares many of the characteristics of the music industry, yet its products often involve even more complicated rights-clearing processes than do typical music products. Some considerations include multiple markets, products, and venues for viewing, both digital and real space, follow-on products such as sequels, and merchandise and tie-ins. A centralized rights management institution could facilitate cross-licensing of rights in the components of films that draw on various cultural resources and references. It could also manage rights in the release of films, starting at launch and continuing through their long trajectory across various markets, including DVD release, international release, second-runs, revivals, and remasterings.[31]

Other creative content industries that have not traditionally relied on IP rights and are currently considering implementing a formalized IP rights regime are also well-advised to consider collective rights management. Implementing a systemized approach to rights management is particularly helpful at the outset of large-scale propertization, as there is an immediate need for an orderly deployment of rights and rewards. Adding a new layer of rights almost inevitably adds complexity relations within an industry. These concerns are only likely to increase as rights-based transactions, such as licensing, proliferate. Were property rights brought to an industry like fashion, the establishment of a collective rights organization could ensure significant economies of scale in enforcement of rights, and might assist individual designers who could not afford to engage in potentially expensive and protracted litigation.[32]

31 While not specifically addressing the exigencies of the film industry, Ruth Towse offers a model for collective rights management in the digital age that would meet many of its needs, such as the ability to manage complicated rights in diverse markets and over time. Ruth Towse, Economics of Copyright Collecting Societies and Digital Rights: Is There a Case for a Centralised Digital Copyright Exchange? 9 *Rev. Econ. Res.* Copyright Issues 3 (Dec. 2012), available at http://ssrn.com/abstract=2216165. It is also noteworthy that some countries have begun to implement centralized collective rights management systems in film rights, including Uganda, see Hillary Muheebwa, Collective Rights Management Takes Root in Uganda, *IP-Watch* (Jul. 24, 2014), available at www.ip-watch.org/2014/07/24/collective-rights-management-takes-root-in-uganda/; Croatia, Collective Management Rights (State IP Office), available at www.dziv.hr/en/intellectual-property-protection/copyright/management-of-crr/collective.

32 Legal commentators have proposed this solution as well. See, e.g., Scott Hemphill & Jeannie Suk, The Law, Culture, and Economics of Fashion, 61 *Stan. L. Rev.* 1147 (2009).

8.7 If You Are a Low-IP or Negative Space: Is IP Good for Your Industry, Is Copying Good for Your Industry, or Is a Hybridized Model Good for Your Industry?

Negative space creative industries, particularly those that have historically existed without multilayered propertization, should consider both the immediate impact and possible longer-term consequences of changing IP allocations and rights. At the outset, they should ask: is changing their present state necessary or likely to be helpful? In some cases, commercial features of the industry can protect business models and keep the road to profitability secure without recourse to additional IP rights. These features can include high product turnover, brevity of periods in which works are most valuable, or widespread reliance on multiple underlying works that require cross-licensing agreements. Maintaining a working environment of extremely fast-paced change, or facilitating collaboration by keeping cross-licensing readily available, are goals that may be hindered by adding IP rights to good commercial conditions. In some circumstances, tweaking other industry features may result in better outcomes than adding layers of legality.

Trademark protection and concerted industry-wide efforts may suffice to address the problems of copying while allowing the industry to generate new works at its usual pace of innovation. In negative spaces like comedy and cuisine, important practices like attribution, homage and apprenticeship might be stifled by imposing copyright on works that have been allowed to widely circulate and enrich the entire industry, such as a shared legacy of jokes and gags in comedy and a trove of classic recipes in cuisine.

Even in higher-IP regimes like video games, where technological protections are strong and user interaction is strongly encouraged, IP protections can be imposed at certain points and not others: software and games are proprietary and protected by IP, but certain characters, avatars, storylines, and uses may sometimes be made freely available for users to play with, modify, and build upon.[33] While the licensing of popular characters may limit some of those uses, the industry may choose not to impose across-the-board restrictions, but rather to implement them in specific cases.

Other higher-IP regimes can also have specific parameters to their protection. In publishing, which tends to be a more low-tech industry, but one with traditionally strong IP protection, copyright protection of fiction will be limited to the telling of the story and not to the characters. These parameters are set by copyright law, which does not allow characters or figures to be copyrighted. But the limitations of copyright can work in favor of publishing, especially with respect to encouraging audience interaction and participation. A rich culture of fan fiction has been flourishing for some time now,

33 See, e.g., Fortnite End User License Agreement, available at https://www.epicgames.com/fortnite/en-US/eula.

as enthusiastic readers create stories involving their favorite characters from well-loved novels, such as the "Harry Potter" and "Twilight" series. Indeed, the author of the Twilight series, Stephanie Meyers, has stated that her work originated as fan fiction following "Fifty Shades of Gray"; and Ms. Meyers has in turn encouraged her followers by creating and supporting fan fiction sites of her work.[34] Similarly, J.K. Rowling, creator of the Harry Potter series, has lauded fan fiction efforts.[35] This generation and support of fan fiction is far from universal. But its emergence, and some of its high-level support, have created a kind of template for user-generated content, which more high-tech industries may want to follow and adapt for their own user communities and audiences.

34 See, e.g., Stephanie Meyer, Twilight Series Fansite, available at https://web.archive.org/web/20111006021434/http://stepheniemeyer.com/ts_fansites.html.

35 See, Darren Waters, Rowling Backs Potter Fan Fiction, *BBC News*, May 27, 2004, available at http://news.bbc.co.uk/2/hi/entertainment/3753001.stm.

9 Tailoring Technological Measures

9.1 Introduction to Technological Issues

Technological protections such as encryption, authentication, anti-circumvention, and anti-counterfeiting measures and devices thwart the appropriation of valuable content. These tools can help secure creative output and mitigate risks to producers and investors. But the advantages of technological protections are not unmixed. Creative industries sometimes overlook the complex but subtle tradeoffs that adding technological protection to creative content or delivery systems may entail. Likewise, they often neglect to consider the long-term effects of content lockup. Creative industries commonly start by asking how effective their proposed technological protections are. But they should go further to ask how much they value features such as interoperability, and they should also ask how much their protective technologies affect any positive externalities.

9.2 What Technological Protection Do You Have in Place and How Effective Is It?

Technological measures can serve as different kinds of bridges between business and legal solutions. A few uses of technology in the creative context include: protecting valuable creative properties from copying and infringement; securing software, algorithms, data, and essential proprietary information, tools and resources; authenticating users and preventing non-authenticated users from access to creative properties; keeping users within a proprietary universe; and managing IP rights and metering IP rewards.

Prior to imposing or implementing new technological solutions, creative industries should ask: Is the proposed technology effective, flexible, adaptive, and cost-effective? Does it achieve its intended purpose? Is it properly cabined to the appropriate level and scope of coverage, or does it exceed its reach and lock up works or uses that should remain accessible or free?

Some technological measures, such as digital rights management (DRM), may result in new restrictions on content that may require some degree of buy-in from users. Thus, creative industries should ask: Will the proposed technological measures eventually be accepted by the user community? This is often overlooked or given short shrift, but it is an important consideration, as the user community is not only the consumer base but can also serve many important purposes.

Users can be valuable resources that give input into creative content, and can help support creative producers as they improve the quality, adaptability, and innovativeness of their content. The roles that users play can be varied, including: spotting errors and inconsistencies and trouble-shooting (particularly in cases where open-source development is encouraged by industry participants); seeking out and rewarding the strongest innovators (which conversely can be problematic for companies that are not wielding their technology effectively or lagging behind in the technological arm's race); and embracing companies and products that have the best balance of technology and openness in the marketplace.

The music industry shows that technological protection can be a double-edged sword. It has not worked particularly well in preventing piracy; nor has it proved a panacea against the loss of content value that has ensued upon industry-wide changes to the music business model, product pricing, and delivery systems. Moreover, it has proven largely unpopular and unaccepted among listeners. When Apple first introduced its iTunes Music Store, it intended to encrypt its recordings with DRM, known as FairPlay.[1] The public reaction against FairPlay eventually drove Apple to remove the encryption, although it did retain certain restrictions on music purchased through iTunes.

The consumer resistance to encryption of music stands in contrast to general consumer acceptance of technological protections in the video game industry. This may be due to the fact that video games have been encrypted since their inception. It may also be due to the fact that video games were first sold in conjunction with proprietary consoles and electronic devices required for their access and use. The tie-in between software and hardware may have inured consumers at the outset to the built-in protections that were part and parcel of video games prior even to the inception of the Internet.

Finding the proper technological balance can be a challenge. On the one hand, technological protection, such as anti-counterfeiting technology, may be required to protect core properties and returns. In the fashion industry, anti-counterfeiting technology has proven at least somewhat effective in curtailing rampant copying of high-end branded goods, although fashion industry participants are still forced to play catch-up with counterfeiters. Examples of anti-counterfeiting technology in fashion include special paper, watermarks, intaglio printing, geometric lathe works, holograms, and microprinting.

1 See Bobbie Johnson, Apple Drops DRM Copy Protection from Millions of iTunes Songs, *The Guardian* (Jan. 6, 2009), available at www.theguardian.com/technology/2009/jan/06/apple-drops-itunes-copy-protection. See also Serenity Caldwell & Joseph Keller, Apple Music Will Now Let You Store Your Music Library DRM-free, *iMore* (Jul. 18, 2016), available at www.imore.com/apple-rolling-out-improved-itunes-match-apple-music-subscribers.

On the other hand, technological openness may contribute to new forms of creativity, new revenue sources, and renewed participation in the creative community. In the case of music, some artists such as jam-bands allow and even encourage copying, forgoing any anti-copying technology or practices. This enables at least a subset of musicians to make a living almost exclusively from live performances and merchandise rather than from recording revenues. It also enables fans to appropriate music creatively by making, recording, and disseminating their own versions of songs, crafting new works that respectfully reference the originals but create imaginative versions that are truly new. These practices follow a tradition that would have been lauded by Mozart and Haydn, and a host of classical composers and musicians, not to mention traditional American roots, R&B, blues, jazz, and rock music.

9.3 How Much Do You Value Interoperability?

When digital innovations facilitate the misuse or appropriation of content, technological protections can offer effective protective measures that are proactive and secure. They are not, however, cost-free, and can be expensive to operationalize and update. Another potential cost is system interoperability. While some creative industries see keeping control of their universe as a net benefit, the cost of interoperability is that it can work against industries or firms that seek to create products across platforms, products, or devices. In an increasingly complex creative landscape, where movies, merchandise, video games, books, TV series, spin-offs, and sequels can span multiple realms and long periods of time, interoperability may be an imperative, even if it comes at the expense of exclusivity and uniqueness of content.

This creates a dual set of incentives that are not always easily reconciled. On the plus side, locking users into a single ecosystem may lead to supra-normal rents, as users are compelled to consume products, services, and resources using one set of devices that are offered by a single manufacturer or closed group of manufacturers. This can lead to consumer loyalty and satisfaction with a given ecosystem, including its providers, creators, and delivery systems.

But systemic lockup may also generate consumer dissatisfaction with the restrictions, perceived or real, of a closed system, such as a lack of access to other distributors, a limitation of content offered (depending, for instance, on the terms of cross-licensing agreements), and a possible curtailment of user rights due to IP protections (for instance, limited copying even for personal use, limited rights to build upon creative output, limited rights to remove or circumvent DRM, or limited rights of repair[2]). The returns that

2 Some of these restrictions are reinforced by law, particularly the DMCA. See, e.g., 17 U.S.C. §1201, available at www.law.cornell.edu/uscode/text/17/1201.

interoperability can generate, therefore, need to be weighed in the balance against the potential costs that it can impose across an industry.[3]

There are other meaningful tradeoffs to interoperability. A closed system may also allow content creators, as well as manufacturers of technology carrying content, to exert considerable control over external providers who want to join the ecosystem, such as offering third-party applications.[4] Even the largest technology companies, including Microsoft, Apple, and Google, share these concerns.[5] Creative industries may be able to leverage their centrality in closed and non-interoperable systems by not only compelling users to consume their content on the terms that they are able to set, but also compelling other participants such as third-party manufacturers or strategic partners to accede to their contractual and licensing terms.[6] Again, this choice may entail a loss of flexibility. By establishing a closed ecosystem, creative industries may commit themselves to a locked structure that is unable to adapt to sweeping outside changes in technology, user preference, and competitive cost and pricing structures.[7]

Disruptive innovation is often driven by technological change, and technological change can be both unpredictable and rapid. Creative industries and firms faced with systemic uncertainty and instability may want to be wary of committing to enclosed ecosystems. They may find that the rigidity of a tightly controlled platform can prevent them from responding to innovation with the same speed and adaptability that smaller, more agile market competitors can marshal.[8] Creative industries that have already been challenged by disruptive innovation have become increasingly aware that flexibility is essential to surviving in an ever-changing world. They should apply the lesson to their own technological measures and assess the value they place on interoperability.

3 See generally Urs Gasser & John Palfrey, Breaking Down Digital Barriers: When and How ICT Interoperability Drives Innovation, Berkman Center for Internet and Society (Nov. 2007), available at http://cyber.law.harvard.edu/interop/pdfs/interop-breaking-barriers.pdf.

4 See, e.g., The Challenge of Cross-Platform Development, *Application Developers Alliance*, available at https://static1.squarespace.com/static/53864718e4b07a1635424cdd/t/579ac09ecd0f68622183782d/1469759648913/The+Challenge+of+Cross-Platform+Development+Paper+and+Case+Study.pdf.

5 For an interesting comparison of Apple vs. Microsoft in this regard, see Fahad Al-Riyami, Interoperability: Pushing Towards a Unified Experience on Microsoft, Apple, and Google Platforms, *WinBeta* (Oct. 22, 2014), available at https://www.onmsft.com/editorial/interoperability-operating-systems.

6 Id.

7 Id. at 17.

8 For instance, size, complacency, and a lack of agility when confronted with digitization are typically cited when describing the demise of the famous maker of camera film, Kodak. See e.g., John Kotter, Barriers to Change: The Real Reason Behind the Kodak Downfall, *Forbes* (May 2, 2012), available at www.forbes.com/sites/johnkotter/2012/05/02/barriers-to-change-the-real-reason-behind-the-kodak-downfall/.

9.4 What Kind of Positive Externalities Do You Have?

Interoperability is often inextricably tied to positive externalities, such as the ability to grow or scale as users are added to the system, creating network effects that can have major benefits for creative industries over time. Nascent industries need to build their user bases from the ground up, and often require a period of time to achieve a certain mass and stability.

Ultimately, an expanding user base can reach a tipping point that leads to an exponential phase of growth, driven by such factors as increased interaction and support from other user bases—for instance, the appeal of a technological device will be compounded by the availability of other linked devices, third-party apps, or related products and services; audience familiarity and shared participation; and exclusion from other incompatible locales. These factors are facilitated by interoperability, which allows both content and users to move between platforms, services, and devices.

Passing the tipping point to rapid growth may also lead to other positive externalities, including the realization of greater economies of scale than could otherwise be achieved among a smaller user base. These efficiencies of scale result in reduced operating costs, enhanced marginal returns, greater services provided at the same or lesser cost, and ultimately larger net profits. Further, the increase in users can actually enhance the utility and value of industry products and services to other users. These network effects, or positive externalities, can generate positive feedback loops that are important to building creative industries, supporting the growth of creative enterprises, and supporting content creation and development.[9]

Creative content industries should ask: Do technological protections advance or impede positive externalities? In some instances, technological lock-in may enable an ecosystem to keep users loyal to one set of products and devices, achieving some of the same goals that lack of interoperability can offer.[10] In other instances, however, technological lockup may exclude users who might otherwise participate in an ecosystem but who do not want to be restricted in their freedom of access and use.[11] This can present some of the drawbacks associated with a lack of interoperability, such as reducing the ability to achieve significant scale or related economies of scale. The tradeoff for creative industries is crucial to their long-term plans for viability and growth, and, they should view technological protections in light of the goal of advancing positive externalities, including enhancing network effects.

9 See generally Cal Shapiro & Hal R. Varian, *Information Rules* (1999).

10 See generally Robert M. Metcalfe, All in Your Head, *Forbes* (Apr. 20, 2007), available at www.forbes.com/forbes/2007/0507/052.html. See also Jospeh Farrell & Paul Klemperer, Coordination and Lock-in: Competition with Switching Costs and Network Effects, in 3 *Handbook of Industrial Organization* 1967 (M. Armstrong & R. Porter, eds., 2007).

11 Farrell & Kiemperer, supra note 10, at 2055.

Creative content industries may differ widely in their technological needs, options, and solutions, as well as in the degree of sophistication they may require their technologies to offer. This may vary depending on the challenges faced, such as the importance of cost effectiveness, the knowledgeability and adaptability of users, pace of innovation in the industry, the often-competing interests of industry stakeholders, and other factors both indigenous and exogenous to the industry. Notwithstanding such differences, however, there are certain business strategies and solutions that will be relevant to virtually all content industries.

From the outset, technological change should be approached conservatively: technological solutions tend to be costly, and are not likely to be a cure-all for deeper industry issues that have been brought to the fore by disruptive innovation. Further, the pace of innovation can add time pressures that do not always yield optimal solutions. Creative firms may find new solutions in the market but may not thoroughly vet such solutions for utility and effectiveness. The necessity of vying in a crowded field does not always align the best-fitting technological choices with the most popular ones.

Historically, critics have pointed to the entertainment industry as an example of suboptimal choices. For instance, it has been argued that the dominance of the recording device market by VHS systems over BetaMax systems was emblematic of the market choosing an inferior product to a better one.[12] More recently, in the music industry, critics have pointed to the emergence of Beats By Dre headphones, which are not especially well-regarded for sound quality, with what many argue to be a marked overemphasis of bass, and which have been argued to typify the music industry's preference for marketing appeal over quality.[13]

Technology is a moving target, as has been amply demonstrated by the emergence of disruptive innovations—including, in the music and entertainment sectors, recording devices ranging from the cassette player, the CD, the DVD, and more recently TiVo, Kodi, and set-top boxes[14]—which argues for caution, rather than precipitate change. The reaction of creative industry markets to technology is equally a moving target, and may not be readily predicted

12 Ian Morris, Format Wars: The Tech That Should Have Won, CNET (Aug. 4, 2008), available at www.cnet.com/news/format-wars-the-tech-that-should-have-won/.

13 See, Are Beats by Dr. Dre Headphones Worth the Money? *Consumer Reports* (May 14, 2013), available at www.consumerreports.org/cro/news/2013/05/are-beats-by-dr-dre-headphones-worth-the-money/index.htm.

14 See, e.g., Rob Cashman, Why Kodi Users Are Being Sued for Infringement, Torrent Lawyer, Aug. 2, 2017, available at www.torrentlawyer.com/2017/08/02/kodi-addons-users-sued/; Richard Bennett, Copyright Office Critiques Set-Top Box Order, High Tech Forum, Aug. 5, 2016, available at https://hightechforum.org/copyright-office-critiques-set-top-box-order/; Annemarie Bridy, Copyright Liability for Streaming Box Distributors: A Comparative EU-US Perspective, The Center for Internet and Society of Stanford Law School, April 29, 2017, available at http://cyberlaw.stanford.edu/blog/2017/04/copyright-liability-streaming-box-distributors-comparative-eu-us-perspective.

or corrected. The optimal strategy is to address the root causes and ramifications of disruption with solid business strategies and well-tailored IP solutions, rather than exclusively resorting to technological protections.

Despite this cautionary notice, many creative industry participants remain persuaded that they require technological protections to prevent theft, unwarranted use, revenue-reducing activities, or other threats to their valuable content, products, and creative incentive plans.[15] But creative industries should recognize that while technological protections may be valuable, they may come at a steep cost.[16]

Several technological measures illustrate the cost-benefit calculus that underlies this approach. For instance, anti-counterfeiting devices such as watermarks and other identifiers are useful, but may function for a limited time period as sophisticated counterfeiters devise new workarounds, copying methods, or other means of subverting or avoiding detection. This is exemplified by the arms race in the fashion industry, where some of the counterfeiting may occur at the originator's manufacturer when it is outsourced to countries that have high degrees of counterfeiting activities, such as China.[17] Similarly, firewalls protect content from illicit access and use to a certain extent, but can be thwarted by third parties that post links to the protected content, or can otherwise be evaded, for instance, by the use of multiple access accounts.

Equally dual-edged are anti-copying protections, devices, or measures, such as limiting access to paid content or forbidding reverse engineering of technological protective software and/or devices. These measures effectively cabin content but run the risk of alienating core consumers, thereby potentially jeopardizing key industry business models. They can be particularly risky when consumers feel as though their rights to content they have purchased,

15 See, e.g., Brian X. Chen, In a Bay Area Courtroom, Lawyers Hit Replay on Apple's History, *N.Y. Times* (Dec. 2, 2014), available at https://bits.blogs.nytimes.com/2014/12/02/in-a-bay-area-courtroom-lawyers-hit-replay-on-apples-history/.

16 See, e.g., Michael Arrington, The Future of DRM, *Tech Crunch* (Dec. 14, 2006), available at http://techcrunch.com/2006/12/14/bill-gates-on-the-future-of-drm/ (quoting Bill Gates as saying that DRM "causes too much pain for legitimate buyers"); Justin Mann, UK Study Claims DRM Encourages Piracy, *Tech Spot* (May 28, 2009), available at www.techspot.com/news/34881-uk-study-claims-drm-encourages-piracy.html; Maira Sutton, Copyright Provisions in the TPP Would Stifle Innovation and Impede the Economy, *Electronic Frontier Foundation* (May 6, 2013), available at www.eff.org/deeplinks/2013/05/copyright-provisions-tpp-would-stifle-innovation-and-impede-economy ("DRM can easily be used to support anti-competitive business practices and hamper innovation that builds upon existing technologies. For example, a company can prevent 'unauthorized' software or digital content from interoperating with their devices by inserting DRM."); Dave Thier, DRM Hurts Companies More Than Piracy, Developer Argues, *Forbes* (Mar. 19, 2013), available at www.forbes.com/sites/davidthier/2013/03/19/drm-hurts-companies-more-than-piracy-developer-argues/ (discussing how DRM can breed apathy in customers toward key products).

17 See, e.g., Hilary-George-Parkin, $1.7 Million in Counterfeit Nike Sneakers Seized En Route to California, *Footwear News*, Dec. 5, 2018, available at https://footwearnews.com/2018/focus/athletic-outdoor/nike-counterfeit-sneakers-seized-1202714529/.

licensed, or otherwise legitimately accessed are being unfairly curtailed, changed, or rescinded. In the music industry, for instance, some commentators have argued that consumers have been alienated by newly imposed restrictions on previously permissible uses, such as unlimited copying of content on one's own personal music devices; restrictions on the ability to "rip" new CDs or copy MP3 digital tracks; proscriptions against sharing music on a noncommercial basis; restrictions on the ability to have access to music on different operating systems and devices; and limitations on music availability in international markets.[18]

Creative content industries offer diverse examples of how technology can be well-utilized, particularly when paired with strong business solutions; but they also offer other examples of technologies that may be poorly executed, intrusive, or unbalanced, and that may have negative repercussions. In the case of protective firewalls, for instance, the computer industry offers several examples of highly functional firewalls, developed and refined over time, that serve to protect data, user privacy, know-how, and proprietary materials. But in the creative industries, the functionality of firewalls, or more commonly paywalls, often used to combat illicit or unpaid access or use of valuable content, has sometimes proven to be more problematic.

The journalism industry, for instance, has struggled to couple paywalls with effective business strategies. Many reputable newspapers and magazines have placed their key content behind paywall protection, seeking to compel longstanding readers to pay for content on a subscription basis for current news and/or a per-article basis for archived content.[19] But many of these news outlets have not succeeded in generating substantial subscription-based readership.[20] One prominent exception of a news publication that seems to have succeeded in protecting its journalistic content is the *Wall Street Journal*, in part because its target market is highly specific and affluent.[21] The *Wall Street Journal* is an interesting exception, however, because while its content is valuable, it does not seem to be so unique that it is not somewhat fungible with its competitors' news, such as that provided by *Bloomberg News* and others. Yet

18 See generally Jessica Litman, Lawful Personal Use, 85 *Tex. L. Rev.* 1871 (2007).

19 See Ryan Chittum, The NYT's $150-Million-a-Year Paywall, *Columbia J. Rev.* (Aug. 1, 2013), available at www.cjr.org/the_audit/the_nyts_150_million-a-year_pa.php; Ryan Chittum, The NYT's New Paywall Products Flounder, *Columbia J. Rev.* (Jul. 29, 2014), available at www.cjr.org/the_audit/the_nyts_new_paywall_products.php; David Kaplan, The Economist's Paywall Rises a Little Higher, *Gigaom* (Apr. 5, 2010), available at https://gigaom.com/2010/04/05/419-the-economists-paywall-rises-a-little-higher/.

20 See, e.g., Derek Thompson, How to Survive the Media Apocalypse, *The Atlantic*, Nov. 29, 2017, available at www.theatlantic.com/business/archive/2017/11/media-apocalypse/546935/.

21 See Michael Nevradakis, Behind the Paywall: Lessons from US Newspapers, *The Guardian* (Mar. 27, 2013), available at www.theguardian.com/media-network/2013/mar/27/behind-paywall-us-newspaper-websites (noting that *The Wall Street Journal* implemented its paywall in 1997 and only registered a 15% decline in print circulation in the following fifteen years).

it thrives, and manages to attain subscription numbers that are the envy of its peers in the journalism industry.[22]

Compounding the problem is that users have found relatively easy workarounds allowing them to obviate the paywall protections, such as reading sites that aggregate and post links to content, using multiple accounts to avoid article limits (typically, newspapers only allow users to access a limited number of articles per month without charge), accessing go-between sites that repost articles and links, and browsing through "private windows" that do not store cookies and user information. Moreover, other content providers, such as online magazines, blogs, or group and political publications, such as *Talking Points Memo* or *Politico*, have joined the online sphere, adding to the competitive pressure on more traditional news sources.

The turmoil that disruption in this industry has seen is well-documented, and has certainly not been quelled by technological means or other more drastic measures. "White knight" rescues, such as Jeff Bezos' purchase of *The Washington Post* or Carlos Slim's purchase of a large share of *New York Times* stock, do not seem to have ensured stability, although they are keeping those institutions afloat at present.[23] Infusions of cash appear to be stop-gaps, but only seem to be slowing, rather than reversing, the demise of even the best-established journalism outlets.

The services and devices that effectively enable newspaper and magazine readers to make an end-run around technological protections, which are intended to keep content proprietary and to retain its commercial value, undermine the business model of the journalism industry.[24] Most major newspapers and magazines are still wrestling with this conundrum, and continue to seek new ways to wield technological protections such as firewalls to support their at-risk business models.[25]

Similar issues have arisen in other creative industries that look to anti-copying devices to protect their content. Illustrative is the publishing industry,

22 See *The Wall Street Journal*, *Nieman J. Lab*, available at www.niemanlab.org/encyclo/wall-street-journal/ (noting that the Wall Street Journal had 917,000 digital subscribers in 2013).

23 See Janet Asteroft, Progress Report on Jeff Bezos Transforming the Washington Post, *PBS* (Jan. 14, 2015), available at www.pbs.org/mediashift/2015/01/a-progress-report-on-jeff-bezos-transforming-the-washington-post/.

24 See Some Readers Will Get Around Paywalls, *Sydney Morning Herald* (Mar. 24, 2011), available at www.smh.com.au/technology/some-readers-will-get-around-paywall-ny-times-20110323-1c70j.html.

25 See, e.g., Ken Doctor, The Newsonomics of the New York Times' Paywalls 2.0, *Nieman Lab* (Nov. 21, 2013), available at www.niemanlab.org/2013/11/the-newsonomics-of-the-new-york-times-paywalls-2-0; Laura Hazard Owen, New York Times Launches 2 New Paywall Products—and Rolls Out Native Ads, *Gigaom* (Mar. 26, 2014), available at https://gigaom.com/2014/03/26/new-york-times-launches-2-more-paywall-products-and-rolls-out-native-ads/; Ravi Somaiya, The New Yorker Alters Its Online Strategy, *N.Y. Times* (Jul. 8, 2014), available at www.nytimes.com/2014/07/09/business/media/the-new-yorker-alters-its-online-strategy.html.

which is contending with the vulnerability of e-books to illicit copying and appropriation.[26] Publishers have attempted to place anti-copying protections on e-books, somewhat analogous to anti-copying mechanisms on digital songs and musical content, as well as on film, media, games, and other entertainment and cultural content.[27] Many publishers are finding, however, that anti-copying measures are proving as unpopular to their readership as they are to music listeners, movie watchers, and game players.[28] This supports the proposition that the public relations problems that Apple experienced with respect to their digital rights management (DRM) protection, FairPlay, was not an isolated incident, but instead is germane to a host of creative industries.[29]

In the publishing industry, an outcry arose among users when publishers not only protected e-books with anti-copying technology but also restricted the release of e-books to public libraries, schools, and other community-oriented venues.[30] Eventually, the publishing industry was compelled by the response of its user community to relent, releasing its e-books to libraries and other such institutions with strict restrictions upon the use and circulation of their published content.[31] The publishers' dilemma—trying to quell appropriation while maintaining adequate access to its materials and satisfaction to its broad user community—illustrates the importance of balancing technological protections of content and related revenue against the need to preserve access, satisfy consumers, and limit incursions on well-established and valid use of materials for educational and enrichment purposes.

The film and media entertainment industries have likewise faced dilemmas when using anti-copying technologies to protect their properties and safeguard their revenue streams. They too are aware of the need to satisfy consumers,

26 See, e.g., Roberto Baldwin, New DRM Will Change the Words in Your e-Book, *Wired* (Jun. 17, 2013), available at www.wired.com/2013/06/new-ebook-drm/.

27 See Id. See also What is DRM (Digital Rights Management)? *Digital Pub.* 101, available at http://digitalpublishing101.com/what-is-drm-digital-rights-management/.

28 See eBook and Digital Rights Management (DRM), for ePublishers, *Tiny Hat*, available at www.tinhat.com/ebooks_epublishing/epublishers_drm.html ("DRM is unpopular with customers, and for good reasons.").

29 Arguably, the unpopularity of the Digital Millennium Copyright Act, Pub. L. 105–304, 112 Stat. 2860 (1998) (codified at scattered provisions in 17 U.S.C.) may also be regarded in this light as part of user resistance to both anti-copying measures and related policies, such as restrictions or bans on reverse engineering of such measures and devices, strict sanctions for attempts to circumvent anti-copying measures, and so on. See generally Aaron Schwabach, Internet and the Law: Technology, Society and Compromises (ABL-CIO, Santa Barbara, CA, 2014).

30 See Ebooks and Copyright Issues, *Am. Library Ass'n*, available at www.ala.org/news/state-americas-libraries-report-2013/ebooks-and-copyright-issues; see also Julie Bosman, Publisher Limits Shelf Life for Library E-Books, *N.Y. Times* (Mar. 14, 2011), available at www.nytimes.com/2011/03/15/business/media/15libraries.html?_r=0.

31 See Matt Enis, With All "Big Five" Ebooks Now Available, Ebook Vendors Assess the Road Ahead, *Dig. Shift* (Aug.5, 2014), available at www.thedigitalshift.com/2014/08/ebooks/big-five-ebooks-now-available-ebook-vendors-assess-road-ahead.

incentivize creativity, and enrich the cultural domain.[32] In the film industry, technological protections can create lock-ups that are particularly problematic for consumers who seek access to content released in both domestic and international markets.[33] DRM protections that are placed on movies domestically often render content incompatible with foreign devices, unavailable in original form in foreign markets, and sometimes inaccessible to foreign consumers.[34] Particularly when films in high demand are released on a "worldwide" basis, global audiences eagerly await access to such products and are liable to be vociferous in their disappointment if access is not immediate.[35]

At the same time, there is a domestic counterpart to the problem: films that are distributed for first release in movie theaters are in high demand, but large audiences will clamor for their early release in second-release formats, such as DVD and Blu-ray, on services such as Netflix and Blockbuster, through distributors such as Amazon Prime, and via online streaming sites. At the initial release of films, the combination of international demand for interoperable works and domestic demand for multiple release and formats of content can render new films especially vulnerable to illicit appropriation and distribution. Often such copying is meant for commercial purposes; however, even when intended for private use, the copied content represents a revenue loss for film producers that they are unsurprisingly loath to assume or forgive.

Historically, the film industry's solution to timing concerns has been to release movies in sequential "windows" which are staggered to maximize viewership, revenue, and audience satisfaction.[36] The first window of release, commonly known as first release, occurs in prime movie theaters, domestically

32 The movie industry is cognizant of this issue, and has made attempts at solving it at various times. See Michael Arrington, Movie Labels to Launch New "Open Market" Play Anywhere Scheme as Last Ditch Effort to Save DRM, *Tech Crunch* (Aug. 26, 2008), available at http://techcrunch.com/2008/08/26/movie-labels-to-launch-new-open-market-play-anywhere-scheme-as-last-ditch-effort-to-save-drm/.

33 See generally Peter Ecke, Coping with the DVD Dilemma: Region Codes and Copy Protections, 38 *Die Unterrichtspraxis/Teaching German* 89 (2005). See also Robert Silva, DVD Region Codes— What You Need to Know, *About*, available at http://hometheater.about.com/cs/dvdlaserdisc/a/aaregioncodesa.htm.

34 Id.

35 See, e.g., Amrisha, Fifty Shades of Grey India Release Date Still Unknown, *Film Beat* (Feb. 24, 2015), available at www.filmibeat.com/hollywood/news/2015/fifty-shades-of-grey-india-release-date-still-unknown-174817.html; Donald Ash, Why Does Japan Get Movies So Late?!? *Japan Guy*, available at www.thejapanguy.com/why-does-japan-get-movies-so-late/. Films are often delayed in Australia for a variety of reasons. See, e.g., Cameron Williams, Why Are Films Always Delayed in Australia?, Junkee, Dec. 7, 2018, available at https://junkee.com/australian-film-release-dates/185655. For a recent example, the film "Ant-Man and the Wasp" was delayed because of the World Cup. See, Lorenzo Tanos, Evangeline Lilly, Paul Rudd React to 'Ant-Man and the Wasp' Worldwide Release Delay Due to World Cup, Inquisitr, June 14, 2018, available at www.inquisitr.com/4941668/evangeline-lilly-paul-rudd-react-to-ant-man-and-the-wasp-worldwide-release-delay-due-to-world-cup/.

36 See Reel Time, supra note 9.

and/or worldwide, and in exclusive showings.[37] At this juncture, films may be fully armored with technological protection, and may not be copied without some loss of quality, so that commercial appropriation is not viable.[38] The second release of films is via other distribution services, providers, and outlets. Second-release movies may also have some anti-copying protection. Yet they may be more susceptible to copying, such as via "ripping" personal copies of DVDs and copying online streams via third-party conversion sites or devices. Further releases may occur in less significant venues, such as second-run movie theaters, release to libraries and other public resource institutions, and releases in smaller international venues. These releases may be susceptible to copying by illicit large-scale ventures such as Pirate Bay.[39] But these sequential windows of release remove some of the pressure to thwart copying felt by the industry. Moreover, they satisfy consumers with multiple opportunities to access their preferred content, and eventually allow content to make its way to more publicly available venues such as libraries, teaching institutions, and resource centers.

Some music streaming services, such as Rhapsody,[40] are beginning to contemplate a similar model of staggered or "windowed" releases, in which music is released first to paying subscribers when it is at the height of its popularity, and thus commercial value, and only later to listeners who do not pay fees but support the service by listening to ad-supported online radio.[41] Book publishers are also considering following suit by staggering digital release dates of e-books, a move which has met with mixed response.[42]

37 Id.

38 Copying via handheld devices such as camera recorders, iPhones, and so on, does not represent a significant threat in most Western countries, partially due to this loss of quality. It does, however, constitute a significant threat in other international markets, particularly in developing countries. And it is possible that technology in personal electronics will evolve to the point where this becomes a more universal concern in the future.

39 See Mike Masnick, Entertainment Industry Demands Swedish ISP Block the Pirate Bay; ISP Says No, *TechDirt* (Mar. 11, 2015), available at www.techdirt.com/articles/20150304/10332430208/entertainment-industry-demands-swedish-isp-block-pirate-bay-isp-says-no.shtml.

40 Note that Spotify originally did not have the windows of release option, which may be part of the reason they are in disputes with the hugely popular artist Taylor Swift, who feels that releasing her music online does not adequately compensate her creativity or protect her revenue stream that, as she claims, represents her livelihood. In 2018, Spotify allowed for windows of release options, with Jason Aldean being the first artist to have his album debuting under this option. Paul Resnikoff, Spotify Unleashes Its First "Windowed" Release—And It's Not for Taylor Swift, Digital Music News (Apr. 13, 2018), available at https://www.digitalmusicnews.com/2018/04/13/spotify-window-jason-aldean/.

41 See Jason Epstein & Rob Glaser, Essay: Why Streaming (Done Right) Will Save the Music Business, *Billboard* (Nov. 21, 2014), available at www.billboard.com/articles/business/6327429/essay-why-streaming-done-right-will-save-the-music-business.

42 See Chris Walters, Hardcover vs. eBook: Why Staggered Release Dates Are a Bad Idea, *Booksprung* (Nov. 7, 2009), available at http://booksprung.com/hardcover-vs-ebook-why-staggered-release-dates-are-a-bad-idea; see also Wylie, supra note 35.

In both these cases, anti-copying technology is used to protect the product, but flexible business models limit the negative impact of content lockup, while providing the means for the creative industry to release content at variable dates. Staggered releases help account for variations in the commercial appeal of creative works, allowing wider audiences to pay for content at rates that are commensurate with their interest in, and willingness to pay for, the creative work.

Offering content at differing points of release and price points is a valuable way to satisfy a wide range of audiences with varying levels of interest in consumption. It also increases exposure to creative content, thereby enabling more potential consumers to become familiar with the work. This has the ancillary benefit of increasing the possibility that creative content can provide a baseline resource for future creators, only some of whom may be able to pay for access. By harnessing technological protection to business plans that maximize the monetization of content but leave room for user enrichment and exposure, creative industries can adopt a balanced strategy aimed at the long-term success of their creative endeavors and commercial viability.

Legal research services and databases offer a different perspective on technological protection. The two main competitors in this field, LexisNexis Group[43] and Thomson Reuters Westlaw,[44] have been battling for market share in the area of legal resources, information, services, and "content-enabled workflow solutions."[45] Both services have highly proprietary models that are technologically protected.[46] Yet they offer a strikingly similar array of data, information, research, resources, and services.[47] It is in the nature of their technological tools that they differ and aim to distinguish themselves among their user base.[48] Each has proprietary search tools and capacities, formats, page delineation systems, organizational devices, and aids to assist legal researchers in managing data and findings.

The materials that Lexis and Westlaw most value are these means and methods that they offer to researchers, rather than any of the underlying information, data, or resources—much of which might be challenging to propertize.[49]

43 See About LexisNexis, *LexisNexis*, available at www.lexisnexis.com/en-us/about-us/about-us.page.

44 See generally, *Thomson Reuters*, available at https://legal.thomsonreuters.com/en/products/westlaw.

45 Id.

46 See, e.g., Electronic Publications Master Agreement, *LexisNexis*, available at www.lexisnexis.com/terms/bender/MasterAgreement/; Terms of Use, *Westlaw*, available at https://lawschool.westlaw.com/pdf/online%20law%20school%20student%20faculty%20user%20agreement.pdf.

47 See Lynn Lenart, *Comparing Westlaw Next, Lexis Advance and Bloomberg Law* (2013), available at www.uakron.edu/law/library/docs/chart_comparing_3_research_systems.pdf.

48 Id.

49 Id.; see also Rob Corrao, Westlaw v. LexisNexis—Which Is Better? *Lac Group*, available at http://lac-group.com/westlaw-vs-lexisnexis-better/.

In relying on their technological innovations to vie for and secure market position, Lexis and Westlaw emphasize their services and research tools as their fundamental value proposition.[50] These legal research services use technology in conjunction with IP rights to protect innovations in search methods, research tools, and organizational aids. These innovations in tools, aides, and an array of supplemental services are a form of creativity akin to creativity in the production of content in other creative industries. The business model of Lexis and Westlaw highlight how important it is for content industries to determine where the value of their products and services inheres, and which of those elements should be protected, propertized, and monetized.

The video game industry offers another model of technological protection balanced against openness. Traditionally, the video game industry offered a closed ecosystem of games and devices, with systemic encryption of both hardware, such as consoles and devices, and software, such as underlying operating systems and platforms. Many gaming systems have continued to follow the closed universe model, such as Sony PlayStation, Nintendo, and Microsoft Xbox.[51] But increasingly gaming is moving online to versions that can be played on any personal computer, mobile phone, or tablet. These games range in their degree of protection, but they are generally covered by IP rights, including copyright and patent of software, trademark of characters and "look and feel," and rights licensed among partners.[52]

The video game industry is careful to protect its valuable properties. At the same time, many video game companies actively encourage participation among their users with respect to creating characters, giving input into potential improvements and changes to games, identifying weaknesses in gaming technologies, and otherwise enhancing the gaming experience.[53] Many video game companies also actively recruit and hire skilled users to assist with software development.[54] The degree of interactive participation that the video game industry has promoted is not only innovative but also extremely effective in building loyal fan bases, and in creating a community that can improve the products and services offered rather than seek to appropriate, commandeer, or arrogate them.

A more recent development in the video game industry is the development of e-sports and e-gaming, which entail large-scale participation in online gaming similar to real world sports, complete with arenas, spectators, lucrative

50 See, e.g., West Pub. Corp. v. Mead Data Cent., Inc., 616 F. Supp. 1571 (D. Minn., 1985), aff'd, 799 F.2d 1219 (8th Cir., 1985).

51 See, e.g., Best Video Game Consoles for 2019, *CNET* (2019), available at www.cnet.com/topics/consoles/best-video-game-consoles/.

52 See, e.g., Lego Video Games, available at www.lego.com/en-us/games.

53 See, e.g., 4 Benefits of Hiring Hackers and Gamers for Tech Roles, Mondo (2018), available at https://mondo.com/blog-benefits-of-hiring-hackers-for-tech-roles/.

54 See, e.g., Isabel Thottam, How We Turned a Love for Video Games Into a Career, Monster (2018), available at www.monster.com/career-advice/article/how-to-break-into-video-game-industry.

rewards, and even e-scholarships.[55] Competitive e-gaming necessitates user lock-in, but by design its complex multi-player and multi-spectator structure call for a centralized mechanism of control. This not only helps manage the flow of activities, and the resulting flow of revenues garnered by e-gaming, but it also staves off potential piracy, cheating, or other illicit uses of creative works. The gaming industry has been extremely agile in turning over materials and generating a rapid flow of new and appealing content to its avid user base. By building in product churn, e-gaming creates and sates demand on an ongoing basis, much like the fashion industry, and makes copying a less attractive moving target for would-be appropriators and imitators. All of these features make the video game industry a lively and deft model that illustrates the potential creative industries can have for yoking technology to innovative content, consumer satisfaction, and commercial success.

55 See Arielle Dollinger, Video Games Are a Waste of Time? Not for Those With E-sports Scholarships, *N.Y. Times* (Nov. 2, 2018), available at www.nytimes.com/2018/11/02/education/learning/video-games-esports-scholarships.html.

10 Tailoring Cultural and Normative Features

10.1 Introduction to Cultural Issues

Creative industries are commercial sectors that generate and produce creative content. Equally, they are cultural ecosystems embedded with norms, values, practices, and features that should be respected and sustained. Many of these values are foundational, such as crediting and rewarding original creative work. They also promote and share some of the central values of intellectual property, including fostering research and scholarship in an open environment, and facilitating collaborative and interdisciplinary work. Creative industries have long been engaged in nurturing artistic communities, supporting longstanding creative practices such as apprenticeship and mentorship. At times they have also been active in encouraging experimentation and exploration. In many cases, they have been engaged in effectively subsidizing work that is worthwhile but that may not yield appreciable benefits or tangible returns.

Cultural ecosystems often share underlying structures that instantiate and express shared norms, including maintaining cultural commons or commons-like spaces, retaining guild or guild-like features, and preserving room for open-source or nonpropertized production. Many creative industries have developed over multiple generations and have evolved to accommodate these underlying structural features and to adapt them to current needs and realities. The balance they strike may be susceptible to change, and may require adjusting when disruptive innovation changes the industry, but cultural durability and depth may depend on preserving that balance rather than expending it in pursuit of more palpable immediate gains.

When seeking to preserve important cultural features, creative industries should first consider the structural elements that support their practices and norms. Their first lines of inquiry should ask: Are they constructed along the lines of a cultural commons or a guild? Do they have some of the necessary features of commons, valuing collaboration and shared working space? Do they make room for creative endeavors that may not end in propertizable rights or commercial reward? Do they emphasize rewarding reputational capital? Do they value broad access to fundamental resources, research, and creative output? And do they have any of the baseline features of guilds, offering apprenticeships or mentoring to emerging artists or artisans, exchanging and passing on traditional knowledge and know-how, and building a shared cultural heritage?

Many creative industries are likely to find that they have at least some of these features. They should recognize that these features are worth preserving and securing for future generations of creators and producers alike. This is not to suggest that they should outright relinquish copyright or other intellectual property rights and resort to nonproprietary and voluntary agreements. But they should consider that in some cases a full roster of property rights may not be essential to protecting creative work. Indeed, propertizing some creative endeavors may stifle some of the predicates that are helpful to keeping creativity rich and diverse. Openness, collaboration, rights in attribution, sharing, gift-giving,[1] and access to creativity's building blocks are all as necessary to the creative process as property rights are to the livelihood of creators.

When trying to distinguish between creative work that should be propertized and work that should be kept free of property rights, creative industries should consider how their underlying structures support nonpropertized work, the value they place on that work, and the safeguards they put in place to keep the theft of work at minimal levels that are neither unsustainable to creators nor undermining to institutions. In that light, creative industries should ask: Do they have important cultural features that substitute for some of the operations of a formalized legal IP system?

Considering the use and effectiveness of cultural features raises several interrelated questions. How strong are cultural capital benefits, such as reputation, attribution, and homage, and how well do they work? Do prizes and rewards confer important advantages, and how well do they work?[2] Are there sanctions within the community or other non-IP mechanisms that functionally inhibit or prevent copyright infringement, plagiarism, or theft? Or are there cultural norms and practices that serve that function?

Another reason for valuing the cultural aspects of creative work is that creativity flourishes best when it actively engages participants on as many levels as possible. Creative content can be passively consumed, but it is more inspiring and meaningful when it is actively engaged. This can occur when creative content consumers and users allow the work to become the source of their own imaginative, innovative, and creative endeavors. In some cases, this may involve transforming the work in keeping with a personal vision, as evinced in such user-generated content as fan fiction, modifications to video game characters and plots, artistic pastiches, parodies and satires, or works intended as homage. In other cases, this may involve adding changes, enhancements, or

1 See generally Lewis Hyde, *The Gift: Imagination and the Erotic Life of Property* (1983).

2 See Joseph E. Stiglitz, Prizes, Not Patents, *Project Syndicate* (Mar. 6, 2007), available at http://www.paecon.net/PAEReview/issue42/Stiglitz42.pdf.; see also Stephen Shavell & T. van Ypserle, Rewards Versus Intellectual Property Rights, 44 *J. L. & Econ.* 525 (2001).

innovations in order to build upon and improve existing work, as may occur in open-source production.

Creative industries should value the active engagement of their user community, in part because it secures user loyalty and ensures user demand for creative products and services, but equally because it taps into a trove of user creativity that can flow back to creative disciplines and enrich them immeasurably. The mutual conferment of creative output and rewards can also yield positive externalities, such as spillover effects in creatively rich communities and network effects within communities that are receptive to creativity.[3] Creative industries should therefore ask: How much room do they make for user-generated content and open-source production? And how much do they bolster and facilitate the spillover and network effects that creativity can generate?

10.2 Do You Have the Features of a Constructed Commons or Guild?

Some creative industries have the hallmarks of constructed commons or guilds. They share certain features including strongly defined and united communities, a communal belief in collaboration and openness, and a commitment to sharing and interdisciplinary or cross-cultural efforts and output. They also share a sense of community membership that may be formally institutionalized or normatively internalized. Their practices may include self-governance rules, principles, and norms, as well as institutional support systems.[4] Creative industries should ask: Are these hallmarks distinguishable and do they operate in ways that construct a commons-like or guild-like environment?

In some cases, creative labor may be premised on, and supported by, established long-term institutional arrangements, some of which may be formalized in contractual agreements, such as tenure or other permanent position or appointment, others of which may be more loosely arranged, such as short-term stays at institutions or affiliations. In education, for instance, long-term arrangements such as tenure-track and tenure positions, administrative roles, and so on tend to be highly formalized and managed within an institution's organizational structure. There are looser affiliations, such as visiting faculty

3 *See generally* Michael W. Carroll, Whose Music Is It Anyway?: How We Came To View Musical Expression As A Form Of Property, 72 *U. Cin. L. Rev.* 1405 (2004); Michael W. Carroll, Creative Commons as Conversational Copyright, in *Intellectual Property and Information Wealth*, 445–461 (Peter Yu ed., 2007); Siva Vaidhyanathan, *Copyrights and Copywrongs: The Rise of Intellectual Property and How It Threatens Creativity*, 1st ed. (NYU Press, New York, NY, 1994).

4 See Elinor Ostrom, *Governing the Commons: The Evolution of Institutions for Collective Action* (1990); Michael J. Madison, Brett M. Frischmann, & Katherine J. Strandburg, Constructing Commons in the Cultural Environment, 9 *Cornell L. Rev.* 657, 659–60 (2010).

roles, adjuncts, and others, but these too are subject to contracts, albeit typically shorter-term and less binding on both sides.

Some creative sectors can inculcate policies that assign rights and responsibilities to their members without recourse to the formalized propertization of content that an IP-based system entails. Working within a well-defined and supportive institutional setting, creators can freely undertake projects that they choose to pursue without determining in advance that the work will result in copyrightable (or patentable) end-products. This allows fundamental resources to be accessed and shared from the outset, and encourages creative output to be made available at the end of the process.

The hallmarks of constructed creative commons can also find more tangible support. They can include powerful institutionally granted financial backing designed to benefit legitimized members of the creative community.[5] This support can prove essential in times of disruption, allowing creative work to be ongoing without necessitating immediate, or possibly even long-term, returns. Such support can include operating budgets earmarked to underwrite innovative projects, new ventures, and creative output that may not be readily marketable or monetizable. In education, this may include institutional support, including financial backing, reducing teaching loads, and coverage of expenses, for the development of online education.

Institutional support may be particularly helpful when such innovations need not be monetized immediately, so that experimental efforts, adjustments, new creative and pedagogical projects, and other output may be generated without immediate justification or recuperation of costs. At the same time, however, this may encourage work that is not likely to be self-sustaining in the long term. Creative industries must, therefore, consider whether or not they consider such work to be compatible with their budgets, time management plans, and priorities. Support can also be extended in the form of non-monetary incentives and rewards, which can be equally gratifying to visionaries spearheading creative projects who have not yet determined the commercial value or viability of their output, but who believe that their work will lead the way to important creative progress.[6] While this work can seem implausible, unrealistic, or unviable in the beginning, it may have the potential to lead to new paths that help counter the inroads that disruptive innovation has made on more traditional creative outputs. Creative industries that support innovative creative production should ask: How can this work be encouraged and sustained, and what institutional underpinnings are required to ensure its ongoing vitality?

5 See Henry Hansmann, The Evolving Economic Structure of Higher Education, 79 *U. Chi. L. Rev.* 161 (2012); see also James J. Duderstadt, Daniel E. Atkins, & Douglas Van Houweling, *Higher Education Faces the Digital Age: Technology Issues and Strategies for American Colleges and Universities* (2002).

6 Penn Online Contract (on file with author).

The educational sector represents a complex creative commons that is deeply entrenched and that has worked out its structure, practices, and norms over several centuries.[7] Other creative industries may have equally deep roots, but may not be as formalized as education. Cuisine is one such creative sector, dating back to practices that began with private chefs hired for wealthy households in England, spanning the emergence of restaurants in France, and proliferating to today's great wealth of culinary offerings.[8] Many of the practices in cuisine stem from those deep roots, including the tradition of apprenticeship among established chefs and culinary aspirants, the handing down of recipes, secrets of the trade, and dishes prepared in open homage to cuisine's great talents and groundbreaking restaurants.[9] These practices and norms serve a greater purpose than solely generating monetary returns. They keep culinary traditions alive and thriving, and contribute to a cultural legacy that is an inherently valuable part of any heritage, touching not only restaurant diners but also private citizens who feel connected to their patrimony through its food, flavors, and culinary arts.

Propertizing cuisine requires ensuring that chefs and restaurateurs are able to make a living by claiming rights in their original work. The incentive to invest in such an inherently high-risk proposition as opening a restaurant must be supported by rights in culinary work that compensate the initial undertaking. But those rights must also be counterbalanced by recognition of the commons-like aspect of work in commercial kitchens: sharing traditional recipes, exchanging ideas and inspiration, and working collaboratively among chefs and sous-chefs are all vital parts of restaurant work. Only some culinary output, therefore, should be propertized. The industry has already recognized this tradeoff in many important respects. Recipes cannot be copyrighted, leaving the foundations of cuisine available and accessible to cooks and chefs alike. Recipe books, however, with their useful trove of information, annotation, anecdote, and other resources are copyrightable, just as any instructional work may be copyrighted, if it meets the requirements for copyright.

In other areas, copyright in cuisine functions just as copyright in any creative work: if a chef performs on television, the recording is copyrightable, or if a restaurant publishes a compilation of its greatest meals with accompanying photographs, the book and photographs will be published under copyright. While certain styles of preparing food, such as "molecular gastronomy" may not be copyrightable as a whole—and indeed, some chefs do not even

7 Michael J. Madison, Brent M. Frischmann, & Katherine J. Sandburg, The University as Constructed Cultural Commons, 30 *Wash. U. J.L. & Pol'y*, 365, 397 (2009); Elinor Ostrom, *Governing the Commons: The Evolution of Institutions for Collective Action* (1990). See also Corynne McSherry, *Who Owns Academic Work: Battling for Control of Intellectual Property* (2001); Henry Rosovsky, *The University: An Owner's Manual* (1990).

8 An Escoffier Biography, Escoffier Society, available at www.escoffier-society.com/biography.php.

9 Christopher J. Buccafusco, On the Legal Consequences of Sauces: Should Thomas Keller's Recipes Be Per Se Copyrightable? 24 *Cardozo Arts & Enter. L.J.* 1121 (2007).

agree that it is a distinct style—books that articulate the principles of the style, such as the encyclopedic "Modernist Cuisine," written by Nathan Myrhvold and Maxime Bilet, are copyrighted.[10] In this distinction, copyright serves its proper function of rewarding original, creative ideas that are "fixed in a tangible medium,"[11] but does not encroach upon the traditions of culinary instruction and lore that contribute to its commons and constitute its lineage and bounty.

10.3 Do You Have Cultural Features That Substitute for or Supplement a Formalized Legal IP System?

Most creative industries share features that incentivize creativity in various ways, only some of which fall into the purview of a formalized legal IP system. These features include a culture that values and rewards reputational capital. In many cases, the obverse of practices that value social capital are those that inhibit or sanction appropriation without consent. Built into the curtailment of appropriation are measures that allow creative communities to express disapproval of bad behavior, including pointing out and shaming copying, plagiarism, outright stealing, and other acts that violate the communal ethos.

In some cases, these cultural features may seem at tension with a creative industry's objectives and operations. Some creative industries may express a commitment to sanctioning appropriation, but at the same time may tacitly allow a certain amount of creative appropriation in order to promote new output, satisfy consumer demand, and generate an economic and creative churn that is commercially helpful and ultimately profitable. As in the case of fashion, some industries require such churn to keep generating products and satisfying rapid, voluminous, and ever-changing consumer demand. Creative industries should consider how central their cultural features and tenets are to their practices, how they mesh with industry policies and directives, and how they are to be reconciled with business strategies and goals.

In fashion, as in cuisine, comedy, and other creative industries that do not have expansive protections, commons- and guild-like practices and norms enable talented young creators to learn from more experienced masters and to build upon the foundations of their artistic endeavors with originality and imagination. But there are also limits to creative sharing and borrowing which may not be set by intellectual property rights. Rather than resorting to litigation over alleged infringement of copyright, creative artists in fashion, cuisine, and comedy can bring deep-seated norms against creative appropriation

10 Nathan Myhrvold, Chris Young, & Maxime Bile, *Modernist Cuisine: The Art and Science of Cooking* (2011).

11 17 U.S.C. §101, available at www.law.cornell.edu/wex/fixed_in_a_tangible_medium_of_expression.

to bear on the practices of rogue designers,[12] chefs,[13] or performers[14] who transgress cultural lines and take original works without permission, attribution, or the right to do so.

Norms that involve public shaming, disapproval among peers, and social sanction are powerful and can be effective without requiring protracted litigation or extensive costs. In science, these norms are evident and familiar, as in the case of discredited scientific research and the reputational damage that retracting work is bound to wreak.[15] But it is not in science alone that reputation plays such a vital role. In the creative industries, where originality is prized and authorship is esteemed[16], the right to have one's work attributed and acknowledged, and the value of one's creative reputation, are enshrined in both practice and in ethos.

10.4 How Much Room Is There for Open-Source Production? Do You Benefit From Open-Source Production?

Creative content industries should consider the value that they place on the generation of work that is unpropertized, non-commercialized, and likely to occur among a wide base of creators, users, and other industry participants. In some creative industries, open-source production can have the potential to add significant benefits to business strategies for growth, development, exploration, R&D, and the generation of new revenue sources.[17] In other cases, open-source production may be a peripheral area of production that retains the possibility of opening new directions, but that still remains largely undefined and untapped.[18] Creative industries must ask: How much do they value the potential benefits that open-source production can offer, and do they choose to centralize it in their organizational planning and practices?

At the outset, creative industries should ask: What exactly are the advantages to open-source production? Among the possibilities include its ability to engage an array of users in fundamental research and innovative work.

12 Laura Snapes, Nirvana Sue Designer Marc Jacobs Over Alleged Copyright Breach, *The Guardian* (Jan. 3, 2019), available at www.theguardian.com/music/2019/jan/03/nirvana-sue-designer-marc-jacobs-over-alleged-copyright-breach.

13 Pete Wells, Chef Sues Over Intellectual Property (the Menu), *N.Y. Times* (Jun. 27, 2007), available at www.nytimes.com/2007/06/27/nyregion/27pearl.html.

14 Dotan Oliar & Christopher Sprigman, There's No Free Laugh (Anymore): The Emergence of Intellectual Property Norms and the Transformation of Stand-up Comedy, 94 *Va. L. Rev.* 1787, 1789–809 (2008).

15 James Meikle & Sarah Boseley, MMR Row Doctor Andrew Wakefield Struck Off Register, *The Guardian* (May 24, 2010), available at www.theguardian.com/society/2010/may/24/mmr-doctor-andrew-wakefield-struck-off.

16 Mark Rose, *Authors and Owners: The Invention of Copyright* (1993).

17 See Yochai Benkler, *The Wealth of Networks: How Social Production Transforms Markets and Freedom* (Yale University Press, New Haven, CT, 2007).

18 See generally Steven Weber, *The Success of Open Source* (2005).

Open-source production may facilitate new approaches to creative production, which in some cases may usefully counterbalance the first-mover advantage that early entrants, who are not necessarily the best innovators, may have garnered. Open-source production also has the potential to stimulate creative innovation to develop in different directions, thereby allowing the best practices and best solutions to rise to the fore without being stifled by competitive forces. It may also draw participants from wide constituencies, reaching into diverse talent pools. It may avoid hierarchies that would otherwise stifle talent, whether through bureaucracy, peer envy, anti-competitive policies, or other potentially harmful organizational and institutional flaws.[19]

Creative industries should consider the practical demands that an open-source production environment may exact. Not only do creative industries need to prioritize keeping open-source values in place, but they also need to have mechanisms in place that will allow open source to thrive and mechanisms to prevent open-source work from being propertized or misappropriated. These measures may include imposing proprietary barriers, oversight, norms, contractual agreements, Creative Commons-type licenses, as well as possible technological measures, such as firewalls. Moreover, creative industries should ask whether the open-source work that they support may eventually be captured both fairly and within reasonable parameters, so that new innovators are able to capitalize on parts of open-source creation while leaving other parts open and accessible.[20] Creative industries should ask whether the long-term prospects of such open-source production point in the direction of openness, propertization, or a hybridized model.

Creative industries should also consider the impact of open-source production on their employees and laborers. One significant concern is how and by whom an industry's workers are paid. In some cases, salaried workers may be paid to perform professionally at their place of employment, and their salaries can support the open-source work that they do, effectively underwriting their unpaid efforts. Here, creative industries should consider the extent to which they are either supporting such efforts or being supported by other institutions. They should also take into consideration the extent to which the creative industry's market structure supports widespread open-source production, thereby effectively spreading the costs of unremunerated production across a market and reducing the burden on any one industry participant.[21]

19 See Id. See also Katherine Noyes, 10 Reasons Open Source Is Good for Business, *Pc World* (Nov. 5, 2010), available at www.pcworld.com/article/209891/10_reasons_open_source_is_good_for_business.html.

20 For instance, the Adobe software makers use, generate, and make available a blend of proprietary and nonproprietary output. See Panos Mourdoukoutas, Adobe's Other Secret, *Forbes* (Dec. 27, 2017), available at www.forbes.com/sites/panosmourdoukoutas/2017/12/27/adobes-other-secret/#328b146e73a5.

21 Some commentators have noticed distinctions between those who create with the promise of exclusive rights and those who do not—as some would say, the difference between professionals and amateurs. *Cf.* Susana Juniu, Ted Tedrick & Rosangela Boyd, Leisure or

Creative content industries should also consider the extent to which workers choose to participate in open-source efforts and the extent to which they feel rewarded by open-source work, whether it satisfies curiosity, interest, or desire to explore in ways that are not directly in line with one's primary employment. Workers may also seek out open source as a way of obtaining peer approval and recognition, participating in creative experimentation, and expanding accessible resources to wider communities than their place of employment.

10.5 How Many Spillover and Network Effects Can Your Industry Produce?

Creative industries should establish positive environments that both support talented work forces and draw outside talent. By concentrating labor forces and driving advances in localized knowledge and skills, they can contribute to creating knowledge clusters that can help generate economies of scale. Taken as a whole, these features may create spillover and network effects that enhance and encourage creative production. Tapping into these spillover and network effects is paramount for creative industries, but the approach to maximizing their utility should be carefully mapped out. In some creative industries, widespread open-source production may be the best means to fostering network effects. In other creative industries, a certain amount of propertization, balanced with a certain amount of "leakiness," or lack of propertization, may prepare the groundwork for wide-scale creative and innovative growth.

Establishing a constructed commons may be challenging to creative content industries, but putting into place some of its features should be manageable, in part because many creative industries are already founded on shared normative principles and values, such as openness, collaboration, and professional autonomy. These norms may be supported by formalized policies that clarify the terms of creative work and its rewards, but they may also be sustained by expressions of commitment that are made at all levels of the industry. Where possible, financial support should be extended as well, which will ensure that industry participants continue to engage in experimentation, cross-pollination, and interactive projects.

Work?: Amateur and Professional Musicians' Perception of Rehearsal and Performance, 28 *J. Leisure Res.* 44, 44 (1996) (finding marked differences between amateur and professional musicians toward rehearsal). Others have observed a distinction between open source software programmers motivated by non-pecuniary factors and those who rely on a proprietary strategy as a basis for their motivation. *See, e.g.*, Jürgen Bitzer, Wolfram Schrettl & Philipp J. H. Schröder, Intrinsic Motivation in Open Source Software Development, 35 *J. Comp. Econ.* 160, 160–61 (2007); Jean Tirole & Joshua Lerner, Some Simple Economics of Open Source, 50 *J. Indus. Econ.* 197, 197–99 (2002). These open questions only underscore the importance of crafting tailoring policies and practices that are flexible and adaptable, so that as more is understood with respect to creativity in a field, better balances in propertization and non-pecuniary incentive strategies may be struck.

Creative industries should strive to encourage localized growth. Productive regions, such as Silicon Valley in California and Kendall Square in Boston, demonstrate the strength of local network and spillover effects, and create critical mass necessary for venture capital and equity funding specialists to thrive. Creative industries can help foster these communities by supporting joint problem-solving, interdisciplinary solutions, multi-tiered grants that support startups, spin-offs, and incubators on various levels, industry-wide conferences that address state-of-the-art issues in the creative landscape, and various efforts aimed at encouraging creators to interact and engage, such as shared office spaces or media labs. These features will help secure skilled and talented workers, who will be drawn to creative sectors and are likely to settle in these areas. Creative industries should also leverage the advantages that their locale may offer, such as established universities and libraries, which offer cultural resources that are well-suited to fortify and further creative production. And creative industries should secure and nurture close ties with user communities, many of whose members hunger not only to consume but also to generate creative content.

Creative industries should recognize the extent to which creativity and innovation, as well as the labor that goes into such creative efforts, are supported by institutional edifices, external funding sources, and safety valves that reduce financial pressures to monetize work. They should further recognize that such support is likely to enhance the prospects for open-source production to thrive, since the drive to propertize, commercialize, and monetize may be balanced against a long-term perspective on commercial viability. Creative content industries should understand that it is unrealistic to expect open source to thrive in an environment starved of financial support: after all, labor needs to be remunerated and employees need to earn their livelihood. But with proper institutional support, creative industries should recognize that open-source production may result in promising work that advances innovation and change.

The software industry illustrates some of the benefits of building open communities with strong, shared norms. It prioritizes professional autonomy, collaborative outreach and efforts, attribution, peer recognition and social and reputational capital. It also accepts a certain degree of self-governance including normative sanctions against appropriation of ideas and output, and other key features that are characteristic of commons-like approaches to creation and its related rewards.[22] Software industry participants generally agree that these features are not only valuable in promoting positive behaviors but also

22 See generally Ashe Dryden, The Ethics of Unpaid Labor and the OSS Community, *Ashe Dryden* (Nov. 13, 2013), available at www.ashedryden.com/blog/the-ethics-of-unpaid-labor-and-the-oss-community; Jeremy Kahn, Open Source Does Not Mean Free Labor, *Jeremy Kahn's Dev Blog* (Oct. 19, 2014), available at http://jeremyckahn.github.io/blog/2014/10/19/open-source-does-not-mean-free-labor/.

constitutive of the strategies that brought the industry long-lasting security and success.[23] One way to consider the open-source movement in the software industry is to see it as an extension of this recognition: normative commitments to openness, peer production, and communal participation in the growth and development of creativity and innovation laid the groundwork for the rise of open-source production and its rapidly expanding acceptance among commercial entities, funders, stakeholders, and the greater user and creator community.

Widespread recognition of the success of the open-source production movement in the software industry has in turn spread to a range of other creative and innovative industries, such as Internet-based systems and services, online privacy and security providers, and other technology sector segments.[24] The development of Internet-oriented products and services, such as Wikipedia, DropBox, and SoundCloud, as well as crowd-sourced sites and resources, offer ample evidence that many facets of the computer industry's approach to creativity and innovation have been embraced and used to build an array of entities, services, and products enabling collaboration in globalized user communities.

Other creative industries have likewise adapted open-source schemes and principles to their content production and delivery. Following the example of the education industry, scholars and researchers are creating a number of repositories, many of which are organized on an open source or "open access" basis, to which creative producers can contribute content, including sites that host scholarly articles such as the Social Sciences Research Network (SSRN)[25], The National Bureau of Economic Research (NBER),[26] and Bepress.[27] These may also include databases of fundamental scientific research or elements critical to research, such as genetic research databases,[28] some of which are

23 See Paola Giuri et al., Skills, Division of Labor and Performance in Collective Inventions: Evidence from Open Source Software, 28 *Int'L J. of Ind. Org.* 54 (2010).

24 See, e.g., *Lasersaur*, available at www.lasersaur.com/ (presenting an open-source laser-cutter); Open Source Malaria: The Story So Far, *OpenWetWare*, available at http://openwetware.org/wiki/OSDDMalaria:GSK_Arylpyrrole_Series:Story_so_far (discussing open source development of a malaria drug); Soft Drink Formula, *Alfredo Octavio*, available at http://alfredo.octavio.net/soft_drink_formula.pdf (providing the formula for an "open source soft drink").

25 *Soc. Sci. Res. Network*, available at www.ssrn.com/en/. It is worth noting that SSRN is now owned by RELX, formerly Reed-Elsevier, as this demonstrates that both nonprofit and for-profit concerns are engaged in open-source efforts.

26 *Nat'l Bureau of Econ. Res.*, available at www.nber.org/.

27 *Bepress*, available at www.bepress.com/. University officials have also shown great support for open-source scholarship. See Richard Wheeler et al., Values and Scholarship, *Inside Higher Ed* (Feb. 23, 2012), available at www.insidehighered.com/views/2012/02/23/essay-open-access-scholarship.

28 See, e.g., An Overview of the Human Genome Project (National Human Genome Research Institute), available at www.genome.gov/12011238.

modeled upon patent pools[29] that provide for the sharing of fundamental scientific research.[30]

There is also a movement afoot to create open-source publications in science, humanities, and the social sciences.[31] These journals can offer nonaffiliated scholars access to foundational work and resources, which can be invaluable to their research and development. Many scholars, academics, and librarians feel that the pricing of peer-reviewed journals in their field can be prohibitive, and open-source journals appear to offer an indispensable alternative to closed-access scholarship. However, many open journals require the author to pay for publication, even though the scholar may retain copyright in the published work. Arguably this represents a cost-shifting rather than the removal of costs from the system: rather than institutions paying for peer-reviewed journals, the publishing academic pays to have the work placed in the journal. Another important caveat is that some open access journals are not peer-reviewed, which subverts the norm in most academic fields. Many critics have argued that this can compromise the quality and authority of the work published and can create a "race to the bottom" in the world of academic publishing. It would seem that open-source and open access journals are promising avenues for making scholarly archives accessible and affordable to all. But how their economics are supported remains to be seen, and their long-term success remains equally an open question at present.

The pursuit of open-source production, its utility to creative communities, and its promise to increase access and affordability, are certainly not limited to scholarship alone. A number of artists are beginning to contemplate creating artistic repositories in areas such as photography, short film, literary works and journalism.[32] In the case of journalism, some joint websites and blogs are created with the free and voluntary contribution of authors, some of whom are employed elsewhere, in a kind of open-source production that is greatly

29 See Josh Lerner & Jean Tirole, Efficient Patent Pools, 93 *Am. Econ. Rev.* 691 (2004), available at www.nber.org/papers/w9175.pdf (providing an overview of patent pools).

30 See, e.g., Arti K. Rai, Open and Collaborative Research: A New Model for Biomedicine (Duke L. Sch., Legal Stud. Res. Paper No. 61, Oct. 2004), available at http://ssrn.com/abstract=574863; Arti K. Rai, Regulating Scientific Research: Intellectual Property Rights and the Norms of Science (Jul. 22, 1999), available at http://ssrn.com/abstract=172032.

31 See Open Access in Humanities and Social Sciences: Visions for the Future of Publishing, 76 *College Research & Libraries News* 2 (2005), available at https://crln.acrl.org/index.php/crlnews/article/view/9262/10312.

32 See, e.g., Open Access Policy for Images of Works of Art Presumed in the Public Domain, *Nat'l Gallery of Art*, available at https://images.nga.gov/en/page/openaccess.html; Open Content Program, *Getty*, available at www.getty.edu/about/opencontent.html; see also, e.g., Latin American & Spanish Videos Freely Available on the Internet: A Guide, Univ. Libraries, available at http://libguides.library.albany.edu/content.php?pid=57045&sid=428759.

enriching the blogosphere.[33] Examples of these include *SCOTUSblog*, *Politico*, *Talking Points Memo*, *Crooked Timber*, *First Monday*, and others.

One more illustration of the widespread effect that the open-source movement has had on creative content production is in the areas of online teaching and learning. Universities and other well-established institutions are not the only entities interested in open source. Jointly led ventures among teachers, educators, instructors, and those simply interested in the exchange of knowledge have contributed to the creation of online language learning blogs, artistic instruction blogs such as teaching music via Skype, and other instructional websites created, supported, and developed by various online communities.[34] In many of these cases, a resistance to propertization may or may not be due to a reluctance to monetize, and thereby commoditize, the output of the creative community. Rather, it may be a recognition that harnessing open source production may help develop areas of creativity that are have wide user interest but limited resources. In these cases, open source may make creative works both affordable and accessible in ways that are not replicated in strictly commercial venues.[35]

For creative content industries undergoing disruptive innovation and searching for the most effective tactical plan for managing change, promoting growth and fostering longevity, the extraction, analysis, and application of the salient factors presented here should prove a useful framework that is readily adaptable to their needs. There are a host of creative content industries that share a fundamental commitment to spurring creativity that will fall into this rubric, including entertainment and media, publishing and journalism, sporting activities, cuisine, and comedy. It is equally relevant to others that are united in pursuit of innovative research, discovery, and production, such as scientific research and commercial sciences such as biotech, software development, computers, electronic gaming and, increasingly, new entrants such as health care and K–12 education. As can be discerned from the broad range of these industries, there is no one-size-fits-all solution: the balance of salient factors must accordingly be developed on a case-by-case basis.

33 Huffington Post prior to its acquisition by AOL in 2011 is a good example of such business model. See Nate Silver, The Economics of Blogging and the Huffington Post, *N.Y. Times* (Feb. 12, 2011), available at http://fivethirtyeight.blogs.nytimes.com/2011/02/12/the-economics-of-blogging-and-the-huffington-post/?r=0 (comparing the business model to "a galley rowed by slaves and commanded by pirates").

34 See, e.g., 10 Sources for Free Online Music Courses, *Study.com*, available at http://education-portal.com/articles/10_Sources_for_Free_Online_Music_Courses.html; Learn 48 Languages Online for Free: Spanish, Chinese, English & More, *Open Culture*, available at www.openculture.com/freelanguagelessons.

35 On commodification, and resistance to commodification, see generally, Margaret Jane Radin and Madhavi Sunder, *The Subject and Object of Commodification* (UC Davis Law, Legal Studies Research Paper No. 16; Stanford Public Law Working Paper No. 97, 2004) (reviewing Rethinking Commodification: Cases and Readings. In *Law & Culture*, Martha M. Ertman & Joan C. Williams, eds., 2005); Margaret Radin, Contested Commodities (Harvard University Press, Cambridge, MA, 1996).

Creative industries should recognize that it is not merely the salient factors but also the interplay among factors that solve the equation. Adding layers of IP, for instance, may cause an industry to place less trust in cultural and normative principles and practices, so that IP enforcement comes to substitute for, if not wholly replace, an ethos of conduct that may be predominantly self-governed and self-sustained. This not only has the potential to transform an industry's entire ecosystem but also has the potential to mutate its communally shared values and mission. Moreover, it has the potential to affect the community itself, which can lead to further upheaval as long-standing members of the creative community struggle to come to terms with the newly emerging culture in which they find themselves embedded. Creative industries should recognize that they will function best when they balance the interests of their stakeholders, even if at times those interests seem difficult to reconcile with the commercial drive to exploit intellectual properties for maximum immediate gain.

11 What Is Exacerbating the Problem

Big Tech: The Thumb on the Scales

11.1 Introduction

The tailoring framework enables creative industries to tackle the challenges that disruptive innovation poses with a methodical, customized, and dynamic response to change. The processes involve evaluating changed situations, identifying weaknesses, and rebuilding toward a more profitable and sustainable future. Responding to a new environment is never easy, and is only made more difficult by the accelerating speed at which commercial and technological progress occurs. But in recent years, even challenges long familiar to creative industries have intensified. The emergence of huge, and hugely powerful, new entrants into the creative landscape is the driving force behind this newly pressurized environment.

A handful of dominant technology companies, known collectively and colloquially, as "Big Tech,"[1] are skewing the calculus of creative production in every dimension and at every significant juncture.[2] The key dimensions in which the Big Tech companies govern interactions and increasingly dictate the commercial terms can be roughly broken down into four categories: pipelines; pricing; policing; and populism.[3] In these critical areas, and across the

1 The definition of "Big Tech" can vary considerably. Broadly, it is used to connote the presence and power of technology giants Google, Facebook, Amazon, Apple, and Microsoft. Admittedly, these companies have different business models: Google derives revenues from ad searches; Facebook derives ad revenues from attention-grabbing content; Apple sells electronic hardware (with tied-in content and services); and Microsoft and Amazon have revenue streams derived from mixed retail, computing, and media. Yet while distinct, these companies collectively represent significant amounts of market share and market power in the digital space. At present, their operations have been granted deferential treatment by regulators and legislators alike. These features ensure that Big Tech will be a critical force with which creative industries must do business if they are to distribute their goods and services online. See, e.g., 'Big Tech' Isn't One Big Monopoly, It's Five Companies All In Different Businesses, The Conversation, March 23, 2018, available at http://theconversation.com/big-tech-isnt-one-big-monopoly-its-5-companies-all-in-different-businesses-92791.

2 See Dante Chinni, From News to Shoes: How Big Is Big Tech?, *NBC News*, Feb. 25, 2018, available at www.nbcnews.com/politics/first-read/news-shoes-how-big-big-tech-n851031.

3 "Populism" is usually defined to mean a sense of support for common people against a real or perceived elite. It is used here to suggest a strain of popular thinking among some

spectrum of creative sectors, the emergence of Big Tech is a game changer that will require creative industries to devise strong, concerted, and sometimes imaginative responses. In addition to the Big Tech companies, a cluster of large and increasingly consolidated companies are also helping to transform the digital space. It is imperative to understand the areas in which these entities are operating and the many ways in which they are exerting unprecedented pressure on creators and upending economic balance.

11.2 Pipelines

In this digital era, creative content is increasingly disseminated not in physical retail stores, but online. The pipelines for making content available—or to the contrary throttling its availability—are as relevant to content distribution as bricks-and-mortar channels, such as stores, newsstands, and rental kiosks historically were. But due both to the ease and the volume that online distribution affords, they are much greater in total import.[4] Another important distinction is that while material goods can usually be obtained through multiple venues (in stores or online), purely digital goods must be conveyed through digital channels. These factors make digital pipelines more central to both purchasing and distributing power than their physical counterparts. In other words, while physical content can be sold in stores or online, digital content can only be conveyed and sold via digital pipelines, making it far more susceptible to their control.

These digital pipelines for conveyance are dominated by a concentrated cluster of entities, which at this point have close to total control over the means, mechanisms, and terms of distribution. It is often not feasible to avoid transacting with the owners of pipelines. They govern the sole means for making content available online. At present, they are also subject to a patchwork of regulations that has proven highly susceptible to lobbying and regulatory capture. Thus, for instance, while television and radio, traditional areas of content dissemination, are subject to fairly strictly regulated standards over the content they can carry (such as restraints on the use of expletives), streaming services, more recent arrivals to the content delivery scene, are much less restricted in

---

digital users which asserts that rights in public access to creative works are paramount and should be promoted even to the detriment of creators and copyright holders.

4 Witness the difference in total music sales per year, which has increased online at a greater rate by far than in brick-and-mortar store sales. See Joshua P. Friedlander, News and Notes On 2017 RIAA Revenue Statistics, RIAA (2017), available at www.riaa.com/wp-content/uploads/2018/03/RIAA-Year-End-2017-News-and-Notes.pdf. This is an account of sales throughout the first half of 2018. There is significant decline in CD sales, even compared to 2017. While this growth may not represent an increase in net revenues, it does show that online sales and purchasing activity easily outpaces brick-and-mortar activity. However, these statistics do not address online music streaming, which is rapidly outpacing sales and may eventually become the industry standard.

the content they can offer.[5] Another contrast lies in the different rates that are levied for broadcasting content versus streaming content. Even the tax treatment of products and content sold in store versus those sold online is variable and non-standardized.

There is little parity or consistency in the differentiated areas of physical and digital content. It is possible that these discrepancies in treatment can be overcome or overturned. But they are magnified when seen as part of a greater imbalance in the regulation of creative content providers and distributors. In part, this may be due to the relatively nascent, yet highly rapid, phases of development that technology has seen in the last few decades. In part, though, it may also be due to aggressive lobbying and advocacy on the part of essential technology companies and providers that have experienced exponential growth, with a concomitant increase in both economic power and political sway.[6] And the disparity is magnified when the investment in lobbying by digital players is taken into account. In 2018, lobbying by Facebook and Google alone amounted to an estimated $33.8 MM,[7] while lobbying by technology companies totaled approximately $64 million.[8] These figures are significant, and are expected by most observers to increase.

The main pipelines of online content distribution can be divided into a few broad groups: Internet Service Providers (ISPs), search engines, and content delivery platforms. The first group consists of a handful of ISPs, which deliver content to the vast majority of online audiences.[9] They have a large and concentrated market share, and therefore dominant market power, in almost any

5 For example, writers on network television shows have struggled to come up with alternatives to words that are banned by censors, whereas streaming service content writers can use the word they had in mind, *see* Whitney Friedlander, FCC Censoreship Rules Are Different for Broadcast, Cable and Streaming, Variety, Aug. 16, 2017, available at https://variety.com/2017/tv/news/fcc-rules-orange-is-the-new-black-american-crime-carmichael-show-1202527318/; Obscene, Indecent and Profane Broadcasts, FCC, available at www.fcc.gov/consumers/guides/obscene-indecent-and-profane-broadcasts (stating "the same rules for indecency and profanity do not apply to cable, satellite TV and satellite radio because they are subscription services").

6 In 2017, the five largest technology companies spent $60 million in lobbying. See, available at Harper Neidig, Tech Giants Spent Record Sums on Lobbying in 2017, *The Hill*, Jan. 23, 2018, https://thehill.com/policy/technology/370252-tech-giants-spent-record-sums-on-lobbying-in-2017.

7 See, Lobbying Database, Center for Responsive Politics, available at www.opensecrets.org/lobby/.

8 See, available at A.J. Dellinger, Tech Companies Spent More Than $64 Million on Lobbying in 2018, Endgadget, Jan. 23, 2019, www.engadget.com/2019/01/23/tech-companies-lobbying-2018-google-facebook-amazon/.

9 See Top Five Most Popular ISPs, Alentus, available at www.alentus.com/articles/top-5-most-popular-isps.asp; see also Number of Broadband Internet Subscribers in the United States from 2011 to 2018, by Cable Provider, Statista, available at www.statista.com/statistics/217348/us-broadband-internet-susbcribers-by-cable-provider/.

given domestic market.[10] These telecommunications companies are essential to disseminating content worldwide via various means, including broadband, cable, and satellite. While subject to some federal regulation, they govern the rate at which content is distributed, the locations that are digitally connected, and now the priority with which some content is speedily delivered and other content is throttled.[11]

The ISPs currently enjoy minimal obligations by law to oversee or engage in active efforts that counter copyright infringement and other incursions on the rights of IP holders. Only upon notice by copyright holders that infringement is occurring are they required to act; and they will not be held liable in conjunction with infringement if they did not actively participate in enabling infringement.[12] ISPs are also not obligated to engage actively in anti-counterfeiting efforts,[13] such as seeking out and thwarting the sale of counterfeit items online.[14]

In some cases, certain ISPs have proven amenable to joining in efforts to police and sanction activities and sites that infringe on copyrighted content.[15] These efforts may be calculated to appease vocal advocates for copyright, but they do not need to be systematic and ongoing, and they are not necessitated by legal obligations. Stakeholders in creative fields have sought to hold ISPs at least partially responsible for monitoring and counteracting infringing behavior, both by lobbying for regulatory change and by trying to put pressure on ISPs to be good actors.[16] To date, however, they have not succeeded in their efforts.

A few channels of dissemination play the role of pipelines on a scale that is almost as comprehensive as the reach of ISPs, despite the fact that choices to

10 Note that "dominant" is used as a term of art, and not a legal term such as the "dominant" market power that would encroach upon antitrust violations. It might, but the definition of "markets" tends to be controversial, so for the purposes of this argument, "dominant" connotes a significant reach among audiences and users.

11 Gary S. Becker, Dennis W. Carlton, & Hal S. Sider, Net Neutrality and Consumer Welfare, 6 *J. Competition L. & Econ.* 497, 519 (2010).

12 See, Mitchell Zimmerman, Your DMCA Safe Harbor Questions Answered, Fenwick & West, available at www.fenwick.com/FenwickDocuments/DMCA-QA.pdf at 23–24.

13 See, David Kravets, ISP Defeats Hollywood Copyright Claims, *Wired,* Feb. 4, 2010, available at www.wired.com/2010/02/isp-defeats-hollywood-copyright-claims/.

14 Katja Weckström, Liability for Trademark Infringement for Internet Service Providers, 16 *Intellectual Property L. Rev.* 1, 35 (2012).

15 AT&T, Verizon, Time Warner Cable, Comcast, and Cablevision Systems were participants in a plan in which infringing members' internet speed would be slowed or their content become redirected to and educational page about copyright infringement. *See,* David Kravets, ISPs Now Monitoring for Copyright Infringement, Feb. 25, 2013, available at www.wired.com/2013/02/copyright-scofflaws-beware/.

16 See, Cecilia Kang, House Introduces Internet Piracy Bill, *Washington Post,* Oct. 26, 2011, available at www.washingtonpost.com/blogs/post-tech/post/house-introduces-internet-piracy-bill/2011/10/26/gIQA0f5xJM_blog.html?utm_term=.8ef429245351; see also Stephen Carlisle, DMCA 'Takedown' Notices" Why 'Takedown' Should Be 'Stay Down' and Why It's Good for Everyone, Nova Southeastern University, July 23, 2014, available at http://copyright.nova.edu/dmca-takedown-notices/.

find and use content may be discretionary, whereas the choice to be online is practically necessitated by modern life. Illustrative is Google and parent company Alphabet: as the preeminent search engine used today, Google cannot be bypassed by any serious creator or creative enterprise, and it has such market power that the terms it sets and the requirements it commands are essentially non-negotiable.

Google controls the terms of dissemination of online goods and services without substantial accountability to purveyors, customers, or regulators. Its search algorithms, closely protected, highly sophisticated, and largely impenetrable determine where a good will be placed relative to its competitors when a customer searches for that good online. Google has the capacity to remove content by fiat, and its decisions cannot readily be appealed to any entity other than Google itself. Neither regulators nor the public can request or mandate reviews of the search engine's operations; and at present no public policy administrator actively oversees Google's practices. Its hegemony is virtually complete.[17]

Similarly, the major content distribution companies are becoming increasingly pervasive and have a critical influence on the content access and consumption of most citizens. They may segment the market to a varying extent, as illustrated by the range of entertainment providers online: Netflix, Hulu, Disney, and a handful of other companies that represent, in aggregate, a huge share of television and film offerings. Even considered singularly, a company such as Netflix commands a strong viewership and growing market share. Further, Netflix controls original and exclusive content that can only be accessed through its channels and on its terms, usually via subscriptions to Netflix services.[18] When Netflix premieres original content on their site, they enjoy total control over the product's release and future licensing revenues.

Other content distributors are likewise demonstrating an interest in generating original content. Apple, for instance, announced that it would spend

17 See, Google Needs Regulation. Republicans Are Too Busy Screaming About Bias, Ed., Washington Post, Dec. 11, 2018, available at www.washingtonpost.com/opinions/google-needs-regulation-republicans-are-too-busy-screaming-about-bias/2018/12/11/eda468fa-fd8b-11e8-ad40-cdfd0e0dd65a_story.html?utm_term=.362da610074c; see also Dipayan Ghosh, Yes, Silicon Valley Needs Regulation. But Trump's Reason Why Is Misguided, *The Guardian*, Sept. 5, 2018, available at www.theguardian.com/commentisfree/2018/sep/05/trump-silicon-valley-regulation-google-fake-news-misguided; see also Allan Smith, 'The Only Answer': An Unorthodox Solution for Regulating America's Biggest Tech Giants Is Gaining Steam on the Right, *Business Insider*, Sept. 5, 2018, available at www.businessinsider.com/regulate-twitter-facebook-google-hearing-trump-2017-10.

18 See, Todd Spangler, Netflix Original Series Viewing Climbs, But Licensed Content Remains Majority of Total U.S. Streams, Variety, Dec. 10, 2108, available at https://variety.com/2018/digital/news/netflix-original-series-licensed-viewing-friends-the-office-1203085230/; Audrey Schomer, Netflix Says 85% of Its Content Spend Will Go to Originals, *Business Insider*, May 16, 2018, available at www.businessinsider.com/netflix-putting-almost-7-billion-toward-original-content-2018-5.

$1 billion in 2018 to generate creative content.[19] Like Apple, companies that generate content will also have increasing ownership and control over the content portfolios they distribute, and will likely mirror versions of the Netflix subscription model that lock viewers into their universe. In this respect, content companies are following trends that have prevailed in the television and cable industries, in which many of the major stations vie to bring out new content seasonally. Further, as content streaming grows in popularity and reach, the Netflix model of content creation and distribution that enables "cord cutting"[20]—that is, when consumers forgo traditional cable network television in favor of alternate streaming services—will grow in tandem, encompassing not only existing competitors such as Hulu and HBO Go,[21] but also formidable newer entrants such as Amazon Prime Video.[22]

The recent re-launch of Amazon Prime Video highlights an important feature of the Big Tech landscape: the domination of content distribution is rapidly melding with the domination of content generation and production. Indeed, it is not hard to see a future in which more and more companies in entertainment, media, music, publishing, and other creative industries unite virtually all aspects of content creation, development, harvesting, distribution, and management under one roof.[23] Already, large-scale mergers and acquisitions have given rise to consolidated entities, such as NBC/Universal/Comcast, and Fox/Clear Channel,][24] that control massive content-rich portfolios. The great majority of these M&A activities have been cleared by regulators, and have not proven susceptible to antitrust challenges. At this writing, several proposed transactions are pending, and the pace of consolidation appears unlikely to abate.

19 See, available at Darrell Etherington, Apple Said to Be Spending One Billion On Original Content in 2018, *TechCrunch* (2108), available at https://techcrunch.com/2017/08/16/apple-said-to-be-spending-1-billion-on-original-content-in-2018/.

20 See, Shoshanna Delventhal, Cord Cutting Is Accelerating Rapidly: New Study, Investopedia, July 15, 2018, available at www.investopedia.com/articles/investing/102015/4-best-ways-cut-cord.asp.

21 See, Trevir Nath, Hulu, Netflix and Amazon Video Comparison, Investopedia, Oct. 23, 2018, available at www.investopedia.com/articles/personal-finance/121714/hulu-netflix-and-amazon-instant-video-comparison.asp.

22 See, Dan Moskowitz, Who Are Netflix's Main Competitors? (NFLX), Investopedia, Oct. 12, 2018, available at www.investopedia.com/articles/markets/051215/who-are-netflixs-main-competitors-nflx.asp.

23 While this kind of vertical integration might run athwart antitrust laws, it remains to be seen whether antitrust will be consistently enforced against it. Certainly recent mergers and acquisitions activities have cast the strength of antitrust enforcement into doubt. See, e.g., Daniel Rockower, Antitrust Implications of the Comcast-Time Warner Merger, *Columbia Bus. L. Rev.*, April 11, 2014, available at https://cblr.columbia.edu/antitrust-implications-of-the-comcast-time-warner-cable-merger/.

24 See, Alex Sherman, Wall Street Is Expecting a Two-Year Pause In Big Media and Telecom Deals After a Crazy 2018, *CNBC*, Dec. 9, 2018, available at www.cnbc.com/2018/12/09/wall-street-expects-two-year-pause-in-big-media-and-telecom-ma.html.

The trend to consolidation seems economically rational: digital streaming is growing in popularity, and content businesses that offer original content and varied subscription models are being rewarded by growing consumer bases. The downside for any given creative firm is not immediate or readily apparent, as centralizing content ownership and control promises tethered viewers and steady income streams. But from a larger perspective, it is troubling that the increasing atomization of content seems likely to compel consumers into purchasing more products from a greater number of content providers, requiring them to subscribe to multiple services in order to gain access to the content they desire. This may mean that consumers have to buy more than they want: they may have to buy subscriptions to multiple services simply to get access to a handful of shows.

Just as in the case of bundled cable services, in which consumers typically have to buy access to multiple stations irrespective of how many shows they actually want to watch, digital consumers may have to purchase access to multiple providers to reach the specific content they prefer. Cable content providers have compelled viewers to settle for the bundled model, despite some amount of consumer dissatisfaction. Their model is now being challenged by digital streaming, which offers new content that is less aggregated. But if digital streaming services are disaggregated, their competitive positioning may still compel users to buy more content access than they actually want or need.

It is unclear whether in the long run digital streaming providers can compel viewers to settle for a model in which they must subscribe to multiple services, each of which may have bundled content, in order to gain access to the content desired. Consumers may balk at multiple purchases, or they may choose to forgo some services in order to stay under a certain level of expenditure. Or they may choose to move away from standard cord-cutting services like Roku, and adopt newer services like Kodi set-top boxes, the latter of which are relatively inexpensive but also may operate in the gray area of copyright, bordering if not actually engaging in infringing activities.[25]

None of these are optimal for digital streaming services, unless consumers come to accept a world in which multiple subscriptions and atomized content are standard practice and unchallenged by alternative options. As content production and delivery become more integrated, consumers may find that digital streaming is not the low-cost proposition many anticipated: competition may exert some downward pressure on prices, but divided content offered by separate providers may keep total outlays surprisingly inflated and difficult to contain. From the perspective of consumers, pricing may be the main determining feature of the prospects for success that awaits digital streaming services.

Consumer concerns lie on the demand side of content-related concerns in the new world of Big Tech. But the supply side of the equation may be equally

25 See, Brian Barratt, The Little Black Box That Took Over Piracy, *Wired*, Oct. 27, 2017, available at www.wired.com/story/kodi-box-piracy/.

complicated. From the perspective of artists and creators, consolidation can mean that they are obliged to work with a smaller and smaller handful of gatekeepers. From the perspective of firms that produce content, protection of valuable copyright is always a critical concern. In theory, content-rich companies should be more likely to support and seek out copyright enforcement when they gain valuable content, even if in their prior iterations as pure distributors they showed little heed to respecting copyright. But protecting one's own content and still playing fast-and-loose with the content of others can remain a real possibility. Sites such as Facebook, for instance, may disregard content appropriation by its users if it suits their interest in page views that are bolstered and monetized by advertising. They may yet protect their own content, such as original or sponsored materials, and not protect others' content. It therefore remains a vital part of policymakers' concerns to ensure that all content-rich companies play by the same rules, not only across the playing field but also within their own domains.

Recent years have seen a growing focus on content streaming, and relatedly content licensing, as opposed to content sales. The music industry has long been moving in this direction, with content streaming online via sites such as Pandora and Spotify, rapidly overtaking services that sell content, such as the Apple iTunes Store. Many newcomers, such as Tidal and Google Play, have tried to monetize the streaming space, although only a few have been shown to be profitable thus far.[26] Even sites such as YouTube, which have traditionally been sustained by advertising revenues, are now moving toward offering streaming services.[27] But music, too, is susceptible to being exploited by Big Tech companies that derive revenues not from the sale or licensing of content but rather from advertising aimed at digital users, irrespective of their use of content to build and retain viewership. Indeed, the early iteration of YouTube offers an example of this conundrum: when first launched, it paid scant attention to copyright in creative works, including videos and music, precisely because it was focused on building viewership and maximizing page views.[28] Moreover, the fact that online advertising is increasingly concentrated in the hands of two Big Tech companies—in 2018, Facebook and Amazon represented over 65% of the digital advertising market—only exacerbates the concern that the driving impetus to maximize advertising revenues may lead

26 See, Lizzie Plaugic, Tidal Is Reportedly Having Money Problems, *The Verge*, Dec. 12, 2017, available at www.theverge.com/2017/12/12/16768650/tidal-money-problems-sprint-investment; Alan Martin, Apple's App Store Made 93 Percent More Money Than Google Play in Q3, The Inquirer, Oct. 12, 2018, available at www.theinquirer.net/inquirer/news/3064452/the-app-store-made-93-more-money-than-google-play-in-q3.

27 See, Megan C. Hills, YouTube Music, A New Music Streaming Service, Will Launch Next Week, *Forbes*, May 17, 2018, available at https://www.forbes.com/sites/meganhills1/2018/05/17/youtube-music/#490f7058376b.

28 See, Sam Gutelle, The Long, Checkered History of YouTube's Attempt to Launch a Music Service, TubeFilter, May 22, 2018, available at www.tubefilter.com/2018/05/22/youtube-music-service-history/.

Big Tech companies to give lower priority to respecting and protecting copyrighted content.

ISPs, search engines, content production and delivery conglomerates, and streaming services are pipelines that will no doubt shape the future of content. Another important set of players is social media sites, whose extensive scope and reach are bound to have an impact on content dissemination. Illustrative are some of the largest social media sites operating today: Facebook, Instagram, Twitter, Reddit, and various other social media sites are accessed by an aggregate 2.6 billion users annually.[29] Increasingly, these users are relying on social media as primary outlets for their news and information.[30] For instance, logged-in users spent an average of more than one hour per day watching YouTube videos just on mobile devices.[31] And while YouTube users have primarily relied on the site for various forms of content, including music, film, videos, and other forms of entertainment, they are increasingly turning to it as a source for news and journalism.[32]

Ever-greater numbers of social media users turn to these outlets to access, consume, share, and enjoy creative content. Coupled with the fact that these social media sites have such enormous reach, it is clear that these venues represent important pipelines for content delivery. The array of creative industries, including journalism, music, film, and entertainment, must take social media into serious consideration when seeking to expand both their means and modes of communication, and their venues to monetize and disseminate content. But the promise of expanded access to users also comes with a daunting caveat: the scale of these social media sites, which threatens to dwarf even the collective size of content industries, suggests that the bargaining power between content and pipelines may well be increasingly skewed in favor of the

29 In 2017, Facebook logged over 2 billion users. See, available at Number of Social Media Users Worldwide from 2010 to 2021, Statista (2019), available at www.statista.com/statistics/278414/number-of-worldwide-social-network-users/; see also Josh Constine, Facebook Now Has 2 Billion Monthly Users . . . and Responsibility, TechCrunch (2018), available at https://techcrunch.com/2017/06/27/facebook-2-billion-users/. Reddit had over 1.66 billion unique visitors from April 2017 to December 2017. See Combined Desktop and Mobile Visitors to Reddit.com from February 2018 to March 2019, available at www.statista.com/statistics/443332/reddit-monthly-visitors/. Twitter had over 328 million active monthly users in 2017. See Daniel Sparks, How Many Users Does Twitter Have?, The Motley Fool, April 27, 2017, available at www.fool.com/investing/2017/04/27/how-many-users-does-twitter-have.aspx.

30 One recent Pew study revealed that a majority of American adults, 62%, get news on social media, and 18% do so often. Jeffrey Gottfried and Elisa Shearer, News Use Across Social Media Platforms 2016, Pew Research Center, May 26, 2016, available at www.journalism.org/2016/05/26/news-use-across-social-media-platforms-2016/.

31 In 2017, YouTube had 1.5 billion logged-in users that visited the site every month See, Lucas Matney, YouTube Has 1.5 Billion Logged-In Monthly Users Watching a Ton of Mobile Video, TechCrunch (2018), available at https://techcrunch.com/2017/06/22/youtube-has-1-5-billion-logged-in-monthly-users-watching-a-ton-of-mobile-video/.

32 See Pew study, supra note 30, available at www.journalism.org/2016/05/26/news-use-across-social-media-platforms-2016/.

latter. This means that creative industries will have to fight to ensure that their content is licitly circulated, fairly compensated, and consistently supported by users and carriers alike.

The control of digital pipelines inherently bears risks of overly concentrated control in the content markets. But these risks are compounded by mergers and acquisitions (M&A) activities that empower a single entity with the ability to control delivery pipelines, services, and content itself. In the digital space, such vertical integration is particularly powerful for several reasons: the major players that control broadband tend to dominate a given region, affording consumers little or no ability to seek alternatives; they can establish and effectively lock in prices, terms, conditions, and services that cannot easily be challenged by competitors or new entrants; and they can determine the payment for content, which they can impose variably depending on whether it is their content or their competitors' content.

While in theory antitrust regulators may frown upon vertical integration, in practice it has infrequently been thwarted even after protracted litigation.[33] As seen in many hotly contested digital arenas, some M&A ventures will succeed and have a direct impact on the immediate landscape.[34] If some of the largest pipeline companies are able to prevail in recent attempts at vertical integration through mergers and acquisitions, they will be able to imprint their terms on the digital marketplace and set the terms and conditions of content consumption and access for years to come.

The recently approved merger of AT&T and Time Warner vividly illustrates both the potential impact and the complicated nature of the concern.[35] AT&T owns the service U-Verse, which provides broadband to its users. AT&T also owns DirecTV, a major satellite distributor of video service. As a major player

33 See Tara Lachapelle, From Comcast to Viacom, Media Mergers Take More Twists, Bloomberg, April 2, 2018, available at www.bloomberg.com/gadfly/articles/2018-04-25/from-comcast-to-viacom-media-m-a-takes-more-twists.

34 Examples from 2017 include Discovery's purchase of Scripps Network; Disney's acquisition of most of 21st Century Fox, including a significant share of Sky network; and Disney's acquisition of the streaming technology company BAMTech. See, Matt Pressberg, Nine Biggest Billion-Dollar Entertainment and Media Deals in 2017, The Wrap, Dec. 26, 2017, available at www.thewrap.com/9-biggest-billion-dollar-entertainment-media-deals-2017-photos/. One of the biggest examples of vertical integration that will transform the media market is Sinclair Broadcasting's proposed purchase of Tribune Media Company, which as of this writing looks poised to clear regulatory approval in 2018. See, Dade Hayes, Sinclair CEO Chris Ripley Says FCC's OK of Tribune Buy Still 'Likely,' But Deal Could Also 'Just Expire,' Deadline, May 9, 2018, available at http://deadline.com/2018/05/sinclair-tribune-media-fcc-chris-ripley-1202386133. Also interesting are less conventional M&A activities that may have some features of vertical integration, such as Microsoft's acquisition of LinkedIn in 2017. See Greg Dool, Media Industry M&A Activity Remains Steady, While Deal Value Spikes, *Folio*, July 6, 2017, available at www.foliomag.com/media-industry-ma-2017/.

35 See e.g., April Glaser and Will Oremus, The Case for Fearing the A&T-Time Warner Merger, *Slate*, May 22, 2018, available at https://slate.com/technology/2018/05/at-and-t-and-time-warner-trial-the-case-for-fearing-this-merger.html.

in the broadband and video distribution service sectors, AT&T is comparable only to Comcast in size and scope. Following its upcoming merger with Time Warner, AT&T will comprise a major studio that owns and controls numerous television channels, including CNN, HBO, TBS, and TNT, as well as a vast amount of television programming.

The controversial, yet now-approved, vertical integration of a giant broadband provider and a massive content company has the potential to fundamentally change the competitive dynamic. The combined entity has enormous control over the prices, terms, and conditions of content delivery in any given market in which it plays—a particularly troublesome prospect in specific markets or regions where AT&T is the dominant provider. Further, AT&T's content component is likely to see a significant advantage over competing content companies, including news, movie, or entertainment channels. This raises the question of whether AT&T, which under the ratified deal would own programming, will be afforded both the opportunity to discriminate against its competitors and the incentive to favor its captive content divisions over their competitors.

The precedent for the AT&T-Time Warner merger was set by the acquisition of NBCUniversal by Comcast in 2011, valued at approximately $30 billion.[36] That merger was equally sweeping in scope, and while initially approved with certain conditions, has been followed by an ongoing phase-out of those conditions.[37] But the AT&T-Time Warner merger is more than double in size, valued at approximately $85 billion.[38] Moreover, while Comcast has a broad scope, it does not reach all markets. DirecTV, which is owned by AT&T, has a far wider reach; whereas DirecTV Now, its streaming service, can be used over any Internet connection. This would give AT&T much more power over its competitors than any carrier in the market.

The ramifications of this merger, which has few parallels in scale or scope, raise diverse concerns comparable to those levied against Comcast in earlier transactions. On those occasions, Comcast has generally prevailed. Given the current environment, it was not inconceivable that AT&T would similarly prevail. But while the full ramifications of these combinations have yet to play out, it is evident that the digital media landscape will be significantly dominated and shaped by these two giants. The implications for competitive content companies, and creative industries more generally, could not be clearer: they will be forced to transact with the owners of major pipelines that also own and control content, making them competitors with all the means, incentives, and market power to skew the playing field to their own advantage.

36 See Klint Finley, The Comcast-NBC Merger Offers Little Guidance for AT&T-Time Warner, *Wired*, April 3, 2018, available at www.wired.com/story/the-comcast-nbc-merger-offers-little-guidance-for-atandt-time-warner/.

37 See Jon Brodkin, Comcast To Be 'Unleashed' on Rivals When NBC Merger Conditions Expire, Ars Technica, Dec. 15, 2017, available at https://arstechnica.com/tech-policy/2017/12/comcast-to-be-unleashed-on-rivals-when-nbc-merger-conditions-expire/.

38 Id.

But for the content companies that are constituents in the AT&T-Time Warner merger, the advantages of having preferential access to pipelines, and the heft of a powerful market player behind them, may appear life-saving in a world in which Facebook, Amazon, Netflix, and Google (sometimes collectively referred to as "FANG") seem ever more dominant. Even the leaders of behemoths like AT&T openly speak of their need to invest in M&A activities that consolidate their market power. This perspective was elucidated by Randall Stephenson, the chief executive of AT&T, whose strategy includes yoking together a combination of content libraries, mobile networks, and advertising technology that would be able to compete successfully with the tech giants. As Mr. Stephenson recently stated:

> Well, I believe if you don't create a pure, vertical, integrated capability, vertically integrated capability — from distribution all the way through content creation and advertising models — you're going to have a hard time competing with these guys. And the statistic we throw out, and since we announced this deal in November of 2016, the FANG market caps have gone up over $1 trillion. You better figure out how to vertically integrate here if you want to compete with those players.[39]

The AT&T-Time Warner merger is also highly likely to herald a further wave of M&A activity among carriers, content companies, and intermediaries, particularly those whose scale will create enormous market advantages when combined. The highly anticipated, if contested, efforts by competitors Walt Disney Comcast to acquire 21st Century Fox are currently escalating, and have gained momentum in the wake of AT&T-Time Warner.[40] Similarly, Verizon in recent years has also sought to acquire content, purchasing AOL and then Yahoo in separate deals intended to monetize their respective technologies and user bases.[41]

There are also strong signals that vertical integration will include control over digital advertising as well as content. For instance, fresh off its merger, AT&T has moved to purchase AppNexus, one of the world's largest Internet advertising exchanges, which marketers use to buy advertising space from

39 See AT&T CEO Randall Stephenson at Code 2018 (full video and transcript), Recode, May 30, 2018, available at www.recode.net/2018/5/30/17397164/att-randall-stephenson-time-warner-transcript-code-2018. See also, In Tech, Life Is Hard on the B-List, New York Times Bits, May 31, 2018, available *at* https://www.nytimes.com/2018/06/01/technology/kevins-week-in-tech.html/.

40 See Mark Sweney, Disney Raises Offer for 21st Century Fox to $71.3 Billion and Outflanks Comcast, *The Guardian*, June 20, 2018, available at www.theguardian.com/film/2018/jun/20/disney-raises-offer-for-21st-century-fox-to-713bn-and-outflanks-comcast.

41 See Brian Fung, Fresh Off Its Time Warner Win, AT&T Is Buying Another Company, *Washington Post*, June 25, 2018, available at www.washingtonpost.com/technology/2018/06/25/fresh-off-its-time-warner-win-att-is-buying-yet-another-company/?utm_term=.808d94893941.

online publishers.[42] If approved, the deal is scheduled to close in 2018, and will consolidate AT&T's position as a significant contender in the online advertising space. This would bring AT&T into direct competition with the most powerful Big Tech companies that currently dominate online advertising. Facebook and Google are the leaders in this space, together controlling approximately 58% of digital ad investment, with Amazon following closely at their heels as it grows rapidly in strength and position.[43]

Creative industries will be divided when considering the implications of these mergers and acquisitions that will involve increasingly integrated control over content, pipelines, and networks. But in a world where a handful of companies are asserting their dominance and placing their thumbs on the scale, such considerations will be imperative to confront, sides will have to be taken, and competitors will have to position themselves advantageously to ensure that their content reaches across platforms and consumer bases.

11.3 Pricing

It is well established that with dominant market share and position comes the ability to have a strong influence on, if not actually to determine, pricing. In a monopsony market condition, one buyer controls a large proportion of the market and drives prices down.[44] Each of the major Big Tech companies can arguably be called a monopsony in its own market sector, particularly with respect to advertising rates. Each controls the prices and rates that advertising commands on their site, as well as the nature of advertisements—for example, pop-ups, click-throughs, banner ads, and so on—and the total marketing environment.[45] These rates are critical to creative industries, as they remain a significant source of revenue when creative works are released, licensed, or sold online. The strength of Big Tech companies is not infinite: they still must negotiate advertisers' rates. But their negotiating power is more than sufficient to ensure that they will command a premium commensurate with their ability

42 Id.

43 See, Data Suggests Surprising Shift: Duopoly Not All-Powerful, eMarketer, March 19, 2018, available at www.emarketer.com/content/google-and-facebook-s-digital-dominance-fading-as-rivals-share-grows.

44 See, Julie Young, Monopsony, Investopedia, April 29, 2019, available at www.investopedia.com/terms/m/monopsony.asp ("A monopsony, sometimes referred to as a buyer's monopoly, is a market condition similar to a monopoly. However, in a monopsony, a large buyer, not a seller, controls a large proportion of the market and drives prices down. . . . In situations where monopsonies occur, sellers often engage in price wars to entice the single buyer's business, effectively driving down the price and increasing the quantity. Sellers that get caught in a monopsony can find themselves in a race to the bottom and losing any power they previously had over supply and demand").

45 See, Susan Young, Getting the Message: How the Internet Is Changing Advertising, Harvard Business School Working Knowledge, May 16, 2000, available at https://hbswk.hbs.edu/item/getting-the-message-how-the-internet-is-changing-advertising.

to promise online views, or "eyeballs," to advertisers eager to reach online audiences.

The market dominance of Big Tech companies in their given sector enables them to exert pressure on the price that online advertising commands, keeping it high when advertising revenue works to their interest, as in the case of Facebook. At the same time, some Big Tech companies may find it strategically advantageous to exert downward pressure on advertising when they want to reach large audiences and not pay external advertisers, as in the case of Google's search engine. The vast disparity between ad rates in physical media versus online venues is notable and has not significantly changed over time. What is becoming ever more evident is the impact of depressed advertising rates on creative industries.[46] For creative industries, which have historically relied on advertising as a significant source of revenues and support, this is nothing short of a disaster. The effects can be seen already in many creative industries and ventures, such as journalism, music streaming, and online magazines: diminishing advertising rates are resulting in sharp decreases in revenues, leading to losses of profits, enterprises, and jobs.[47]

Beyond driving advertising rates, Big Tech companies have long-term plans to increase their profitability and scope. The leaders among these companies are creating or acquiring an increasingly sophisticated arsenal of technologies that allow them to track and target the right audiences, to measure responses instantaneously, to calibrate the effectiveness of ad campaigns, and to "package" user data that is immensely valuable and in demand.[48] The results of such large-scale data mining may be a mixed blessing for creative industries. On the one hand, the ability of Big Tech to develop data mining may be useful to content creators seeking to establish and promote their brand, to reach particular audiences, and to measure and recalibrate their product in response to measurable consumer data. Such brand building has been argued to be more important than ever in a competitive online environment that rewards differentiation and audience recognition and loyalty.[49] On the other hand, while quantifiable advertising data is immensely valuable to Big Tech as a product, it may be only of limited value to creators and creative content industries as a revenue-generator and a consumer-oriented tool. And it may prove costly if

46 See Jonathan Taplin, *Move Fast and Break Things: How Facebook, Google and Amazon Cornered Culture and Undermined Democracy* (Little, Brown, New York, NY 2017).

47 See, e.g., Netflix: Bringing Data Analytics to a Creative Industry, Harvard Business School Digital Initiative, Nov. 17, 2015, available at https://digit.hbs.org/submission/netflix-bringing-data-analytics-to-a-creative-industry/.

48 See, e.g., Christian Hagen, Marco Ciobo, et al., Big Data and the Creative Destruction of Today's Business Models, AT Kearney (2013), available at www.atkearney.com/documents/10192/698536/Big+Data+and+the+Creative+Destruction+of+Todays+Business+Models.pdf/f05aed38-6c26-431d-8500-d75a2c384919.

49 See, e.g., Scott Goodson, Why Brand Building Is Important, *Forbes*, May 27, 2012, available at www.forbes.com/sites/marketshare/2012/05/27/why-brand-building-is-important/#5b8f15ba3006.

Big Tech companies are able to use attractive creative content as a loss leader without recognizing the inherent value of the content itself.

11.4 Policing

The online appropriation or piracy of creative content has long been active and lucrative to pirates; and it continues to threaten the viability of creators and creative industries.[50] The music industry presented one of the first and largest examples of industry-wide losses that followed, and to a great extent were triggered by, the development of free online music sharing services. Although recent data suggest that the music market may be trending slowly upward,[51] most observers agree that it will likely never regain its robust revenues preceding the digital age.[52] Merchandise sales, "360 contracts," and newer sources of revenue are likewise not adequate to replace lost revenues resulting from both piracy and waning music sales. It remains to be seen whether online music streaming can offer a sustainable income source for musicians and industry stakeholders, but the prospects at present are mixed at best.[53]

As a warning to creative industries of the challenges to come, the music industry's free fall at the onset of digitization could not have been clearer. Equally, the responses it engendered showed that creative industries would be hard-pressed to recover their footing after digital disruption had changed their landscape indelibly. Rampant file sharing and massive losses by traditional content companies did not lead to a new paradigm in the sale of music until Apple, a technology company seen by some as an interloper, was able to set prices of digital music tracks at a level that consumers would support in a market upended by the availability of pirated content. Meanwhile the music industry lost significant consumer support upon trying to bring its infringers to heel. The loss of revenues that ensued from these blows spurred creative industries to seek broad legislative initiatives and technical strategies to thwart piracy, or at least to stanch its losses. But infringement persisted, and the losses mounted. A downward slide that would take decades to correct had been set into motion.

The loss of revenues from online activities has found parallels in other creative sectors. In journalism, for instance, works have been freely copied, linked,

50 See Jonathan Barr, Netflix, Amazon and Hulu Are Paying a Steep Price to Battle Piracy, *Forbes*, Oct. 31, 2017, available at www.forbes.com/sites/jonathanberr/2017/10/31/netflix-amazon-hulu-are-paying-a-steep-price-to-battle-pirates/#2532a5fd3501.

51 See, Jesse Kirshbaum, It's 2018 and the Music Business Is Better Than Ever, *AdAge*, Jan. 2, 2018, available at https://adage.com/article/agencies/2018-music-business/311771/.

52 See, Mark Sweney, Slipping Discs: Music Streaming Revenues of $6.6 Billion Surpass CD Sales, *The Guardian*, April 24, 2018, available at www.theguardian.com/technology/2018/apr/24/music-streaming-revenues-overtake-cds-to-hit-66bn.

53 See, Victor Luckerson, Are Artists Finally Profiting from the Streaming Era?, The Ringer, March 16, 2018, available at www.theringer.com/tech/2018/3/16/17126048/lil-pump-record-industry-revenue-streaming-era; available at www.cnbc.com/2018/01/26/how-spotify-apple-music-can-pay-musicians-more-commentary.html.

circulated, and used, all without payment. In photography, digital prints have likewise been open to unremunerated appropriation. Both these industries continue to struggle to find strategies for protecting their content and stanching piracy-related losses. New technologies have made creative goods ever more susceptible to being illicitly copied, such as the proliferation of set-top boxes that may enable users to stream works gratuitously. Thus, piracy has only grown in scale and sophistication. Even now, the scale of infringing activities and sites has proven both daunting and elusive: no industry has found a way to monitor online theft efficiently and comprehensively.

Creative industries have only seen mixed results in their efforts at policing their content. Among the strategies they have pursued are making active searches for potentially infringing content, sending cease-and-desist letters, and litigating against the largest and most egregious infringers. Yet many creative industry stakeholders have compared their efforts to a game of "Whack-a-Mole,"[54] which entails one offender being thwarted for a short time, only to spring up anew, to be recreated by imitators, or to be reinvented by competitors.[55] Without being able to rely on active intervention by the carriers of content, creative industries are forced to play a defensive game, only being able to respond after their content has already been appropriated and drained of value. Their woes are only compounded by a lack of coherent regulation in the digital landscape, which affords room for infringers to operate from distant jurisdictions and often under dubious or virtually lawless regimes. Even the most diligent of policing cannot be made effective without proper enforcement mechanisms and some deterrent effect. These realities have left the creative industries exposed to rampant piracy and effectively powerless in its wake.

In their efforts to police activities that infringe creative copyright and/or steal creative works, many industry stakeholders have called on Big Tech companies for assistance in large-scale policing efforts. Some have further called for policies that would require Big Tech companies to both monitor potentially or actually infringing activities and to impose sanctions on offending sites, actors, and agents.[56] There are currently provisions in place to facilitate

54 See definition, "whac-a-mole," available at https://en.wikipedia.org/wiki/Whac-A-Mole.

55 RIAA CEO: Piracy Notices Are Costly & Increasingly Pointless, *Torrent Freak* (Sep. 24, 2015), available at https://torrentfreak.com/riaa-ceo-piracy-notices-are-costly-increasingly-pointless-150924/. RIAA CEO Cary Sherman criticizes the DMCA takedown system, arguing that "[T]he result is a never-ending game that is both costly and increasingly pointless." The main problem is the "whack-a-mole" issue. When service providers receive a takedown notice, they are in compliance if they remove the content from the site. Users can add the content again; then another takedown notice needs to be sent and the provider would remove the content again to be in compliance. This is what is considered the "whack-a-mole" process.

56 See, Kim Hart, Policing the Policies of Tech Giants, Axios, June 15, 2017, available at www.axios.com/policing-the-power-of-tech-giants-1513302767-acd31a83-d517-463f-8a97-a3ed645caa36.html; Yue Wang, Is Alibaba Doing Enough to Fight Fakes, *Forbes*, March 10, 2017, available at www.forbes.com/sites/ywang/2017/03/10/is-alibaba-doing-enough-to-fight-fakes/#762455e95587; Rana Foroohar, Facebook's

the monitoring of potentially offending content, notably the key sections of the Digital Millennium Copyright Act ("DMCA") that attempt to balance creators' rights against users posting infringing content and the rights and responsibilities of service providers. These provisions remain controversial, however, and the evidence of their efficacy in curtailing infringement is, at best, inconclusive.

The Digital Millennium Copyright Act was crafted by Congress with an express purpose of putting into place policies and practices that might help creative industries combat the problems arising from digital copyright infringement.[57] It attempted to set in place procedures to enable copyright holders to notify Internet service providers[58] (ISPs) when they considered copyrighted materials to be infringed.[59] These "notice and takedown" provisions were intended to be "a cost-effective, quick, and powerful tool to remove material that infringes your copyright."[60]

Section 512 of the DMCA creates a "safe harbor" for ISPs that shields them from their own acts of copyright infringement[61] as well as from potential secondary liability for the infringing acts of others.[62] The actions of the ISPs that

---

Self-Policing Needs an Update, *Financial Times*, Sept. 10, 2017, available at www.ft.com/content/f5d04d7e-9481-11e7-a9e6-11d2f0ebb7f0.

57 WIPO Copyright Treaties Implementation and On-Line Copyright Infringement Liability Limitation, H.R. 551, 105th Cong. § 401("The digital environment poses a unique threat to the rights of copyright owners, and as such, necessitates protection against devices that undermine copyright interests. In contrast to the analog experience, digital technology enables pirates to reproduce and distribute perfect copies of works—at virtually no cost at all to the pirate. As technology advances, so must our laws (The House Commerce Committee).")

58 The term "service provider" is broadly used here and comprises any entity offering transmission, routing, or providing connections for online communication. Among the main functions of service providers that are covered by the safe harbor include such activities as serving as a conduit, caching, hosting, and offering information location tools (e.g., the primary role of search engines).

59 17 U.S.C. § 512.

60 Ken Lui, The DMCA Takedown Notice Demystified, *Science Fiction & Fantasy Writers of America* (Mar. 6, 2013), available at www.sfwa.org/2013/03/the-dmca-takedown-notice-demystified/.

61 Section 512 of the Digital Millennium Copyright Act shields online service providers from liability for (i) copyright infringements by users of online sites and (ii) provision of links to material that infringes copyright drawn from other Internet sources. The safe harbor attaches when a service provider meets certain requirements: (i) it has effective notice-and-takedown procedures; (ii) it promptly removes content when a copyright owner notifies it that material is infringing; and (iii) it has no actual or effective knowledge that the posted material is infringing. 17 Code Section 512, available at www.rcfp.org/browse-media-law-resources/digital-journalists-legal-guide/protection-infringing-material-posted-oth.

62 There is some dispute over the extent to which ISPs are shielded from directly infringing activities. See, R. Anthony Reese, The Relationship Between the ISP Safe Harbors and the Ordinary Rules of Copyright Liability, *Columbia J. of Law and the Arts* (2009), available at www.law.uci.edu/faculty/full-time/reese/reese_ispsafeharbors.pdf.

might otherwise trigger liability claims typically include storing digital users' material or providing digital users various information location tools. Sections 512(c) essentially immunizes ISPs from liability for copyright infringement[63] as long as the provider does not have certain kinds of knowledge regarding the infringing material or activity.[64] While Section 512(c) applies to materials posted by site users, often referred to as "user-generated content" ("UGC"),[65] Section 512(d) protects ISPs from damages arising from copyright infringement when they refer or link users to an online location containing potentially infringing materials.[66]

Creative industries generally laud Section 512 for its attempts at creating a mechanism for addressing the responsibilities of ISPs vis-à-vis infringing materials, but they also tend to be dissatisfied with its many shortcomings. For one, it primarily places the onus of finding and flagging potential copyright infringements on copyright holders—a burden that may be particularly

63 It is worth emphasizing that the safe harbor provisions are not copyright exceptions; they are limitations on liability for service providers.

64 Under Section 512(c), an online service provider is not liable for money damages for user-generated content that infringes another copyright, if (i) it is not aware of any infringing content on its site, nor is aware of any "red flags" that would make an infringement apparent; (ii) it does not receive a financial benefit directly attributable to the infringing activity, if it has the right and ability to control that activity; and (iii) it acts expeditiously to remove the infringing content from its site once it has received proper notice of the infringement. (It should be noted that this protection extends only to service providers that merely transmit or temporarily store digital information for their subscribers. If a service provider selects or alters the content, for example, it will likely have to pay the copyright owner monetary damages for the infringements of others.) See The Basics of the Digital Millennium Copyright Act, The Reporters Committee for Freedom of the Press, available at https://www.rcfp.org/journals/news-media-and-law-winter-2012/basics-digital-millennium-c/.

65 David Oxenford, Copyright Office Reviews Section 512 Safe Harbor for Online User-Generated Content—The Differing Perceptions of Musicians and Other Copyright Holders and Online Service Providers on the Notice and Take-Down Process, Broadcast Law Blog (Apr. 12, 2016), available at www.broadcastlawblog.com/2016/04/articles/copyright-office-reviews-section-512-safe-harbor-for-online-user-generated-content-the-differing-perceptions-of-musicians-and-other-copyright-holders-and-online-service-providers-on-the-noti/.

66 Under Section 512(d), an online service provider that links to material without knowing that it infringed another's copyright, will not be liable for money damages if (i) it is not aware that the material it linked to is infringing, nor is aware of any "red flags" that would make the infringement apparent; (ii) it does not receive a financial benefit directly attributable to the infringing activity, if it has the right and ability to control that activity; and (iii) it acts expeditiously to remove access to the infringing material from its site, most likely through removal of the link, once it has received proper notice of the infringement. Id. (A noteworthy clarification is offered by the Citizens Media Law Project: if a complaining party does not include several pieces of information statutorily required to appear in the notice, such as information reasonably sufficient to permit the service provider to contact the complaining party for example, such notice will not serve as "actual notice" for the purposes of Section 512, available at www.dmlp.org/legal-guide/protecting-yourself-against-copyright-claims-based-user-content.) Supra, note 61.

onerous for smaller creators or enterprises.[67] It also does not respond to the "Whack-A-Mole" problem discussed earlier, insofar as offending sites are able to avoid any real liability for their actions by closing down and reappearing under a newly assumed name and URL. This has led some advocates of enhanced liability to argue for a "take down and stay down" system that would require ISPs, upon notification of infringing activities, to search their entire content to determine whether and where the infringing material might reappear. Many creative industry representatives argue that a "notice and stay down" process would compel providers to proactively block copies of infringing content from being uploaded multiple times and across multiple venues.

There is, however, some resistance to the idea that notice and stay down would work in a manner that preserves some important features of the Internet. One argument is that automated takedown notices run the risk of overcompensating for potential infringement by challenging content usage that is actually legitimate.[68] Another concern is that it may be onerous for small businesses and startups to innovate, compete, and thrive if they are required to engage actively in policing content.[69] And some policymakers have argued that caution must be taken with respect to the First Amendment rights of the online user community.[70]

Notwithstanding these concerns, the notice and takedown system alone, while imperfect, could certainly be strengthened and improved to help creators and creative industries when confronting large-scale infringing activities and content. Various proposals are being considered by policymakers,[71] and the Copyright Office, cognizant of the pressing need for improvement, is undertaking a vital reconsideration of Section 512 today.[72] Further, some advocates of notice and stay down argue that such an approach would benefit individual creators and small creative enterprises, primarily by offering them an effective and permanent recourse that would not involve multiple, and

67 See, e.g., Kevin Madigan, Despite What You Hear Notice and Takedown Is Failing Creators and Copyright Owners, Center for the Protection of Intellectual Property, Aug. 24, 2016, available at https://cpip.gmu.edu/2016/08/24/despite-what-you-hear-notice-and-takedown-is-failing-creators-and-copyright-owners/.

68 See, e.g., Mike Masnick, DMCA's Notice and Takedown Procedure Is a Total Mess, And It's Mainly Because of Bogus Automated Takedowns, Techdirt (Mar. 30, 2016), available at www.techdirt.com/articles/20160330/01583234053/dmcas-notice-takedown-procedure-is-total-mess-mainly-because-bogus-automated-takedowns.shtml.

69 Corynne McSherry et al., In the Matter of Section 512 Study: Docket No. 2015–7, *Electronic Frontier Foundation* (Apr. 1, 2016), available at www.eff.org/files/2016/04/01/eff_comments_512_study_4.1.2016.pdf.

70 Id.

71 See, e.g., Chris Castle, Safe Harbor Not Loophole: Five Things We Could Do Right Now to Make the DMCA Notice and Takedown Work Better, *The Trichordist* (Sep. 10, 2012), available at https://thetrichordist.com/2012/09/10/safe-harbor-not-loophole-five-things-we-could-do-right-now-to-make-the-dmca-notice-and-takedown-work-better/.

72 See, available at www.copyright.gov/policy/section512/.

possibly costly, efforts to protect their work.[73] Lastly, and notably, at least one major study offers evidence that the notice and takedown system works effectively, if one accepts the premise that a relatively modest number of filed counter-notices demonstrates that notices are being properly issued and not subject to chronic overuse.[74]

An overarching concern of the DMCA Safe Harbor provisions is the balance it strikes between protecting creators' rights and affording users latitude in online activities and speech. There are real fair use concerns that underlie the objections to Section 512 being raised before the Copyright Office today.[75] But these issues cannot be allowed to obscure the very real threat that online piracy poses to creators and creative industries, and the very real need that they have to hold ISPs responsible for their fair share of monitoring, policing and, where necessary, sanctioning infringing behavior. Already proposals for such measures as site blocking and de-indexing have been raised and are, again, proving contentious in both broad and granular perspectives. Yet for policing to be successful, the remedies that are available to the infringed parties must

73 See, e.g., Stephen Carlisle, DMCA "Takedown" Notices: Why "Takedown" Should Become "Take Down and Stay Down" and Why It's Good for Everyone (Jul. 23, 2014), available at http://copyright.nova.edu/dmca-takedown-notices/.

74 See Robert Atkinson et al., RE: Section 512 Study: Notice and Request for Public Comment, Docket No. 2015–7, Information Technology & Innovation Foundation (Mar. 21, 2016), available at http://www2.itif.org/2016-section-512-comments.pdf. In its response to the U.S. Copyright Office's request for public comment concerning the impact and effectiveness of the Section 512 Safe Harbor provisions, the Information Technology & Innovation Foundation (ITIF) asserts that the DMCA are effective and balanced, and should remain unchanged. The evidence that the takedown process is succeeding, according to the ITIF Study, is an appreciable lack of counter-notices filed, as well as data indicating that few takedown notices are issued inappropriately. ITIF also points to a provision in the DMCA that provides for monetary damages when a party knowingly misrepresents information in a takedown notice. Further, ITIF addresses what it believes are the two main errors, which may arise in the notice and takedown process: "false positives" and "false negatives." False positives occur when a takedown notice is inappropriately used to request a takedown for materials that qualify for an exemption. False negatives occur when infringing content is not identified, and therefore not taken down. ITIF argues that demonstrably few false positives and negatives occur in the current system. Lastly, the ITIF Study purports to show that there are few signs that speech is being impeded or otherwise negatively affected by notice and takedown. But cf. Benjamin Wilson, Notice, Takedown, and the Good-Faith Standard: How to Protect Internet Users from Bad-Faith Removal of Web Content, 29 *St. Louis U. Pub. L. Rev.* 613 (2010) (Proving that a copyright owner has acted in bad faith when filing a takedown notice may prove challenging to Internet users who have posted allegedly infringing content).

75 Article 1. See, David Oxenford, Copyright Office Reviews Section 512 Safe Harbor for Online User-Generated Content – The Differing Perceptions of Musicians and Other Copyright Holders and Online Service Providers on the Notice and Take-Down Process, The Broadcast Law Blog. available at www.broadcastlawblog.com/2016/04/articles/copyright-office-reviews-section-512-safe-harbor-for-online-user-generated-content-the-differing-perceptions-of-musicians-and-other-copyright-holders-and-online-service-providers-on-the-noti/.

be practical, potent, and effective. In the end, the perfect solution may prove elusive, and an ever-evolving set of remedial measures is the best that can be achieved on behalf of those engaged in creative work.

11.5 Populism

The changes to the digital landscape outlined here have been compounded by a shift in consumer expectations: many users resist paying for content, no matter how original or artistically valuable the works they enjoyed might be, and no matter how much effort and investment went into producing them. Some see no need to pay for creative content, regardless of the long-term consequences on artists and the industries in which they are so crucially embedded. Some users contend that "information wants to be free"[76] and "copyright is obsolete." They argue that intellectual property is a form of control of a valuable resource that would better serve humanity by being freely shared, openly accessible, and unfettered by demands for remuneration or other rewards.

The argument that information should not be propertized, and should be free, seems an inherently sympathetic one. After all, information is a valuable and value-conferring resource. A closely analogous argument can be made for creativity and its fruits as well. Users who argue for a digital world free of constraints on information and creativity are, however, necessarily compelled to ignore, dismiss, or explain away the costs and risks that generating information and creative works entail. They cannot explain how those who assume the costs and risks of creative generation and information production are to be compensated for their efforts. Nor can they explain why anyone would assume such risks, or undertake such efforts, without the promise of being rewarded for their work. In sum, they cannot argue away the entire premise of intellectual property rights—the incentive motive that underlies the constitutional grant of rights to creators and inventors in the first place. Nonetheless, there remains a coalition of digital citizens who believe that the right to access should trump the right to control over, and rewards in, creative output. There is also a fraction of users who believe that access should always be free, irrespective of the costs to creators and their supporters. While their disregard of the rights of creators seems far less sympathetic, their voices continue to be heard and to resonate with many users who are unaware of or indifferent to the consequences to artists that their position implicates.

76 Recognizing that "information wants to be free" can mean many things to many people, the phrase has been used by a significant group of digital citizens who believe that free and open access to information is and should be the leading feature, if not the foundational principle, of the Internet. For an excellent discussion of this postulate, and a critique of where its advocates can go astray, see Wagner, R. Polk, Information Wants to Be Free: Intellectual Property and the Mythologies of Control, *U. Penn. L. Rev.* 995 (May 9, 2003), available at www.law.upenn.edu/fac/pwagner/wagner.control.pdf.

This shift in fundamental assumptions among certain consumers of creative content[77] was reflected in the largely negative response that consumers expressed when music industry representatives, particularly the Recording Industry Association of America (RIAA), brought legal action against several potential infringers.[78] The public relations damage was severe, but arguably would not have been so acute had there not been a shift in consumer mores and expectations that had been coalescing around the idea that content ought to be free and freely available. This continues to exacerbate the problems that creative industries face when trying to police their content online and continues to press upon the range of possible solutions that they have at their disposal in the ongoing battle against content infringement.

Populist assertions may gain momentum through a groundswell of views among digital users, as seen in online petitions, organizations, and activist campaigns. But populist movements may also be fomented and harnessed by political forces for various reasons and motivations, ranging from strategic to philosophical. The parameters of influence in all politicized debates are always subject to dispute. Yet inevitably, copyright and creative work is subject to politicization, given the stakes and the outcomes that are at play in the enormously lucrative creative industries.

It is hard to substantiate, or to quantify, the influence of advocacy on IP policies and populist positions. But there are instances that make a strong case for the ability of stakeholders to sway the opinions and decisions of lawmakers and community members alike. How the changes that arise from political movements are perceived also frequently lends itself to debate, and may depend on a stakeholder's position. In the digital space, the influence of lobbyists behind the scenes that are able to shape and mobilize opinion, and the outcome of those efforts, may be hard to discern and rationalize.

Recent controversies that are emerging, such as those involving Facebook, Twitter, and other sites that increasingly offer news and reportage, reveal that political influence does indeed play a role in the construction, and at times distortion, of digital users' experiences and understanding. More immediately relevant to creative industries is the often-raised contention that Big Tech companies will underwrite initiatives that purport to be driven by grass-roots efforts but that are in fact directed by their own interests and objectives. This practice, commonly known as astroturfing, has been alleged in the recent efforts to oppose key copyright legislation in the E.U., which appear to have received the support and funding of Google.[79] Similarly, earlier movements to defeat proposed legislation against online copyright infringement, known

77 And it is a change: few consumers of physical goods would argue that creative works and resources found in brick-and-mortar stores is, or should be, "free."

78 See Humes, supra at note 19.

79 See David Meyer, Google Is Being Critized Over Its Copyright Stance in Europe. But the Company Is Right, *Fortune*, June 26, 2018, available at http://fortune.com/2018/06/26/google-eu-copyright-directive/.

as Stop Online Piracy Act ("SOPA") and the Protect IP Act ("PIPA"), were heavily backed and funded by Google and Wikipedia, and led to the defeat of those proposals in 2012.[80]

The long-term consequences of populist movements that are funded and directed by any given group of interested stakeholders can change entire ecosystems and end in unforeseeable costs and benefits. The Big Tech companies have already learned to harness populist appeals that appear to support a wide range of users' objectives, but that inevitably further their own aims. When the apparent and ulterior motives align and create net gains, populist-driven change can be beneficial. But when other vital stakeholders are disrupted or undermined by the outcome, their losses may be felt across the landscape, and may result in diminished resources that are not readily found elsewhere or replaced.

80 See Larry Magid, SOPA and PIPA Defeat: People Power or Corporate Clout?, *Forbes*, Jan. 31, 2012, available at www.forbes.com/sites/larrymagid/2012/01/31/sopa-and-pipa-defeat-peoples-power-or-corporate-clout/#12839d3e33c7.

12 What to Do When Tailoring Doesn't Suffice

Countervailing Strategies

12.1 Introduction: Finding Strategies or Workarounds When Big Tech Skews the Field

Creative industries constantly face disruptive innovation in their own creative realms. To name just a few instances, disruption can occur: when business priorities or consumer tastes change; when technology lowers the price of content production but also drives down profit margins in content sale and delivery; or when cultural and behavioral preferences shift from valuing creators' livelihoods to valuing access to free content. When market forces, legal sticking points, technological changes, and cultural revolutions unite, the new set of challenges can prove overwhelming even to industry participants that consider themselves well-prepared for change. Critically, working from the four-factors framework to craft a carefully tailored solution helps equip creative industries with a road map that charts a course to survival and success.

These challenges are significant enough in themselves. But disruption can also occur on a massive scale, as in the changes that Big Tech has wrought and continues to wreak, changing not only the creative landscape but also commercial vectors across the board. Disruptive innovation on such an extensive scale presents a new level of challenge that cannot be managed by creative industries alone; nor can it be confronted on a single front alone. The fast and unpredictable pace of change, coupled with an uncertain political and legislative landscape, make offering proactive strategies difficult to gauge. Still, there are a host of options available, and choosing among them may become clearer for creative industries to discern as technologies evolve and attain a relatively mature and stable state.

As discussed, the influence of Big Tech occurs at multiple points in the digital world, affecting the flow of information and resources, the provision of goods and services, and the rights of entry, access, and use. Four main areas affected are pipelines, pricing, policing, and populism. Creative industries can use the tailoring framework to address several concerns even in these broad areas. They can zealously seek out new ways to monetize creative work, counterbalancing the need for advertising-driven revenue with other potentially rewarding income streams, such as the sale and licensing of exclusive works in diverse venues. This kind of product diffusion already occurs in film and entertainment, where movies and television series are often released in multiple venues, at varied times and subject to differentiated pricing. When large creative firms undertake strategic alliances with large telecoms, technology companies, or platforms, the importance of original creative work can be amplified. This can graphically bring home the need for Big Tech companies to work with creative industries, rather than to treat them either as enemies or as repositories of freely available materials and resources.

Creative industries can also address consolidation and the blurring of boundaries within industries by actively pursuing opportunities to engage in M&A, strategic alliances, centralization of control over content, and other activities that help position them favorably in highly competitive markets. These efforts can help firms realize important economies of scale and positive network effects, promote first-mover advantages, and circumvent interoperability issues. They can also garner useful infusions of capital, generate market activity in new niches or among new consumer bases, and enable firms to hone their pricing strategies in differentiated markets.

At the same time, M&A, consolidation, and alliances can be risky ventures: among other possibilities, they risk running afoul of antitrust concerns, they can be so expensive that they may require leveraging assets or taking on unwarranted debt, they can require long periods of run-up to positive returns on investment, or they can lose momentum in the process of bringing together incompatible company cultures. Even if those hurdles are successfully navigated and cleared, however, creative industries may find that their efforts are not substantial enough to counteract the operations of Big Tech. Nonetheless, the battle to maintain creative enterprise must be fought on multiple fronts, and may well require a number of both victories and failures to determine what the best approaches might be and how creative industries are to prevail in the digital age. Already there are interesting signs of newly energized ventures that are rising to meet the challenge of digitization. Following are three approaches that are noteworthy. The first approach involves scaling up, or securing access to pipelines and market position through M&A, consolidation, and strategic alliances. The second approach involves centralizing and taking control of content at multiple points in the creative process, from generation to production to delivery. The third approach involves keeping content fresh and interactive and keeping users engaged, and thereby appealing to popular tastes, demands, and interests. While all of the examples are recent and therefore still emerging, they represent some of the imaginative efforts that creative industries are making to stay relevant and to remain competitive in spite of the incursions that Big Tech is making on their creative ecosystems and in the greater landscape.

12.2 Scaling Up: Mergers and Acquisitions

The first set of options aims to build size, scale, and capacity that can effectively counter the strength of Big Tech. Obviously, only a few creative industry participants are already large and robust enough to be able to consider taking on the tech superpowers. These companies can enter strategic alliances with comparably sized companies, or they can join the firms that are increasingly looking to mergers and acquisitions to build their market share and position. Examples now abound in several recent unions, such as AT&T's acquisition of DirectTV,[1] Verizon's purchase of Straight Path (one of the largest owners of millimeter wave spectrum),[2] and Charter Communications' acquisition of Time Warner Cable.[3,4] Some of these M&A deals represent vertical integration among creative companies that are uniting complementary content, such as movies, television, and media. Others represent horizontal integration, bringing together creative companies with distribution channels, delivery platforms, telecom carriers, and satellite networks.

Related options for a few of the largest creative companies are to build capacity in-house, or to branch out into activities that can tie in with creative output and build real economies of scale. One instance is the recent announcement by the Walt Disney Company of its plans to build a distribution channel, Disney Plus, which will be the exclusive purveyor of its extensive and enduringly popular content.[5] This option may be available only to a few other creative firms, such as Marvel or DC Comics; and it will be interesting to see if it gains adoption by any of Disney's rivals. Another possibility is illustrated by the emergence of Pixar, a computer animation studio that was purchased by Disney in 2006, but was begun as an independent spin-off of LucasFilm.[6] The acquisition of Pixar enabled Disney to grow its market share, capacity to create highly sophisticated and popular films using state-of-the-art film technology, and to compete on an equal footing with the largest creative companies in the world. Indeed, the Pixar studio has consistently produced and released many of the highest-grossing films to date.[7]

By engaging in M&A, creative industries can bulk up their strength and amass the kind of market power that poses an effective counterweight to some of the forays that Big Tech has made on creative content. The power to check Big Tech may not occur only in commercial spaces; it can also occur in lobbying activities, regulatory measures, audience capture and retention, and other

1 See, Press Release, AT&T Completes Acquisition of DIRECTV, July 24, 2015, available at https://about.att.com/story/att_completes_acquisition_of_directv.html.
2 See, Nine Biggest Billion-Dollar Entertainment and Media Deals in 2017, The Wrap (2017), available at www.thewrap.com/9-biggest-billion-dollar-entertainment-media-deals-2017-photos/.
3 See, The Five Biggest Media Mergers of All Time, *Fox Business News*, Dec. 3, 2018, available at www.foxbusiness.com/features/the-five-biggest-media-mergers-of-all-time.
4 See Tara Lachappelle, From Comcast to Viacom Media Mergers Take More Twists, Bloomberg, April 25, 2018, available at www.bloomberg.com/opinion/articles/2018-04-25/from-comcast-to-viacom-media-m-a-takes-more-twists.
5 See Rick Marshall, Disney Plus: Here's What We Know So Far About the Upcoming Streaming Service, Digital Trends, April 23, 2019, available at www.digitaltrends.com/movies/disney-plus-streaming-service-news/.
6 See Pixar: Our Story, available at https://www.pixar.com/our-story-1.
7 Id.

areas. It can also change the nature and scope of certain kinds of interoperability among content providers, delivery systems, devices, and online providers and services. While net neutrality remains an uncertain proposition at best (as of this writing it has been repealed, but efforts are being made to restore it[8]), creative industries must retain as much control as possible over the dissemination of content, and must fight for the ability to stream their content without being disadvantaged by telecom companies that are allied with their rivals, competitors, or in-house brands. The larger creative companies will likely have a major advantage when negotiating for streaming rights and bandwidth. Although antitrust is and will remain a concern, M&A activities are liable to persist in creative sectors, in part because the necessities of size and scale will mandate growth, consolidation, and ongoing attempts to capture market share.

12.3 Strategic Alliances With Big Tech

Creative industry firms can merge with big tech companies, or they can form strategic alliances or partnerships of varying scope and scale that achieve their objectives without locking them into a fixed relationship and a closed (or non-interoperable) universe. The range of potential partners includes telecom carriers (Comcast, Sprint, Sky), large-scale platforms (Google, Facebook), firms that offer hosting services, content delivery, B2B or B2C web services, e-commerce, and other services (Amazon, GoDaddy, Alibaba), and technology companies that offer computer electronics, software, online services, content delivery, and related goods and services (Apple, Samsung, Microsoft). Obviously, the choices may exceed even the greatest of ambitions that creative firms may harbor when seeking out strategic alliances. But they can provide much-needed financial backing that can empower creative firms to deliver content profitably and sustainably. Relationships with big tech players can also enable some firms to reach audiences that would otherwise be beyond their scope, to develop new business models that may suit their needs, and to push the boundaries of interactive content in cutting-edge technological mediums.

The meteoric growth of popularity of e-sports is one of the most significant recent phenomena on the Internet, giving rise to participatory and spectator gaming, competitive matches, and even e-sports scholarships.[9] Its increased visibility, appeal, and commercial potential has been met by growth in streaming companies that offer innovative products and services to online audiences,

8 See David Shepardson, Democrats to Push to Reinstate Repealed 'Net Neutrality' Rules, *Reuters*, March 4, 2019, available at www.reuters.com/article/us-usa-internet/democrats-to-push-to-reinstate-repealed-net-neutrality-rules-idUSKCN1QL1W0.

9 See, John Koetsier, Esports: The New Football Scholarship: Gaming Scholarships for College Grew 480% Last Year, *Forbes*, May 12, 2018, available at www.forbes.com/sites/johnkoetsier/2018/05/12/esports-the-new-football-scholarship-gaming-scholarships-grew-480-last-year/#752d57b222a1.

and the newcomer Twitch is illustrative of the inventive and attractive options available to e-sports players and fans.

Twitch[10] is a streaming service that allows content creators to share videos with audiences and share revenues associated with their streams with Twitch.[11] While the platform is primarily used for video gamers to showcase how they play a certain game, the platform also allows for streamers to showcase other forms of content. Twitch was recently acquired by Amazon, but had previously partnered with major web platforms and sites, such as the Twitch streaming company, Ninja.[12]

As is the case with most content streaming services, Twitch generates the bulk of its revenues from advertisements. But it also derives meaningful revenue through its relationships with video game producers, who stream their content on Twitch in exchange for a percentage of returns on video game sales garnered through the service.

Twitch also strategically aligns its interests with those of its content producers. Not only does it share ad revenue and game sales revenue associated with a particular stream, but it also allows for individual donations from viewers to a specific streamer. Twitch has introduced a subscription model that allows a user to donate certain amounts of money at fixed intervals to a particular streamer, which the streamer then shares with Twitch. This share rate can be negotiated more favorably to the streamer if the streamer is exceedingly popular. Moreover, Twitch streamers actively control how many ads they air during their streams, which gives them greater autonomy over the production of their content. This system, which allows for specific subscription to content producers and individual donations, may allow content producers to realize greater revenues for their unique products, as opposed to fixed monthly subscription costs which are typically distributed widely across content producers as a whole.

10 See, Brad Stephenson, Twitch: Everything You Need to Know, Lifewire, May 6, 2019, available at www.lifewire.com/what-is-twitch-4143337; Brad Stephenson, Everything You Need to Know About Twitch Subscriptions, Lifewire, May 6, 2019, available at www.lifewire.com/twitch-subscriptions-4147319.

11 See generally, Scott Alan Burroughs, A Twitch In Time: Legal Issues Catch Up With Popular Game-Broadcasting Platform, Above the Law, Sept. 5, 2018, available at https://abovethelaw.com/2018/09/a-twitch-in-time-legal-issues-catch-up-with-popular-game-broadcasting-platform/; Roman Brtka, Intellectual Property: The World of eSports, IP Watchdog, April 2, 2018, available at www.ipwatchdog.com/2018/04/02/intellectual-property-esports/id=95245/; Sam Machkovech, Nintendo Announces Plan to Share Ad Revenue With Streamers, Ars Technica, May 27, 2014, available at https://arstechnica.com/gaming/2014/05/nintendo-announces-plan-to-share-ad-revenue-with-youtube-steamers/; Mike Futter, Microsoft Studies New Let's Play-Friendly Monetization Rules, Game Informer, Jan. 9, 2015, www.gameinformer.com/b/news/archive/2015/01/09/microsoft-studios-announces-new-let-s-play-friendly-monetization-rules.aspx; Willie Clark, The (Still) Uncertain State of Video Game Streaming Online, Ars Technica, Jan. 28, 2018, available at https://arstechnica.com/gaming/2018/01/to-stream-or-not-to-stream-how-online-streaming-game-videos-exist-in-an-ip-world/.

12 See Twitch Ninja, available at www.twitch.tv/ninja.

Twitch's revenue-sharing program with its streamers represents a way in which the company can ensure greater profits for its streamers or content producers as well as promote cooperative copyright relationships. Twitch streamers work cooperatively with music producers to avoid copyright infringement.[13]

However, as Twitch gains popularity, some participants have begun to call into question whether a streamer's specific content is copyright protectable. While streamers who air live video games do not own the video game gameplay, they may be able to protect the specific way they interact with the game and how they broadcast and comment on it. Whether or not streamers can protect their streaming style from others is not clear and may be subject to dispute. A further dispute may also arise with the video game producers if streamers attempt to copyright this information, but to date video game companies have avoided any claims due to their mutually beneficial relationship with streamers. Nonetheless, some large video game producers, such as Nintendo, are more likely to police the use of their games in Twitch streams, and are still evincing some resistance to the Twitch model of individualized streaming.

12.4 Creating a Global Media Company

Increasingly, creative firms that are essentially content conglomerates are beginning to embrace, if not expand, their diverse roles. This phenomenon is highlighted by Universal Media Group's self-characterization as a "global media company."[14] The business paradigm that underlies this characterization involves an extensive reach and control over content generation, distribution, and communication, which is permeating virtually every aspect of creative industries. Spotify also calls itself a "global media company," and has sought to expand its role in recorded music as well as video,[15] ticket sales,[16] live concerts,[17] and podcasts.[18] In some of these ventures, such as the introduction

13 See, Kyle Orland, Twitch Licenses Legal Music Library for Use by Streamers, Ars Technica, Jan. 15, 2015, available at https://arstechnica.com/gaming/2015/01/twitch-licenses-legal-music-library-for-use-by-streamers/.

14 See, Universal Music Group Is Making TV Shows in Tandem With Lionsgate, Music Business Worldwide, Aug. 6, 2018, available at www.musicbusinessworldwide.com/universal-signs-deal-to-make-tv-projects-with-lionsgate/.

15 See, The Exclusive War Between Apple Music and Spotify Is Back On . . . But This Time, It's Video, Music Business Worldwide, March 29, 2018, available at www.musicbusinessworldwide.com/the-exclusives-war-between-apple-music-and-spotify-is-back-on-but-this-time-its-video/.

16 See, Spotify Generated $40M+ In Ticket Sales Last Year. Now It's Accelerating Its Presence in Live Music, Music Business Worldwide, June 26, 2018, available at www.musicbusinessworldwide.com/spotify-generated-40m-in-ticket-sales-last-year-now-its-accelerating-its-presence-in-live-music/.

17 Id.

18 See, Richard Trenholm, Desert Island Discs and Other BBC Podcasts Wash Up on Spotify, *CNET*, Aug. 13, 2018, available at www.cnet.com/uk/news/desert-island-discs-and-other-bbc-podcasts-wash-up-on-spotify/.

of video, Spotify is contending with challenges from an array of competitors, some of which have established market power, such as Apple Music. The magnitude of Spotify's efforts, and the rivalries it is taking on, speak clearly to its ambitions to position itself in the ranks of global media contenders.

These organizations are seeking to anchor control over their valuable brands, as well as to extend that control to a wholly integrated cultural influence, thereby securing their long-term financial growth and sustainability. Even Sony Corporation, historically known for its portfolio of technology and consumer products, is shifting its focus to its entertainment subsidiary, Sony Productions, and to its in-house production and distribution of creative entertainment content.[19] Sony is planning to bring more of its content online via the company's online PlayStation Network, ensuring that its content remains entirely under its ownership and control. Sony is aggressively mining its rights to Marvel characters such as those in the Spider-Man family, and creating new content such as the hugely popular film Spider-Man: Into the Spider-Verse. It is also creating tie-ins with video games, as in the recently launched Spider-Man game, which sold 3.3 million copies in the first three days of its release. These powerful ventures are clearly aimed at competing with the strength of insurgents such as Netflix, Amazon, and Apple.[20] Interestingly, Sony is squarely taking aim at the disruptor Netflix, which has disrupted moviemaking by mastering the art of generating original content and launching it digitally and independently, to great success. It remains to be seen whether Sony and its fellow global media companies can yoke their competitive advantage of enormously valuable content portfolios to the agility and innovativeness of the newcomers. But these are both important steps for the creative industries as a whole, as they position themselves for long-term success in the digital age.

12.5 Taking Control of Content Development, Content Production, and Delivery Systems

Another way to scale up, gain market power that can contend with the big tech players, and exert control over creative work is to build a powerhouse organization in-house. This approach can work for some of the largest creative industry participants, such as The Walt Disney Company (Disney), whose entrenched power and extensive back catalogue ensure a competitive standing that is a helpful counterweight to the behemoths of Big Tech. As noted previously, Disney is seeking to remove its creative works from external

19 See, Brooks Barnes, Sony's Chief Plans to Make Entertainment Assets a Priority, New York Times, Jan. 6, 2019, available at www.nytimes.com/2019/01/06/business/media/sony-movies-television-ces-playstation.html?action=click&module=News&pgtype=Homepage.

20 See Brooks Barnes, Netflix's Movie Blitz Takes Aim at Hollywood's Heart, *New York Times*, Dec. 16, 2018, available at www.nytimes.com/2018/12/16/business/media/netflix-movies-hollywood.html?module=inline.

delivery services, bring all of its content in-house, and centralize its dissemination through a wholly owned streaming service called Disney Plus (styled Disney+).[21]

But Disney's consolidation of control is not limited to the content it produces. It is also centralizing the delivery of content it owns from providers it has acquired. This process is illustrated by its rollout of content via a new cable channel for distribution, ESPN+.[22] Disney had previously purchased ESPN and typically aired its content through cable or satellite subscriptions to ESPN. More recently, Disney moved a significant amount of its content to ESPN+, which charges a monthly subscription rate. Similarly, Disney is buying up sports programming and pulling it off competitor platforms. This model allows Disney to offer audiences more specific, choice-driven subscriptions to desired content, as opposed to blanket subscriptions to content, only some of which audiences may appreciate or want to consume.

By segmenting content, Disney achieves two objectives: it can price discriminate more finely, and it can target specific creators and offer their content to specific audiences. This may yield greater returns to those specific creators, as opposed to blanket subscriptions to all content which when spread out to all producers within a platform may result in lower revenues to those producers. In sum, Disney is attempting to disengage from competitor services by promoting its own streaming service with its own producers. This differs from the model of simply selling streaming rights to other providers and is potentially more lucrative to both the company and its content producers.

Disney and large corporate entities can consolidate power by exerting new forms of control over their content at various points of production, commercialization, and delivery. But in the creative industries, artists are the engines of content generation, and their power need not exclusively be constrained to the earlier stages of creative work. The music streaming service Tidal[23] is attempting to offer a relatively new example of artists trying to consolidate control over creative output. Tidal is a music streaming service that is currently owned, and recently re-launched, by popular music star Jay-Z and a selected

21 See Mike Sorrentino, Disney Plus Streaming Service: Release Date, Price, Shows and Movies to Expect, *CNET*, April 16, 2019, available at www.cnet.com/how-to/disney-disneyplus-streaming-service-name-release-date-shows-movies-to-expect-punisher-jessica-jones-cancelled/.

22 See generally, Jeremy C. Owens, Disney's Approach to Streaming ESPN Could Determine the Future of Television, Market Watch, May 9, 2018, available at www.marketwatch.com/story/disneys-approach-to-streaming-espn-could-determine-the-future-of-television-2018-05-08; Christopher Harris, ESPN+ Acquires FA Cup Rights for U.S. Market, Source Confirms, World Soccer Talk, Aug. 13, 2018, available at http://worldsoccertalk.com/2018/08/13/espn-acquires-fa-cup-rights-for-us-market-source-confirms/; Max Willens, How ESPN Is Marketing ESPN+, *Digiday*, Sept. 12, 2018, available at https://digiday.com/media/espn-marketing-espn/.

23 See, available at Ben Popper, JayZ Relaunches Tidal With Music's Biggest Artists As His Co-Owners, The Verge, March 30, 2015, www.theverge.com/2015/3/30/8314833/tidal-jay-z-streaming-music.

number of major popular music artists.[24] Its business model de-emphasizes the more standard advertising-based revenue in favor of subscription-based revenue, and allows its artists-owners to retain a substantial share in equity in the company. It also purports to pay artists a significantly higher rate of streaming royalties than competitor sites such as Spotify and Pandora. Tidal also promises to offer exclusive content from its stable of artists, which has proved popular but may not be of enduring value, as the window of exclusivity appears to be fairly limited.[25]

Tidal has its counterparts in other creative industries: for instance, Vessel, a relatively new video streaming service, follows the same model as Tidal,[26] offering a subscription-only service that features original and exclusive content. Yet in both the music and video sectors, these ventures face formidable competition. In music, the subscription service recently launched by Apple has the potential to overshadow Tidal with a vast and established consumer base and the ability to raise prices on Tidal artists' output when those works are released on the Apple iTunes site.[27] In videos, Vessel faces stiff competition from Netflix as well as Disney, AT&T (the largest pay-TV distributor in the U.S., which bought Time Warner in an $85 million deal to form the foundation of a new video streaming service), and Apple, which purportedly has a video streaming service in the works.[28] It will be a challenge for Tidal, Vessel, and their progeny to distinguish themselves from their competitors, but the very fact that these creative industry participants are devising new ways of taking control of their creative works and seeking improved rights and remuneration to artists is a positive and promising development that may well find success in the long run.

The business model that Tidal, Vessel, and their progeny represents is a new amalgam of artists and rightsholders trying to take control of the production and distribution of their content. This is increasingly evinced by such new ventures as PEOPLE, an artist's collective co-founded by members of The National (Aaron and Bryce Dessner) and Bon Iver (Justin Vernon), which is

24 See Andrew Flanagan, Andrew Hampp, It's Official: JayZ's Historic Tidal Launches With 16 Artist Stakeholders, Billboard, March 30, 2015, available at www.billboard.com/articles/news/6509498/jay-z-tidal-launch-artist-stakeholders.

25 See Jem Aswad, JayZ's New Album '4:44' Has Dropped – But Sources Say Tidal's Exclusive Will Only Last a Week, Variety, June 29, 2017, available at https://variety.com/2017/digital/news/jay-z-new-album-444-tidal-exclusive-1202483883/.

26 See Andrew Hampp, Vessel to Debut New Blake Shelton, Hunter Hayes, Boyce Avenue Videos: Exclusive, Billboard, March 24, 2015, available at www.billboard.com/articles/business/6509502/vessel-to-debut-new-blake-shelton-hunter-hayes-boyce-avenue-videos.

27 See Nina Ulloa, Apple Will Charge You 30% More If You Subscribe to TIDAL on iOS, *Digital Music News*, April 29, 2015, available at www.digitalmusicnews.com/2015/04/29/apple-will-charge-you-30-more-if-you-subscribe-to-tidal-on-ios/.

28 See Joshua Warner, Netflix vs Disney vs AT&T: The Battle for Video Streaming, IG Group, Nov. 19, 2018, available at www.ig.com/au/news-and-trade-ideas/shares-news/netflix-vs-disney-vs-at-t--the-battle-for-video-streaming--181119.

structured as a noncommercial digital distribution platform intended to centralize the artists' control of music consumption and fan engagement.[29] As these online music media brands struggle to diversify their revenue streams beyond advertising, several of them are increasingly taking on the marketing role of record labels and adopting a more integrated approach to service artists' release campaigns. They are also seeking increased cross-media and cultural impact beyond sales alone.

There are, of course, inherent risks to the artist-owned business model of content ownership and distribution. Digital streaming economics are comprised of many small payments, requiring up-front investments in electronic infrastructure that may take years to recover absent significant scale. Further, up-and-coming artists may feel pressured to prioritize immediate exposure and revenue over ownership, and may be driven to fund immediate creative projects and earn a daily living. As a result, these artists often opt to secure audiences on third-party social media sites like Facebook, Instagram, and Twitter, rather than build their own media and distribution platforms from scratch. This may mean that while artists can build valuable connections with their fans, and interact with fans via these platforms, they also relinquish important rights of control to the platforms that deliver their content, thereby undermining somewhat the point of artist-owned ventures.[30]

Another challenge that some commentators have pointed out is that the rise of automated discovery channels such as Spotify's algorithmic playlists may be making music reviews and criticism seem less relevant and less able to convince potential buyers to make a "purchase" (i.e., a stream) of a song or album.[31] As a consequence, artist-owned ventures will have to work hard not only to persuade listeners to join their network but also to purchase the music from their site. This may not be easy: in the case of Tidal, for instance, a hit song by singers Jay-Z and Beyonce, "Everything Is Love," was placed exclusively on Tidal for the first 48 hours after it dropped, but was then released on Apple Music and Spotify's paid tier.[32] If exclusivity continues to be so limited, it seems doubtful that Tidal will be able to position itself as a power player in

29 See What Happens When Artists and Record Labels Build and Buy Their Own Companies?, Music Business Worldwide, Aug. 16, 2018, available at www.musicbusinessworldwide.com/what-happens-when-artists-and-record-labels-build-and-buy-their-own-media-companies/.

30 Aside from PEOPLE, a few artists and developers are working on building software that brings control of context into artists' hands. For instance, Saga software, created by Mat Dryhurst, enables artists to control how their work is represented on third-party sites (displaying a sad face or error message over a video if it's embedded on a website in a way that the artist never approved). See, History of Saga, available at https://github.com/matdryhurst/Saga#saga.

31 See Adam Clair, All Ears: Streaming Music Services Have Made Record Reviewing Superfluous. But Are We Better Off Without It?, *Real Life Mag.*, Nov. 8, 2017, available at https://reallifemag.com/all-ears/.

32 See David Turner, How Tidal Got So Fucked, Gizmodo, June 20, 2018, available at https://gizmodo.com/how-tidal-got-so-fucked-1826870560.

the digital music distribution market. It remains to be seen if Tidal, PEOPLE, and similar artist-owned ventures are initial attempts that will lead to sustainable models—whether of these sites or in improved, follow-on enterprises—but the business model still has the potential to enhance creative industries' control over their content in the long run.

Artists are not the only creative industry participants seeking to extend control over all aspects of creative content. Several music magazines are trying to expand from covering the culture to engaging in, managing, and deliberately creating it. The FADER, a well-respected music publication, has long been operating under the same ownership as the creative agency Cornerstone.[33] These entities are now actively engaged in converging their creative staff and bringing their two halves, which were historically kept apart, under one umbrella.[34] Another major urban music site based in the U.K., GRM Daily,[35] also maintains its own marketing agency, GRM Agency,[36] and is seeking to offer what they describe as a "complete 360-degree solution" to artists whom they cover on the editorial side.[37]

Other creative industries are also extending their ventures to the editorial/agency hybrid model. *The New York Times* has created T Brand Studio,[38] which has worked for over 100 brands to date (including Spotify) on advertising products. And *The New York Post* has created an in-house creative agency, Post Studios, which has featured the streetwear brand Supreme on the *Post*'s cover.[39]

Other more unconventional efforts have been made in journalism as well. *The Players' Tribune*,[40] for instance, is a multimillion-dollar sports media platform founded by star baseball player Derek Jeter that gives its athlete-subjects final approval of their own coverage, as well as the only listed byline on the article (staff writers essentially serve as ghostwriters for their subjects). While this approach certainly cannot be considered traditional "journalism," it does create a venue and a platform that allows fans to connect with valued content. *The Players Tribune* is also actively seeking to expand and diversify its revenue

33 See generally, The Cornerstone Agency, available at www.cornerstoneagency.com/.

34 See KC Ifeanyi, How Fader Magazine and Its Creative Agency Are 'Bucking Traditions' to Shape Culture, Fast Company, Aug. 17, 2017, available at www.fastcompany.com/40454019/how-fader-magazine-and-its-creative-agency-are-bucking-traditions-to-shape-culture.

35 See generally, GRM Daily, available at http://grmdaily.com/.

36 See generally, GRM Agency, available at http://grmagency.com/.

37 See What Happens When Artists and Record Labels Build and Buy Their Own Companies?, Music Business Worldwide, Aug. 16, 2018, available at www.musicbusinessworldwide.com/what-happens-when-artists-and-record-labels-build-and-buy-their-own-media-companies/.

38 See generally, T Brand Studio, available at www.tbrandstudio.com/.

39 See Jonah Engel Bromwich, Today's Supreme Drop Is All Over the New York Post, *New York Times*, Aug. 13, 2018, available at www.nytimes.com/2018/08/13/style/supreme-new-york-post.html.

40 See generally, *The Players Tribune*, available at www.theplayerstribune.com/en-us.

streams through deals with partners like Amazon Prime and Amazon Prime Video.[41]

Record labels are likewise seeking to expand their control over creative content, in an opposite but parallel direction to these media companies. Record labels have traditionally been in the business of creating culture, in the form of music. Recently, they have been seeking control over the narratives that surround music culture, and to extend that control to the ways in which the narratives of music culture are disseminated across various media platforms. Illustrative is a multi-year agreement announced between Universal Music Group (UMG) and Lionsgate, articulated by UMG's management as a new impetus to "expand the definition of music-driven stories—whether that means narratives set against entire scenes or eras of music, or projects driven by our artists' catalogues."[42] These efforts may include building partnerships with platforms such as Snapchat, which has been actively seeking out such opportunities through its Lens Studio app and Discover feature.[43] Or they may include building relationships with Spotify, which has integrated with Instagram Stories precisely with a view to bringing new revenue opportunities to "music stories" and music culture writ large.[44]

12.6 Keeping Content Fresh, Interactive, and Engaging

An innovative model for building growth in the creative industries draws from many elements of the tailoring framework but adds new, important features that enhance the strengths of each aspect of tailoring as well. Fortnite, a novel addition to the online gaming universe, has seen skyrocketing growth, currently garnering approximately $318 million per month in gross revenues.[45]

41 See Darren Heitner, The Players' Tribune Finds New Revenue Stream Through Deal With Amazon Prime Video, *Forbes*, July 17, 2018, available at www.forbes.com/sites/darrenheitner/2018/07/17/the-players-tribune-finds-new-revenue-stream-through-deal-with-amazon-prime-video/#280fe88ccd74.

42 See Universal Music Group Is Making Shows in Tandem With Lionsgate, Music Business Worldwide, Aug. 6, 2018, available at www.musicbusinessworldwide.com/universal-signs-deal-to-make-tv-projects-with-lionsgate/.

43 See Leila Cobo, At Midem Snap and Geffen Executives Sing Praises of Snapchat Promotion; Scooter Braun Playfully Prods, Billboard, June 6, 2018, available at www.billboard.com/articles/business/8459744/midem-snap-geffen-neil-jacobson-ben-schwerin-scooter-braun.

44 See Instagram Stories Now Offers Its 400M Users Thousands of Licensed Songs, Music Business Worldwide, June 28, 2018, available at www.musicbusinessworldwide.com/instagram-stories-now-offers-its-400m-users-thousands-of-licensed-songs-to-soundtrack-their-videos/.

45 See David Turner, Fortnite Is a Video Game Phenomenon. The Music Business Could Learn a Lot From Its Success, Music Business Worldwide, Oct. 17, 2018, available at www.musicbusinessworldwide.com/fortnite-is-a-video-game-phenomenon-the-music-business-could-learn-a-thing-or-two-from-its-success/.

Fortnite is a battle royale game in which players can create worlds, buildings, arenas, and personae. A strong share of its revenues is derived from the sale of digital goods, but its core profits flow from its tiered subscription model. At the outset, Fortnite is free to play. But every ten weeks, it introduces a new season replete with a new theme, new map changes, and new items. Access to new features requires the purchase of a "Battle Pass," which also offers access to additional goods and services. Fortnite strongly encourages its players to maintain access and to pay for the enhanced version, not only to remain competitive but also to remain au courant with other players, friends, and the Fortnite community.

The subscription, or more accurately recurring fee model, would seem to resemble a more traditional model that is familiar in the music industry, such as the Spotify model. But it moves beyond the standard model in several respects. With respect to content, it offers new and actively refreshed content on a weekly basis for players to unlock. It also offers a fast-changing array of limited-run items for purchase, which secures ongoing revenue streams in new merchandise. And it features "loot boxes" that enable users to obtain consumable virtual items, which can be redeemed to receive a randomized selection of further virtual items, ranging from simple customization options for a player's character or avatar, to game-changing equipment such as weapons and armor.[46] Moreover, Fortnite regularly makes sweeping changes to its larger narrative, ensuring player and audience attentiveness. This differs significantly from the more static and limited music model. Spotify, Apple, Pandora, and SoundCloud do offer personalized playlists as incentives to retain users and to ensure their ongoing return to the sites. Yet these playlists are neither actively refreshed nor based in new content. Rather, they are simply the repurposing of existing catalogues.

Music playlists are essentially passive, and they offer no monetary transaction for additional content on music streaming services. Further, music streaming does not offer users or fans the opportunity to interact directly with artists. Spotify, Apple, and Pandora give no means of displaying fandom. In contrast, Fortnite offers an abundance of ways in which fans can express their enthusiasm and support for various aspects of the game, its players, and its related products. The commitment to fostering, responding to, and rewarding its online community has served Fortnite extremely well, building extremely loyal audiences that support each other and spread the gospel to new entrants and curious onlookers. Audience engagement serves to build out the site's user base and contributes to positive network effects that are vital to scaling up. Still further, Fortnite draws heavily from the contributions of other creative enterprises and artists, bringing in guest musicians, making direct allusions to popular games, songs, dance moves, and memes (although sometimes at the risk of copyright

46 This practice is controversial, however, and may come under regulators' scrutiny over time. See, e.g., Benjamin Pu, What Are Loot Boxes? FTC Will Investigate $30B Video Game Industry, *NBC News*, Nov. 28, 2018, available at www.nbcnews.com/tech/tech-news/loot-boxes-gambling-video-games-ftc-look-it-n941256.

transgressions[47]), and engages users in expanding their creative experience across genres, disciplines, and an array of cultural reference points.

All of these features not only capture users' attentions but also retain their interest and their willingness to pay for access to ever-changing materials. When contrasted with the static model of other creative industries, such as music and publishing, it is easy to see that the recurring fee model is particularly well suited to the attractive forum of interactive experience that Fortnite represents. But Fortnite and its progeny in the gaming world need not stand alone and unreplicated. The music industry has had some success in emulating certain features that Fortnite has mastered, such as offering users the ability to reward their favorite individual players with "tipping" or "micropayments" that are made easily and securely online. In music, this model was developed by the early adopter Bandcamp, and its success has been reflected in overseas markets by large-scale music streaming services such as Tencent in China and WAV Media, a US-based media platform that is owned by the South Korean Internet company Naver.[48]

Not only individualized payments, but also individualized and dynamic experiences, are design decisions that creative industries across the board can learn from the videogaming industry and shape to their own specifications and objectives. As video games begin to explore online game-streaming, the potential for new, fluid models can only expand, offering adaptable business strategies and user engagement approaches.[49] Many of these innovations dovetail perfectly with the tailoring framework, offering novel business solutions and engaging user communities just as prescribed here: to fit the needs and objectives of the creative industries, including their participants and their creators. And where they expand the parameters of the four factors, they demonstrate not only their own flexibility but also the adaptability of the tailoring framework to the ever-evolving creative landscape.

But it is with respect to their legal ramifications that ventures like Fortnite appear to be pushing up against traditional copyright constraints. Fortnite has been accused by various artists, game makers, and celebrities of appropriating copyrightable elements of their creative work.[50] Whether the dance moves are

47 See Gregor Pryor, Fortnite and Copyright: Can You Steal a Dance Routine?, Gamesindustry.biz, available at www.gamesindustry.biz/articles/2018-12-04-when-does-a-homage-become-a-rip-off.

48 See Cherie Hu, Tencent Music Uses 'Tipping' to Rack Up Revenues. Why Aren't Western Music Streaming Platforms Doing the Same, *Music Business Worldwide*, Oct. 3, 2018, available at www.musicbusinessworldwide.com/tencent-music-uses-tipping-to-rack-up-revenues-why-arent-western-music-streaming-platforms-doing-the-same/.

49 See Keza MacDonald, What Lies Ahead For Video Games in 2019?, *The Guardian*, Jan. 8, 2019, available at www.theguardian.com/games/2019/jan/08/video-games-2019-preview-harry-potter-last-of-us-kingdom-hearts-streaming.

50 See, e.g., Nick Statt, Fortnite Keeps Stealing Dance – And No One Knows If It's Illegal, The Verge, Dec. 20, 2018, available at www.theverge.com/2018/12/20/18149869/fortnite-dance-emote-lawsuit-milly-rock-floss-carlton.

themselves copyrightable, and whether they are infringing when replicated by Fortnite into figures known as "emotes," are both open questions that may well require resolving through litigation, negotiation, or regulation (including bringing copyright laws up to speed on new technologies). Another open question is whether some of these elements might constitute violations of the rights of publicity of those who created and popularized the originated works.[51] Some artists have also alleged that Fortnite has engaged in cultural appropriation of dance moves made prominent by African American creators.[52] These too are matters to be resolved as Fortnite and other popular, interactive, and culturally trenchant creative properties grow, mature, and attain both commercial and cultural authority.

12.7 Conclusion: Taking Control

Taking control of content at multiple points in the production-to-delivery pipeline need not be relegated to established companies, startups, or artists alone. The preceding examples demonstrate that efforts to consolidate and harness control over content are underway in a number of creative sectors, from music to e-sports to video games. They also seem especially promising when they harness features drawn from the tailoring framework offered here—including changing business models, wielding copyright protections in innovative ways, building in technological defenses, and securing consumer appreciation and participation—with other management and operational practices.

Whether these strategies and ventures succeed over the long term remains to be seen. But creative industry participants are urgently seeking new approaches to attaining healthy and sustained growth. Their efforts in launching a host of promising ventures can only be welcomed and appraised as they evolve. These startups share a common trait: they are seeking to shift the paradigm away from more traditional models, in which different entities in creative commercial sectors specialize in well-defined but limited roles, and toward more innovative approaches, in which these ventures undertake newly diversified and fluid roles, often coupled with innovative approaches to commercialization, IP rights, and cultural norms, mandates, and expectations. It will be interesting to see if they can lead the way forward, and not just whether but also how they can shift the tailoring framework with unexpectedly innovative changes and meaningful results.

51 Rights of publicity are the personal rights that govern how an individual can control and profit off the use of their own likeness, name, and other identifiable traits. Id. They constitute a rapidly evolving and hotly contested area of intellectual property that is fascinating, but outside the scope of this work.

52 See Jonathan Band, Fornite, Copyright and Cultural Appropriation, DisCo, Dec. 20, 2018, available at www.project-disco.org/intellectual-property/122018-fortnite-copyright-cultural-appropriation/#.XCdTe_x7ndc.

13 Copyright, Democracy, and Art

13.1 The Democracy Paradox: How Protecting Copyright Enhances Democratic Flourishing

Fundamentally, art has always been democratic: anyone can whistle, sing, play, make or create music; most people can pick up a pencil, or a piece of chalk, and draw, sketch, outline, design, or doodle; or they can use that same implement to write stories, poetry, histories, recipes, or comedy routines; some can grab a camera or video camera and make photographs and movies; others may prefer to grab a chisel and make a piece of sculpture. Not everyone has had access to all forms of art, but in virtually every culture, at any given time, people have made art and shared artistic endeavors and creations. In many senses, art is democratic—and universal.

But art has also been undemocratic across many cultures. In the Western classical tradition, much of "high" art was produced under patronage, and much of it was enjoyed, consumed, and reserved primarily for the elite. Eastern high arts were also at times based in exclusivity: elite castes were meant to pursue learning and the fine arts. These culturally determined preserves of "high" art and culture have been fiercely criticized and contested, and resistance to these artificial, class-based constraints remains a part of why popular movements against cultural elitism are so powerful. Few today believe that art should belong only to a small, elite cluster—and even if certain arts still seem to operate that way, creators in general want to make art available and accessible to as wide an audience as they can reach.

Contemporary culture is in some respects moving away from the idea that artistic production is or should be relegated to a select few creators producing works that aesthetically appeal to limited audiences. The breakdown between "high art" and "low art"[1] reflects an increased awareness that art can come in many forms and appeal to many audiences. Equally, the question of who can and should create has been expanded to embrace a broad array of people who engage actively with artworks and who may generate works of their own.

1 See Berys Gaut & Dominic McIver Lopes, *The Routledge Companion to Aesthetics* (Routledge, 2nd ed., Abingdon, Oxon. 2005).

Indeed, many creative industry participants are increasingly aware of the creative work that occurs in their audiences and user communities, and welcome new contributors to cultural production.[2]

But in contrast with these moves toward more egalitarian artistic principles there exists another recognition that seems to underscore the more undemocratic aspect of art: serious art, the kind that creators dedicate their lives to making, typically requires huge up-front investments and considerable risk. Serious art tends to demand hard work, deep learning and meticulous honing of a craft, repeated effort, and slow development, often resulting in works whose quality—whether greatness, mediocrity, or futility—cannot be known until the entire process of rendering them has been completed. The lifetime of investment that creators make is what makes them "professionals," rather than amateurs, however impassioned amateurs can be. And the reward for that professionalism has been, in the case of some creators at least, the ability to earn a livelihood from one's artistic production.

Is professional art "democratic"? It is, in the sense that making livelihood by selling art in the open market is a basically democratic endeavor: anyone can try to do it, and it is reasonable to assume that in a capitalist economy the market will reward the work it values accordingly. The fact that not everyone who tries to purvey his or her art will succeed does not render it an undemocratic system. Democracy in an economic context necessarily involves the judgment of creative producers, intermediaries, customers, and critics, all of whom will determine whether creative works succeed or fail. What does make it less than wholly democratic, however, is that not everyone will be able to pursue professional artistry.[3] Not everyone, that is, can assume the costs of investment and the risks that making art entails. Without a system of patronage or, in more recent terms, subsidization, a creator must be able to make the long-term gamble on living from art.

The up-front investments, and the potential for an unpredictable payoff, as well as the possibility of having a career that never actually pays the bills, may bar some aspiring creators from the start. This is a serious concern. Yet it does not, and should not, stand as reason for opposing the professionalism of creative endeavor. Nor should it fortify the claim that professional art is indefensibly undemocratic. It may mean that we should consider how to make the system of identifying and supporting creators more fair, more expansive, and more meritocratic.[4] At the same time, however, we must recognize that

2 The interest in fostering creativity among users is an important rationale put forward by advocates of keeping copyright restrained and fair use expansive. See, e.g., Michael B. McNally, Samuel E. Trosow, Lola Wong, et al., User-Generated Content: Policy Implications, 17 *First Monday* 6 (Jun. 4, 2012).

3 The issue of economic inequality writ large is outside the scope of this book. But it is, of course, a factor in determining whether individuals have the assets to pursue concentrated artistic endeavor.

4 E.g., supporting artistic enterprise by outside funding such as scholarships, offering emoluments to emerging artists, and subsidizing public creative works.

professionalism by definition is, and likely will always be, pursued by only a fraction of creative people. Even in a democracy, even given a degree of subsidization, creative professionalism is bound to be rare.

These claims implicate another aspect of democracy: access to art. This consideration falls not on the production side, but on the consumption side.[5] It is virtually indisputable that access to art is vital and should be as expansive as possible. The richness of art that precedes a creator inevitably serves to inspire, teach, motivate, and nourish his or her strength and vision. "It is only by standing on the shoulders of giants that I have been able to see so far" is a memorable summation. And in intellectual property lore, Jefferson's great metaphor of passing the torch also illuminates how creators feed each other's work. A creative heritage likewise inspires and sustains audiences who are equally important and deserving of access. And creators who strive to reach wide audiences know the value that access confers and the legacy that access may secure for them.

But access to art cannot come at the expense, literally, of the professional creator. Some have argued that there is a vital First Amendment right to the full and unfettered dissemination of expressive work. But while expressiveness is secured by the First Amendment, dissemination is not so clearly granted. Moreover, certain key principles oppose the claim that works must be freely disseminated. There is a fundamental and societally agreed-upon right to earn a livelihood from what John Locke called the "fruits of one's labor, the sweat of one's brow."[6] The right of the creator to render a concrete, identifiable work, defined as a work of intellectual property, is also a right granted by Congress under constitutional authority. Further, it is an "exclusive" right that enables a creator to derive value from creative output, and to derive a livelihood from that extraction of value. As the Constitution posits, that very grant of exclusive rights itself promotes the "progress of Science and Useful Arts": intellectual property rights add to the foundation of artistic works on which a culture is predicated, and therefore are not antithetical to the goal of keeping art and culture rich and diverse, but are rather central to the entire premise.

Where does that leave access? When works are granted "exclusivity," their access may well be curtailed while the period of statutory coverage runs. That is the deal that is struck with creators: you keep your work for a period of time, and you have the right to recuperate your investment and to reap your rewards for the risks you took in making it; but after that time, your work will

5 That it is urgently necessary to strike a balance between rights and access is the essential concern at the heart of Justice Steven Breyer's seminal work, Stephen Breyer, The Uneasy Case for Copyright: A Study of Copyright in Books, Photocopies, and Computer Programs, 84 *Harv. L. Rev.* 281 (1970). See also Stephen Breyer, Copyright: A Rejoinder, 20 *UCLA L. Rev.* 75 (1972).

6 There is considerable debate, however, over whether Locke's view would encompass a broad construction of copyright law. See, for e.g., Herman T. Tavani, Locke, Intellectual Property Rights, and the Information Commons, Ethics and Info. Tech., vol. 7 (June 2005).

be added to the public domain.[7] Creators can also choose to make their works freely accessible, and not to limit or charge for access.[8] But the crucial point is that the choice is theirs.

That tradeoff seems unfair to those who argue that greater, or immediate, access is necessary, that the term of exclusivity is being prolonged far past the investment time, and that rewards are granted to those who may not even have made an investment, such as heirs and assigns. Those arguments may well be worth having. But how does that implicate "democracy," unless "universal access" is being used as a proxy for enhanced democracy? And is the term "democracy" then meant to stand in opposition to a right in one's work? Does a proposed right to access supersede a granted right to exploit one's labor? If so, is it acceptable if it undermines the entire viability of creators?

It seems untenable, and profoundly unfair to creators, that their right to make a living could be entirely undermined, even in the interest of making creative works immediately and universally accessible. But this is another concern that recent debates over democracy and art are unwilling to confront directly. Indeed, few who argue for expanded access are truly willing to say that they are fine with the rights of creators being eviscerated and deprived of value. That, however, is the logical endpoint of total access without exclusive intellectual property rights in creative work. If enhancing democracy means expanding access without regard to such rights, that proposition should be advanced forthrightly, and creators should be able to respond to it and to defend their rights as they choose. But the cost of increased access—the expense that is borne by professional artists, and the loss of livelihood that will be the outcome of access without compensation—cannot be elided or simply swept away by appeals to democratization as an invincible good and goal.

This, then, is the framework for controversies regarding the "democratization" of art in the digital age that is often overlooked or misused. Central to its false premises are the conflation of the term "democracy" with "artistic efforts by the many," and the conflation of "elitism" with "professional art (by the few)." Central to its conclusion is the undermining of the value of creative work that should be conferred upon and enjoyed by the creator. Indeed, the core idea that creators should be able to earn a living from their professional work, which had been universally agreed upon, has been challenged—if, that is, the implications of full and free access are understood. This challenge to the very viability of artists is unprecedented, but it also arises from the muddy waters of the debates that swirl around democracy and art. And no one is

7 There are many advocates of the public domain who argue that its scope has already been seriously compromised and remains under assault. See, for e.g., James Boyle, The Second Enclosure movement and the Construction of the Public Domain, 66 *Law & Contemp.* Probs., 33 (2003); Larry Lessig, Free Culture: The Nature and Future of Creativity (Penguin, New York, NY 2003).

8 For e.g., creators can make their work available under a Creative Commons License. See www.creativecommons.org.

really willing to answer the basic question: if artists cannot make a living from their work, how can they pursue a creative profession in a serious and sustained way?

The point of this book is to recognize that professional creativity, undertaken by creative artists and supported by creative industries, is critically important to our cultural heritage. Creative work has been constitutionally granted the right to be owned, protected, and used on the terms that the owner of its copyright determines are necessary and appropriate. On the other side of the balance, there are public welfare demands on creative work: it is meant to enrich culture, and it constitutes the building blocks on which culture will be constructed and enlarged. In our time, the access that digital users have to creative work is unprecedented and exciting. New uses of creative work are emerging and reshaping collective visions of what transformative work can be. Many creators encourage these developments, and many creative industries welcome the chance to bring them on board and add new works, and new kinds of work, to their portfolios. The sticking point is that the original works must remain protected, and retain their value, as promised by the grant of rights that copyright conveys. When copyrights work effectively, they both protect creative output and defend democracy's strengths—its professional artistic community, its amateur artists, and its users and consumers of the creative arts. Striking that balance is what leads to creative sustainability; and equally, it is what best supports democratic flourishing[9].

9 Theories of human flourishing have deep roots in many philosophies. A current strand is the Capability Approach, built on the pioneering works of Martha Nussbaum and Amartya Sen, among others. The capability approach posits that the freedom to achieve well-being is lodged in what people are able to do and be, the lives that they are effectively able to lead, and their ability to realize themselves fully in their lives. For some seminal works on the Capability Approach, see Martha Nussbaum, Creating Capabilities (Harvard University Press, Cambridge, MA 2011); Amartya Sen, "Capability and Well-Being," in The Quality of Life, Nussbaum and Sen, eds., at 30–53 (Clarendon Press, Oxford, UK 1993). See also The Capability Approach, Stanford Encyclopedia of Philosophy, available at https://plato.stanford.edu/entries/capability-approach/.

Index